Social Life in School

Dedication

To Kate and Jack

Social Life in School
Pupils' Experience of Breaktime and Recess from 7 to 16 Years

Peter Blatchford

UK The Falmer Press, 1 Gunpowder Square, London, EC4A 3DE
USA The Falmer Press, Taylor & Francis Inc., 1900 Frost Road, Suite 101,
Bristol, PA 19007

First published in 1998

**A catalogue record for this book is available from the British
Library**

**Library of Congress Cataloging-in-Publication Data are
available on request**

ISBN 0 7507 0743 7 cased
ISBN 0 7507 0742 9 paper

Jacket design by Caroline Archer

Typeset in 10/12pt Garamond by
Graphicraft Typesetters Ltd., Hong Kong

*Printed in Great Britain by Biddles Ltd, Guildford and King's Lynn
on paper which has a specified pH value on final paper manufacture
of not less than 7.5 and is therefore 'acid free'.*

Contents

Acknowledgments   vii

Chapter 1   Introduction   1

Chapter 2   Pupils' Experience and Behaviour at Breaktime:
             A Review and Description of Research Approach   11

Chapter 3   Pupils' Views on Breaktime at 7, 11 and 16 Years   26

Chapter 4   Changes in Breaktime Activities from 7 to 16 Years   41

Chapter 5   Playground Games at Junior School: Changes over the
             School Year   58

Chapter 6   Friendship Formation after Entry to Junior School   72

Chapter 7   The Experience of Friendship at Breaktime at 16 Years   90

Chapter 8   Pupils' Views on Teasing and Name Calling at 7, 11
             and 16 Years   109

Chapter 9   Fighting in School   136

Chapter 10   Conclusion   159

References   178

Index   184

Acknowledgments

It is my great pleasure to thank a number of people for their help with this book. I would like to thank first of all Tony Pellegrini, Colin Rogers and Joy Coughtrey for giving so unselfishly of their time, and commenting so helpfully on an earlier version of this book. They should not be held responsible for any remaining difficulties.

I want to also thank colleagues who worked on various components of the research reported in this book: Paddy Walls, the Research Officer on the 16 year follow up, Clare Sumpner, the Research Officer on the Breaktime national survey, Ann Mooney and Rose Creeser who conducted the 11-year-old interviews with me, Jessica Burke and Clare Farquhar who conducted the 7-year-old interviews with me, and Charlie Owen who helped with the statistical analysis.

Over the years a small international group of researchers, interested in research on breaktime/recess behaviour, have made contact and shared interests and ideas with each other. I would like to acknowledge their various contributions to this field. They include Mike Boulton, John Evans, Craig Hart and Tony Pellegrini.

It was a marvellous and poignant experience to interview the same children at 7, 11 and then 16 years, at the end of each of the three main stages of their school careers. For each child there was often some particular defining feature which seemed constant through the seeming metamorphoses at each visit. I felt I got to know at least some of them well, and can still bring to mind — at the time of writing, thirteen years on, in the case of the 7-year interviews — a look or turn of phrase. I wish all of the pupils success in their lives after school.

It is also my pleasure to thank the children and staff of Tillingbourne Junior School, Chilworth, Surrey, especially the Headteacher Paul Wood, and two class teachers Jan Weston and Debbie Baker.

I would also like to offer thanks where it is sometimes taken for granted. The following funding bodies made the research reported in this book possible: Economic and Social Research Council (ESRC) for funding the longitudinal study and the 16-year follow up, and The Nuffield Foundation for funding the national survey.

Finally, I would like to thank Anna Clarkson, of Falmer Press, for her support and advice.

Chapter 1

Introduction

Breaktimes in schools are ubiquitous. Almost every school — primary and secondary — has some form of compulsory recreational break. In schools in Britain there will be a morning break and a longer lunchbreak and in some schools an afternoon break as well. Pupils' experiences at breaktime can figure large in their overall feelings about school. As adults, when we bring to mind our school days, it can be images of the playground and events there that come to mind, as much as events in the classroom.

Despite my best efforts at recall, I have very few memories of my years in an east London primary school. I do, though, have an enduring memory of the midday break during the infant stage. I must have been about 6 years of age. The memory is of a seemingly endless time on a large playground. Most children appeared to have gone home for dinner because there were few other children around. There seemed little to occupy me except a concern, still tangible today, that an older and presumably wayward boy, should go home soon, or stand to lose his dinner and get into trouble. I am not sure why this memory is still with me, but I think it owed much to the contrast between the purposeful, supervised and safe activities of the classroom and my first experiences of the sometimes desultory, unsupervised and rather frightening time on the playground.

I cannot be alone in finding that conversation with my own children, when it turns to their day at school, is as much about their social lives and breaktime activities, as it is about more obvious school concerns. (It is true that my children know I am interested in breaktime behaviour; but this appears to *reduce* the likelihood of them discussing their own experiences!)

The main theme of this book can be stated at the outset: activities and social relations at breaktime are important because it is during this part of the school day that pupils are relatively freed from the attention of adults and the structure of the classroom. It is true that conflicts and petty squabbles can arise, and teasing and name-calling can occur. It is also true that some pupils can be taunted and bullied. But breaktime is also a time when friends, not always in the same class, can meet; a time when they can have fun and construct games in a relatively safe environment; a time when important social networks are formed; a time when they can fall out, but can also develop strategies for avoiding conflict. It is time when pupils can find freedom and a social life independent of the classroom, where the rules of conduct are more their own, and where activities stem from their own initiative.

It is therefore at breaktime that pupils reveal much about their social lives and their interests, and this is why I feel it is of interest to researchers as well as teachers and others working in education. Yet until recently breaktime, and pupils' experiences of it, have tended to be taken for granted. There has been little research on the day-to-day experiences of pupils at breaktime and little recognition of the possible social and even educational value of informal and undirected activities in school.

Why 'Breaktime'?

It is important to make the point that this book is concerned with experiences across the school years. In Britain the term 'playtime' is often used at primary level (4–11 years) whereas the term 'breaktime' is preferred at secondary (11–16 years). There has been more awareness of playtime and the use of school grounds at primary level, but we must not forget the continued experience of breaktime over the secondary years, and the important role it can play in pupils' social lives. In this book I prefer to use the term 'breaktime' for all breaks including lunchtime because it is more inclusive and indicates that breaktime issues are of relevance through all the school years. Both are interchangeable with 'recess' which is the term preferred in the United States and some other countries, though recess is only likely to be experienced by the younger grades in US schools.

The Place of Breaktime in the School Day

My memory of a much younger self suggests a long lunchbreak. But, when young, many experiences have a timeless quality about them. How much time does breaktime actually take up? In a recent national questionnaire survey about breaktimes, which I will introduce shortly, we found that the total average time at breaktime, that is, the total time at morning and afternoon breaks and lunchtime was 93 minutes at the infant stage (5–7 years), 83 minutes at the junior stage (7–11 years) and 77 minutes at the secondary stage (11–16 years). This amounts to around 24 per cent, 21 per cent and 18 per cent of the school day for the infant, junior and secondary stages respectively. This means that the youngest children in school have the longest breaktimes. They also have a longer lunchbreak; in nearly half of the infant schools, lunchbreaks were 75 minutes or more long, and in 60 per cent of the infant schools they were 65 minutes or more. These results therefore suggest that my early impression of long infant school breaktimes was not entirely attributable to the tricks that time can play on memory.

There have not been international studies which would enable us compare the situation in different countries, but it does appear that breaktime occupies a bigger part of the school day in the UK than in many other countries and that, unusually, breaktime continues into the secondary school stage. There may be other differences. In the UK, 'recess' occurs at a fixed time and this may allow children to make more of, and even plan, how to use the time to interact with peers, play games and 'work' their social networks. In contrast, in at least some States in the US, the schedule for recess is more variable, and children may not be able to do this sort of planning (Pellegrini, personal communication).

If breaktime takes up a sizeable part of school day, the playground can also occupy a large part of the school grounds. A crow's eye view of many schools would show school buildings dwarfed by surrounding asphalt and grass. For some of the time the school would be relatively peaceful, but at certain times of the day, the crow, who might just have been tempted to land on the school roof, would be made wary by the sudden intensity of action and noise, as children rushed out of the school. Hovering for a moment, the crow would notice children running and shouting, or sitting and talking. From the crow's perspective at least, life in school would be most obviously enacted on the playground.

A Negative View about Breaktime and Breaktime Behaviour

So in temporal and spatial terms, as well as in terms of pupils' experience, breaktime is a significant part of the school day. However, although difficult to quantify, the dominant view of children's behaviour at breaktime appears to be negative, with a stress on unacceptable behaviour that can occur then. Several areas of concern have fuelled this negative view. One is a growing appreciation in recent years of the extent of bullying in schools and the harm that it can do to the victims. Initially inspired by the work of Dan Olweus (1993), there have now been a number of studies and initiatives in Britain (La Fontaine, 1991; Tattum and Lane, 1989; Smith and Sharp, 1994; Sharp and Smith, 1994). Most bullying appears to take place on school playgrounds (Whitney and Smith, 1993). Other worries have centred on racist name calling (Kelly, 1988; Cohn, 1988) and teasing (Mooney et al., 1991), which again can occur at breaktime. Views have also been influenced by violent incidents such as the murder of a British Asian boy in a Manchester secondary school playground. This incident led to the setting up of a public enquiry (Macdonald, 1989), because it showed how violence, possibly racially motivated, could erupt in school playgrounds. A more general influence has been concern about behaviour in schools, particularly expressed by the Teacher Unions and the press, that gathered momentum over the 1980s and culminated in the reporting of the Elton committee of 'Enquiry into Discipline in Schools' (DES, 1989). The Committee identified the lunchbreak as 'the single biggest behaviour related problem that (staff) face'.

I first became interested in breaktime during visits to primary schools during the 1980s, when the subject of breaktime, and difficulties that arose then, often came up in discussions. In order to find out more about these difficulties and to seek some practical solutions, I interviewed primary headteachers and teachers in the south east of England. These were the basis of the book *Playtime in the Primary School: Problems and Improvements* (Blatchford, 1989). I found that staff had a number of concerns with pupil behaviour, for example, with what was seen as a large amount of needlessly aggressive behaviour. Less dramatically, many were aware of lower level but more common problems that can arise at breaktimes and that can spill over into the school. It was felt that problems could arise during the long lunch break.

In our national survey of staff views about breaktime, staff in primary schools appeared to be making more effort than those in secondary schools to improve behaviour, and this might explain why they felt behaviour at breaktime had improved over the past five years. Nevertheless in one in four schools, both primary and secondary, the view was that behaviour at breaktime had declined. There was a perception of less respect toward authority and the environment, an increase in aggression, and more individual pupils with difficult behaviour. There was also a clear view that behaviour *out of school* had declined in the last five years.

There is an allied concern with the quality of outside play — a general perception that children are not as constructive in their play as they once were. In the interviews with teachers, concern was expressed about children idling around the playground — not seeming to know what to do with themselves — and play being described as low level, and, for the boys, mainly tests of physical prowess (Blatchford, 1989). Traditional playground games were commonly seen to be in decline. One head felt that children had 'lost the vocabulary of outside play', and felt it appropriate to 'teach' children supposedly forgotten outside games.

Changes to Breaktime in Schools

What has been the consequence of this negative view about breaktime in schools? During my visits to schools since 1990 it seemed to me that changes were taking place, and that these changes owed something to a view of breaktime as a time when avoidable difficulties could arise. We could find no systematic information on breaktimes in schools, for example, on the time allocated to morning, lunchtime, and afternoon breaks and whether this had changed over the past years, and on supervision arrangements at breaktime, even though it is commonly recognized that major changes took place during the 1980s as a result of teachers' industrial action. We therefore conducted a national questionnaire survey of breaktimes in primary and secondary schools in order to chart changes that had taken place over the five years up to the time of the survey (that is, a comparison of the 1990/1 and 1995/6 school years).

We chose a random sample of one in ten of all primary and secondary schools in England. Altogether we received questionnaires back from just over 60 per cent — representing 6 per cent of all schools in the country. What did we find? In around half of primary and secondary schools there had been changes to the length of breaktime. The main change was a reduction in time spent at lunchtime, along with the abolition of the afternoon break. The overwhelming reason given for this was to increase the amount of time spent on teaching. This was particularly true at secondary level. There is a view that breaktime can use up time during the school day when pupils could be working, and that teachers' time and effort can be expended calming pupils down after returning from vigorous activities on the playground. This view might be expected to grow in strength in the UK in the context of growing competition between schools, school league tables based on examination results, and the consequent move to maximize pupil academic achievements. Interestingly, and even taking into account changes to breaktime, the survey also showed a tendency for the length of the school day to have increased over the last five years.

A second reason, given by staff, for the reduced time at breaktime was in order to reduce behaviour problems in school. Staff, especially at primary level, were adopting more deliberate policies with regard to lunchtime supervision. (Further details on the national survey can be found in Blatchford and Sumpner, 1996, 1997.)

What are the implications of these changes? Whilst it is of course appropriate for schools to be concerned with the amount of time spent on teaching and the demands of the National Curriculum, and on management of behaviour at breaktime, one unexplored side effect may be the impact these developments have on time when pupils of all ages can meet and interact in a relatively undirected fashion. What are the consequences of the current changes on pupils' social lives? In order to answer this question we need a better understanding of a more fundamental question: what do we know about pupils' social experiences in school, especially as manifested at breaktime? This book is an attempt to find some answers to this question. It also seeks an answer to an allied question: What value does breaktime have for pupils, and what might be lost by further reductions in breaktime? It may well be that decisions taken in the interests of improving academic and social behaviour have unexpected effects on pupils' informal, social lives in school.

Before we leave the survey, it is worth recording two other changes to breaktime that have taken place. During the 1980s in England, again especially at primary level, there was a tendency for lunchtime supervision to pass from teachers to ancillary staff. In the national survey we found that 'dinner ladies', as they are often called, are now the main supervisors at breaktime at primary level, outnumbering teachers by six to one. Yet we found that teachers had a number of concerns about the effectiveness of such supervision, and this has no doubt contributed to their sense that problems can arise at breaktime.

Changes to the physical nature of the school grounds have also taken place recently, and these can be expected to have affected pupils' breaktime

experiences in school. Concerns about children's safety have led to the dis-
mantling of some older playground apparatus. Others have sought to improve
the school grounds. With greater awareness of the sometimes bleak nature of
school grounds, and the way this can contribute to troublemaking and boredom, has come an understandable interest in environmental projects, for example, involving the creation of wildlife and nature areas, and the installation
and provision of play equipment (see Blatchford and Sharp, 1994). It is of
course appropriate to consider the school grounds constructively, but improvements to the physical environment may paradoxically decrease other opportunities for pupils, for example, because of a resulting reduction of playground
space, and constraints arising from limited access to equipment. Worries about
school security, heightened by recent tragic events, also seem bound to constrain freedom of movement around school grounds.

Recent changes to the organization of the school day and in some cases to
the school grounds seem, therefore, to have led to growing restrictions on
pupils' traditional freedoms to interact and play in school settings. This has
also been noted in the US (see Pellegrini, 1995) and in Australia (Evans, no
date). These trends can stem from a negative view about breaktime, as we
have seen, which can be expressed in a deliberate anti-breaktime viewpoint
(an anti-recess movement has been identified in the US by Pellegrini, 1995),
but, more generally, they seem to derive from a situation in which breaktime is
taken for granted — 'like the fabric of the building' as I have said before (1989)
— and understandably, given the turmoil in education over the past decade,
not seen as a priority. At primary level there is more appreciation of the value
of outside play experiences at breaktime, but by secondary school an indifference toward breaktime appears more widespread, perhaps because the value
to pupils is less clear.

The situation with regard to breaktime in schools needs to be seen along-
side changes to the opportunities for peer interaction *outside* school. There are
signs in England and elsewhere that children of primary school age (5–11
years) have less opportunities out of school for interacting freely with peers
(Hillman, 1993), and thus developing friendships and social skills. Children are
far more likely to be driven to school, rather than walk. This emphasizes the
likely importance of interaction at breaktime in schools, which for a growing number of pupils may be the main opportunity for them to interact and
develop friendships.

Pupils' Activities and Experiences at Breaktime: This Book

There have therefore been important cultural and social changes that appear
to be influencing the nature of pupils' free activities and social relations, both
in and out of school. Though still relatively neglected by researchers and
school policy, there are signs of a growing appreciation that much can be
learned from studying children's behaviour and experiences at breaktime (see

Blatchford and Sharp, 1994; Hart, 1993; Smith, 1994, Special Edition on Role of Recess in Schools in *Journal of Research in Childhood Education*, 1996).

It is important to ask whether pupils' behaviour and experience at breaktime support the generally negative view I have just described. But in seeking to find out what we do know about breaktime activities and experience we face a difficulty — not only has there been little research, but existing research is fragmented and only provides a partial and at times indirect account.

In this book my aim is therefore, first, to provide an integrated account and analysis of pupils' experiences and activities at breaktime, and, second, to then draw out implications for school management and policies on behaviour. It represents (at least to me) a logical development in my research on breaktime. This began, as I have said, with an account of teachers' views and recommendations for managing breaktime (Blatchford, 1989), and was followed by an account of new initiatives at breaktime (Blatchford and Sharp, 1994) and the national survey, as described above. In these projects, school staff have been the main respondents and informants; but throughout we have been following closely the pupils' perspectives of breaktime. As part of a longitudinal study of pupils' educational progress in London schools, based at the Institute of Education, we have interviewed the same children at 7, 11 and 16 years. The book draws heavily from these children's accounts. I also draw from a case study of the breaktime activities and experiences of one class of 8–9-year-olds, after entry to junior school.

This book stays close to the pupils' own descriptions, and stems from the view that pupils are the experts on breaktime, and have privileged access to it. I felt that a focused study of such experiences could tell us much about the social value of breaktime and also address issues that have important implications for efforts to improve school behaviour. Although, as we have seen, recent changes threaten to alter and constrain pupils' social lives in school, we know surprisingly little about experiences during this part of the school day.

The book, then, has two main aims. The first is to better understand pupils' experiences, activities and peer relations at breaktime, which is the main opportunity for social interaction in school. (I will say more about the second aim shortly.) In line with the review to be found in the next chapter the book will look at selected aspects of breaktime experience. I will list these areas now with main research questions, and then in the next chapter I will amplify and ground them in an integrated review of previous research.

Pupil Views on Breaktime

How do pupils feel about breaktime at each age, about staying in the school or going out to the playground? Why do they like and dislike breaktime, and how do they feel breaktime could be improved? What do they feel about the school grounds and locations allotted to them?

Activities at Breaktime

What do pupils do at breaktime and how do activities change from the primary to secondary years? At primary level what role do breaktime activities and games play in social relations between pupils after entry to school; where do games come from and what social processes explain how the games change after entry?

Friendships at Breaktime

What can we learn about the nature and composition of friendship groups, what factors affect friendship choices, and how do friendships change in the short term after entry to school, and in the long term between primary and secondary stages? What factors are associated with individual differences and group differences in friendship formation?

Teasing and Name Calling in School

How prevalent is it and how significant is it to pupils, why and how are pupils teased and how do they react to it, how does it change with age and how is it affected by ethnic and gender group differences?

Fighting in School

How prevalent are fights at school, what is the significance of fights for pupils, how do fights begin and how are fights affected by age of child, personal characteristics of pupils and situational factors?

Background literature and theory relevant to each of these topics is given in the next chapter and also at the beginning of each subsequent chapter. Each topic can be read separately, but they are linked and the aim is to build up an overall picture of pupils' social experiences at breaktime. Given the large amount of attention given to bullying recently, and the way that this has now been extensively studied (e.g. Olweus, 1993; Smith and Sharp, 1994), in this book I deliberately concentrate on less explored, but more commonly experienced, aspects of breaktime experience.

Breaktime Experience, Peer Relations and School Policy

The second main aim of this book is to discuss implications of the analysis of breaktime experiences for school policies, management of breaktime and attitudes to pupils' social lives during the school years. There are some important issues that need to be addressed. Here I raise two that have a particular bearing on breaktime experiences. A first main issue concerns the appropriate stance schools should adopt with regard to pupils' social experience in school. To a large extent the stance has been one of indifference and at best toleration. Current developments though, as we have seen, are leading to a reduction of opportunities for social interaction, and we may need to consider more deliberately what the role of breaktime might be and how schools can provide an appropriate context within which pupils can contact each other.

Reference has already been made to increased initiatives to improve breaktime in schools. These are commonly designed to deal with a perceived problem of poor behaviour in school and playground (Blatchford and Sumpner, 1996; see also Blatchford and Sharp, 1994). Concern about bullying in schools has also led to a number of initiatives (see Sharp and Smith, 1994). Much of this work is well meaning but some will have the effect of constraining behaviour at breaktime. To what extent should we be concerned that the time for unsupervised free association and the development of a distinctive children's culture, and the development of friendships between children, are being constrained? If current developments are moving us more toward an interventionalist approach to breaktime, there is also a view, found particularly at primary level, and supported by the Opies' books (e.g. 1969), that the best adults can do is to leave pupils to their own devices. I will return to this issue after I have considered evidence on breaktime experiences, and I will attempt to assess the appropriate degree of intervention schools should adopt with regard to breaktime.

A second issue concerns the role of breaktime and peer culture in the context of current concerns with school effectiveness and improvement. Over recent years there has been a good deal of research and initiative devoted to understanding school effectiveness and bringing about school improvement. There is not space here to review this work (see Mortimore, 1991; Reynolds, 1991; Stoll and Mortimore, 1995). A common feature has been an attempt to list factors associated with more effective schools. Stoll and Mortimore (1995), for example, identify 11 factors: participatory leadership, shared vision and goals, teamwork, a learning environment, emphasis on teaching and learning, high expectations, positive reinforcement, monitoring and enquiry, pupil rights and responsibilities, learning for all, and partnerships and support. These factors are based on extensive research, and similar factors are found in other reviews in this field. The main stress is on learning factors and positive relations within the classroom in service of higher school achievement.

This work is necessary and desirable but has tended to leave to one side pupils' informal and social experiences at school. Though there is a growing appreciation of the importance of pupil perspectives when considering school effectiveness and improvement — for example, Barber (1994), and more recently the chief HMI Chris Woodhead (*Times*, 6 March 1996), have commented on the negative effect of boys' anti-school attitudes on their relatively poor motivation and achievements at school — pupil perspectives tend to be seen in terms of the management of classroom learning. Even in a recent study specifically directed at the relevance of pupil perspectives for school improvement (Ruddock et al., 1996), there is an absence of comment on the effect of and importance of pupils' social lives in school. It is the aim of this book to provide such an account of social experiences at breaktime in school.

Plan of the Book

In Chapter 2 I review what is known about pupil behaviour and experience at breaktime and draw out main research questions addressed in the book. Each following chapter is then directed at the areas of pupils' experience at breaktime, identified above and in the review. Chapter 3 provides a context for the rest of the book by examining pupils' views at 7, 11 and 16 years on breaktime. In Chapter 4, and again drawing on the main longitudinal study, there is an analysis of how breaktime activities changed over the school years and how pupils explained changes in activities from primary to secondary school. In Chapters 5 and 6 the attention shifts to the case study of one class after entry to junior school (aged 8–9 years). Chapter 5 complements the data in Chapter 4 by examining in more detail how and why games changed after entry to school. Chapter 6 continues with an analysis of friendship relations in the 8–9-year-olds. We then return to the main longitudinal study and in Chapter 7 there is an analysis of friendship relations in the 16-year-old pupils. In Chapters 8 and 9 the data examined are still from the longitudinal study and I look at teasing and name calling, and fighting respectively. Finally, in Chapter 10 main themes arising from the book are reviewed and implications for schools are discussed.

Chapter 2

Pupils' Experience and Behaviour at Breaktime: A Review and Description of Research Approach

As said in the last chapter, existing research, relevant to an understanding of pupils' experience and activities at breaktime, is fragmented. This is not surprising given relevant areas include play, inter-group relations, peer relations and friendships, aggression and fighting. Each of these topics has been studied from different conceptual frameworks, and this makes it difficult to use a common theoretical framework to help organize a study of breaktime behaviour and experience. Inevitably authors and researchers will be selective in terms of their own background and interests; in my own case this lies more in psychology than other disciplines, and this will no doubt be apparent to the reader. But I feel it is important to seek to provide an integrated review of the relevant literature, because it is of interest in its own right, and in order to provide a basis for the research questions addressed in the subsequent chapters.

There have been perhaps two main approaches of relevance to pupils' breaktime experiences: firstly, descriptions of peer culture stemming from sociological and ethnographical perspectives, and typically based on qualitative research methods, and, secondly, a concern with features of peer relations such as social competence and friendships, stemming from a psychological perspective, and typically based on quantitative research methods. Each approach comprises a disparate set of research agendas and studies, and have evolved in parallel with each other, with little cross referencing. This is unfortunate because I will argue there is surprising consensus about some main features of peer relations in school and at breaktime.

I will draw on these two areas of research, and others where relevant, in order to discuss some main themes relating to pupils' experience and activities at breaktime, which will be at the heart of this book. There is not space for a complete review of all topics and readers are referred to Blatchford (1994; and in press), Boulton (1992), Evans (1989), Pellegrini (1995), Smith (1994) for other accounts.

Pupils' Views on, and Experience of, Breaktime

Recently I was discussing breaktime behaviour with a colleague, and she said, with little thought to the contrary, that children at 7 years of age did not like playtime. During discussions with teachers, I have often heard stories of play-ground mischief and pupil distress. The recent awareness of bullying in schools might also lead the casual observer to assume that breaktimes are not enjoyed by many pupils. Yet how much of this is an adult view from a distance, as it were, rather than based on pupils' own experience? When we first interviewed the children who are the main source of data in this book — when they were 7 years of age — most said they liked breaktime, particularly the long lunchbreak (Tizard et al., 1988).

There are a number of suggestions that the pupils' experience of break-time and recess can be of a different culture to that of the classroom. A general context is the conceptualization of pupil cultures, arising out of sociological and ethnographical approaches, of a sub-culture that stands apart from, and sometimes in opposition to, the mainstream culture of the school and classroom. In an early and influential series of studies, an anti-school culture was seen to arise in reaction to having low status in the school (Ball, 1981; Hargreaves, 1967; Lacey, 1970), or have its roots in working class culture outside school (Sharp and Green, 1976; Willis, 1977). An alternative view stressed the need to attend to pupils' own changing constructions of school and the way these could alter in relation to different school situations (Furlong, 1984).

These studies of pupil perspectives have concentrated on secondary schools. Some studies in this tradition have been located in primary schools. Pollard (1985), for example, argued that pupils' interests and rules varied according to school situation. Peer culture may appear more informal than the parallel school culture but it has nonetheless its own hierarchy, rules and criteria of judgment. Different pupil sub-groups — which Pollard called 'good', 'joker' and 'gang' groups — vary in the degree to which they draw on peer cultures, and there-fore the degree to which they run counter to classroom-based school culture. Pupils strive to maintain their self image, and 'having a laugh' is a main feature of an oppositional pupil culture.

These studies, therefore, suggest a different and sometimes oppositional, pupil culture away from the classroom. Sutton-Smith (1990) has been almost alone among them in seeking to capture, and indeed champion, the particular character of primary school playground culture. He concludes that 'there is a culture of school playground play, just as there is a culture of schooling . . . Further, the school-playground child culture is apparently one of the most important as far as the children are concerned . . .' (p. 5). He goes on to con-ceive of school breaktime events as 'festival' occasions, by which he means the participation of all in 'cultural events with their own traditions, rule systems, sanctions, forms of periodicity and endurance, and spatial boundaries . . .' (p. 6). He argues that practically all children talk of their 'public joy' (the Latin definition of the term *festum*) as they burst out of the school buildings on to the playground. 'There is an immediate intensification of action and interaction in the games that are available . . . the playing of many roles . . . loud verbal barracking . . . There are stylizations of language, paralinguistics, and behavioral gestures . . .' (p. 6). In a powerful statement, which runs counter to the negative climate of thought about breaktime, which I have described above, he concludes that 'the school playground festival is one of the few places where a distant and non-intrusive supervision is possible so that children's political rights can be guaranteed consistent with an adult concern with their safety. The school playground still provides the one assured festival in the lives of children.'

Sutton-Smith's view may be seen as over romantic. It is significant that almost all the research on playground life is based in primary schools, and a more positive view may be fostered by the prevalence of playful activities at this age. Some accounts of pupil culture at primary level do stress more negative aspects. For example, Kelly has drawn attention to the extent of racist name-calling in the playground (1988), and to racist and sexist harassment that can take place on school playgrounds (1994). Troyna and Hatcher (1992) have pointed to the way peer cultures express tensions between a desire for domination as well as equality, and can support racial teasing even when children themselves are not racist. They argue that a theory of children's relationships has to be able to account for both friendship and hostility. As we shall see, this neatly sums up the direction of much recent developmental psychology toward peer relations. Pollard (1985) also recognized tensions in children's culture; on the one hand it offers children security from the teacher dominated classroom and their weak structural position in school, and this is largely centred on the playground, and on the other hand it offers constraints and expectations which bear on, and can be harmful to its members.

So, to summarize, the view of playground cultures stemming from sociological and ethnographical studies is of a different culture to the school, with its own rules, structures and sense of festival, as well as conflict, domination and harassment. But these studies are for the most part not directly about breaktime. One of the first things I was keen to do was to obtain the pupils' own descriptions of breaktime — what they liked and disliked about it, and their own explanations for these feelings. I was also keen to examine whether attitudes changed as pupils moved through school and left behind the more obviously playful, and presumably enjoyable, activities of their younger school days. It also seemed likely that pupils' experiences would vary — with some liking and some disliking its vigour and freedom. In our first interviews with the children in the longitudinal study (see below), when aged 7 years, we found some differences in the educational and breaktime experiences of the four main groups studied — black (in the sense of Afro-Caribbean origin) and white girls and boys (Blatchford, 1997; Tizard et al., 1988). I wanted to see if the pupils' experience of breaktime differed as these children progressed through primary, and into secondary school.

Breaktime Activities

Teachers might be expected to have a close acquaintance with the nature of playground activities, but they can be the first to admit to only a general idea of what goes on. This can be said by primary teachers — who can engage more directly with playground activities, and when playground games can be clearly visible — as well as secondary teachers, who can find breaktime activities more covert and hidden, sometimes deliberately so. Teachers, of course, need a break themselves, and are likely to supervise morning breaktime on a rota, and therefore intermittent, basis. We have seen that lunchtime break is now supervised by ancillary staff rather than teachers.

So what has research shown about the nature of breaktime activities? As with other areas of breaktime experience, there have been two disparate types of research. The first is qualitative research. Perhaps the most compelling, and certainly most often cited, study of outdoor play is the Opies' (1969). Although they were not social scientists ('folklorists' is a preferred term) the detailed catalogue and analysis of games and language, and the portrayal of children's play culture from the pupils' own perspectives, has some of the features of ethnographic enquiry. Their commentary has provided much insight. They argued that control of games has to be with children themselves; adults have no role in this culture. The world of childhood games is passed on from child to child, and is restricted to the primary years, disappearing as children become self conscious about the games.

> Older children may be remarkably poor informants about the games . . . Fourteen year olds . . . from whom we wanted further information about a game they had showed us proudly a year before, have listened to our queries with blank incomprehension. (Opie and Opie, 1969, pp. 5–6)

Historians have indicated that the existence of a separate children's culture has roots deep in history. Writing about childhood in the nineteenth century Walvin (1982) has said:

> . . . they belonged to an independent cultural world of childhood which owed allegiance only incidentally to the world of adults. Furthermore, these games were played by both sexes and all classes. For most children it was the informal games of the street and field which provided the enjoyments of childhood and which, though they did not realize it, linked them to the pastimes of generations past and of others yet unborn. (Walvin, 1982, p. 89)

Though influential, the Opies' research is mostly not based on events in school playgrounds, which they dismiss as a 'restricted environment'. Sluckin's (1981) pioneering study was one of the first studies to concentrate on the school playground. He argued that the playground offers children the opportunity for peer interaction in the context of which many lessons relevant to adult life are learned. More recently, Grudgeon (1993) argued that playground culture is as complex, structured and rule bound as that of the classroom, and that the culture is learned from other children. Like Sluckin she sees the playground as a site of cultural transmission and socialization into adult roles, though she more clearly shows that the culture of the playground, and the socialization processes, are different for boys and girls. For girls, playground games and language contribute to gender identity, and a form of empowerment against boys. Thorne (1993) has provided a thoughtful analysis of the degree to which boys and girls in school can be said to have separate cultures and argues that gender identity needs to be seen not as abstract and fixed but as it arises in school contexts. Gender relations can differ in school and playground.

A few researchers have studied breaktime behaviour from a psychological perspective, most notably Tony Pellegrini (1995) and Mike Boulton (1992), and their studies point to the vigour and involvement shown in the play of primary school children at breaktime. But in general, psychological research has tended to treat breaktime behaviour more as an outcome variable than of interest in its own right.

A more general topic of research of relevance to breaktime, at least at primary level, is research on play. I ought to make it clear that interest in this book is not in the overall role of play in the school curriculum and learning (Moyles, 1989; Smith, 1990) but children's play in the context of informal experiences which take place not in the classroom but usually on the playground. There is a general view, as we have seen, that the quality of play and outside activities, have been in decline, but what does closer study, based on the pupils' perspective, say about the nature of breaktime activities? There has been research on outside play (Smith, 1994) but what about breaktime activities other than play? And how do activities change as children progress from primary to secondary school? At what point, if at all, do games and playful activities decline, and to what extent are these attributable to developmental factors or the influence of school-based factors such as the influence of other children? In the longitudinal study, we were able to interview the same children at points throughout their school careers, and this seemed to me a golden opportunity to hear from those most likely to know. As with other aspects of their experience of breaktime, I was also interested in how activities varied between individuals and between groups, particularly boys and girls.

Friendships, Social Status and Peer Relations

Breaktime more than anything is a social occasion — it is a time when pupils meet, play and talk with each other. To use the jargon, it is prime site for 'peer' interaction. There is a large body of psychological research that makes the point that peer relations and friendships play a significant part in children's development. In an influential book, Youniss (1980) adapted the theories of Piaget and Sullivan to show how peer relations were qualitatively different to adult–child relations. In contrast to adult–child relations, peer relations are characterized by equality, cooperation, reciprocity and mutuality — all of which make a contribution to social development. Youniss did not argue that adult–child and peer relations were better or worse than each other; rather that they served different functions and had different effects. Piaget's theory — not usually seen as stressing the social context of development — has been recently pains-takingly re-evaluated in order to highlight the role he saw for peer interaction in cognitive development (DeVries, 1997). This general position, regarding the value of peer relations for social relations, underlies much social developmental psychology (Hartup, 1992).

As I have said, there have been few psychological studies directly focused on breaktime behaviour, although studies in the areas of friendship develop-ment, social skills and competence, and popularity and rejection are relevant.

Children's Friendships

There has been an impressive body of psychological research on children's friendships (see reviews in Dunn, 1993; Hartup, 1992; Parker and Gottman, 1989), and there are signs that this interest is still growing (Hartup, 1996). It is important not to lose sight of possible negative effects. Savin-Williams and Berndt (1990) point out we should not neglect ways in which friendship groups can support rejection and stereotyping, and how they can lead to insecurity, jealousy and resentment. More recent psychological research on children's friendships has sought to understand ways that friendships can be destructive as well as positive. Hartup (1996), in his recent presidential address to the United States *Society for Research in Child Development*, began his talk by citing a case in which two friends conspired to kill the mother of one of the boys.

But there has also been progress in understanding the positive signific-ance of friendship for young children and the importance of friendship as a support in adjusting to school (Ladd, Kochenderfer and Coleman, 1996; Savin-Williams and Berndt, 1990). Pellegrini (1995), in the US, found that a measure of the extent of sixth grade peer network predicted adjustment to school in seventh grade. Friendships also play a role in social and communicative skills, and school work (Faulkner and Miell, 1993). More generally, Hartup (1996) con-cludes that friends 'provide one another with cognitive and social scaffolding . . . and having friends supports good outcomes across normative transitions' (p. 1). For primary aged children, play has been credited with a central role in friendships (Dunn, 1993). Sociological research, too, has expressed a view in line with psychological research: 'friendship groups form the structural basis of the child's extra-curricular life from a very early stage' (Woods, 1983, p. 96). In a similar fashion, Davies (1982) has highlighted the importance of friendships in school to 10- and 11-year-old Australian pupils.

One of the main functions of breaktime is the opportunities it provides for friends to meet. Friends can be contacted in school and classroom of course, but there are more constraints on their activities and expression. Breaktime offers the sense of 'festival', as Sutton-Smith puts it, which allows friends to talk and play more freely. This is easily taken for granted — even by pupils — but may be important, perhaps especially now that opportunities out of school for self directed activities with friends seem to have declined.

I have used the literature on friendships as a starting point but I wanted to find out more about friendships, and friendship development, particularly in relation to breaktime: what are the characteristics and composition of friendship groups then, and how do friendship groups change after entry to school and in the long term? In what ways are breaktime activities, for example, games and play, related to the experience of friendship? What factors influence friendship choices at breaktime, and what factors are associated with individual differences and group differences in the friendship experiences? If boys and girls engage in different activities at breaktime, what effect does this have on friendship groups?

Popularity and Rejection by Other Children

Psychological research has been able to shed light on individual differences between children in the success of their peer relations. This is seen in studies, allied to those on friendships, concerned with social 'status', competence and skills. There have been considerable advances in understanding factors associated with rejection by, and popularity with, other children. This literature is too vast to be summarized here, and I just mention several findings of relevance to breaktime behaviour. It has been found that children who are popular with their peers tend to engage in more pro-social behaviour, while rejected children engage in more aggressive behaviour (see review by Williams and Gilmour, 1994). Popular children tend to be more intelligent, more socially skilled, less involved in conflicts with peers, and more sociable (Savin-Williams and Berndt, 1990). Ladd and Price (1993) showed that rejected children are less likely to play with friends, have less consistency in play partners, gravitate to younger play partners, and play preferences are less likely to be reciprocated. Parker and Asher (1987) in a widely cited review, have identified the long term consequences of peer difficulties (in terms of peer acceptance, aggressiveness, and shyness/withdrawal) on later personal adjustment (in terms of dropping out of school, criminality and psychopathology). Strongest support was for a link between peer adjustment, in terms of aggressiveness and peer acceptance, and later adjustment in terms of dropping out of school and criminality.

The relevance of these findings is that one of the main settings in school for peer rejection and other social difficulties is breaktime. Children throughout school place a lot of importance on being in a group and not feeling left out, or rejected. Children are likely to express their social feelings most freely on the playground, and any difficulties children have with peers are likely to be most evident there and have most effect. It seems likely that children who are rejected by their peers are likely to be left out of games and other breaktime activities, and have more limited social networks, but these possible associations need closer investigation. Such information will be of value to schools in considering difficulties faced by some pupils at breaktime. Children who experience difficulties with peers may come to hate breaktime and seek to avoid it and stay in. Boulton (1992) found that some children habitually spend large amounts of playground time alone, and that such children can be overlooked by supervisors.

I was interested in finding out more about the relations between the popularity and rejection by peers and experience of breaktime, and breaktime activities. Research has tended, for understandable reasons, to concentrate on children who are rejected by peers, but I wanted to find out more about children who appeared to be popular with peers and how this related to their breaktime activities. At primary level, for example, do popular children play a particular role in the origins and development of playground games?

Conflicts at Breaktime: Teasing and Name Calling, and Fighting

School playgrounds at breaktime are crowded places. At primary level, activities and language tend to be vigorous and playful, and in the form of public display. At secondary level, action can sometimes be vigorous, as in a team game like football, but activities and language can appear more measured, sometimes less visible, and carry more weight. Breaktime can be a time for testing and protecting self esteem in the eyes of others. It is a time when conflicts, verbal banter and teasing can occur, and when conflicts sometimes lead to fights.

As I have already said, there is a recognition, in both the sociological and psychological literature, of a tension in peer relations between positive and negative features, and this is likely to be seen most forcefully at breaktime. As Hartup and Laursen (1993) have argued, there is a long-standing tradition of work in psychology which stresses the importance to interpersonal relationships of both 'affirmations' and 'conflict', and children necessarily have to learn to manage both friendships and conflict. Recent research, in fact, has shown many ways in which conflict has a central and productive role in children's social development (see chapters in Shantz and Hartup, 1992).

Breaktime is a significant arena for social development because it is the main time when everyday relationships and conflicts with peers have to be managed, and where adults tend not to be directly involved. There is more freedom for self directed activity and developing friendships, but also more freedom for falling out and conflict. The ability to deal with and negotiate the difficulties that can arise is likely to be important, as Sluckin (1981) showed, and may be the seedbed of social skills necessary for adult life. Cutting back on breaktime to reduce conflict may paradoxically make it more difficult for children to learn how to *avoid* conflict.

When I first became interested in breaktime, I — like many others — was struck by the aggressive use of language, often involving taunts and insults. Some of this no doubt reflects real conflict, but much seemed to me ritualized, albeit abrasive, and in the spirit of *continuing* an encounter, rather than ending it. Interest in bullying in schools has led people to an awareness of verbal forms of bullying but, just as play and real fighting can be confused, so it is possible more playful insults can be confused with language meant to wound and hurt. There has been a tendency to see certain behaviours such as teasing and name-calling in a fixed way, as signs of negative behaviour such as bullying, when the interpretation and meaning of behaviour to the participants will vary according to a number of factors including the nature of the relationships between pupils. It is likely that the same form of words, for example, can have a very different meaning when the participants are friends as opposed to non friends.

Perhaps the most obvious form of conflict between pupils is fighting, which as probably everyone can testify can occur during school breaktimes, when the constraints of the classroom no longer hold. Yet Evans (1989) has also shown how pupils can manage recess encounters in order to minimize the possibility of fights. Some years ago I collaborated with a headteacher of a large primary school in Ealing, who was interested in improving the school grounds and breaktime. We studied a series of fascinating videotapes of breaktime he had made from the roof of one building. In one sequence we sought to trace the events that led up to a fight on the playground. The poor quality of the tapes may have contributed to the sense of a different world, at a distance from the observer, but it was also clear to us that understanding of the perspectives of the participants would be necessary to make the events meaningful.

These early observations led me to an interest in teasing and name calling, and fighting, at breaktime. I was interested in finding out more about their prevalence, changes with age, but also their significance to pupils and why and in what ways they felt teasing and fighting occurred. There has been concern recently with ways racist taunts and name calling can be used by one group of pupils against other groups. I was interested in taking a broader look at ways teasing, name calling and fights on the playground, were used between groups — particularly different ethnic groups and boys and girls.

Is Breaktime of Value to Pupils?

I have argued that a generally negative view prevails about breaktime in schools. In the national survey we asked school staff directly to say what the value of breaktime is for pupils. It was seen as a time for pupils to relax and have a break from classroom activities, to socialize, and to 'let off steam'. These reasons are relatively low-level ones, and do not suggest a fundamental social value. But there is a danger that they may underestimate the importance of breaktime to pupils.

As we have seen, psychological and sociological research can be taken to show ways in which breaktime can contribute to pupils' social development, though the picture is far from clear, and the evidence is largely not directly based on breaktime experience. At breaktime, children develop and experience friendships and wider social networks, manage conflicts and falling out, and learn important social skills. This is a very different picture to the predominantly negative view we saw earlier in this chapter. More particularly, Pellegrini and Smith (1993) have provided a valuable review of the psychological literature in order to show the role of breaktime in social and cognitive development.

> In both correlational and longitudinal research, children's recess behaviour is related, in theoretically predictable ways, to both cognitive and social outcome measures . . . Thus, it seems to have educational value and certainly has considerable educational relevance. (Pellegrini and Smith, 1993)

So breaktime might be important because, in the school context, peer relations can find expression then, and breaktime activities and interactions can have social and educational value. One aim of this book was to examine the possible social value of breaktime.

This Book

In this book, therefore, I attempt to provide a wide ranging but integrated account of pupils' experience and activities at breaktime. As said in the last chapter, and in line with the review in this chapter, I will be exploring the following areas:

- pupils' views on and experience of breaktime;
- activities at breaktime;
- friendships at breaktime;
- teasing and name calling; and
- fighting at breaktime.

Again, in line with the review in this chapter, each topic will be examined in terms of the following main themes.

Changes over Time

Little is known about long term changes in breaktime activities and games. The longitudinal study provided a unique opportunity to study developments in pupils' breaktime experiences throughout their primary and secondary school careers. What changes in pupils' views, activities, friendships, teasing and name calling, and fighting occur over time — from infant to secondary school stages? How can these changes be explained and what do we learn about the value of breaktime at each age?

Individual Differences

General trends may mask considerable differences between children in their experience of breaktime. Most people probably know of someone who disliked school breaktimes, but, as we shall see, many children do like them. In what ways do pupils vary in their breaktime experiences and activities, and in their popularity and involvement in games? Are some children more likely to be involved in teasing and fighting at breaktime, and what factors might explain these differences?

Group Differences

In the Institute longitudinal study, a main aim was to examine the educational progress of boys and girls, and of pupils from white and black (in the sense of Afro-Caribbean) ethnic groups (Blatchford, 1997; Plewis, 1991; Tizard et al., 1988). There were some indications, even when aged 7 years, that children in the four groups (black girls and boys and white boys and girls) differed in their experience of school and breaktime. More generally there has been interest in differences between boys and girls in their play (Evans, 1989; Smith, 1994; Thorne, 1993), and ethnic group relations and racism (Milner, 1997; Troyna and Hatcher, 1992), which has relevance for breaktime experiences. As breaktime is relatively free of adult structure, it is a main setting in which sex and ethnic group differences can have expression and can be observed. There is a possibility that group differences in play and breaktime activities can play a part in laying the foundations for later differences and difficulties between groups.

In this book I examine sex and ethnic group differences in two ways: first, whether boys and girls, and black and white pupils differed in their breaktime experiences and activities; and, second, to what extent do inter-group relations and within-group affiliations affect breaktime activities, friendships, teasing and fighting?

Social and Situational Factors

The notion that behaviour is affected by situation has been basic to social psychology. One early, and formal, expression was in Lewin's equation $B = f(P,E)$; that is, behaviour is a function of the person and the environment or setting. Another expression was in the 'ecological psychology' of Barker and Wright and Gump, who examined the effects of everyday environmental settings on behaviour. Situational factors can be more important in affecting behaviour than is commonly appreciated (Ross and Nesbett, 1991). In this book, I concentrate on the influence of one main setting within the school day. Pollard (1985) uses the term 'interests at hand' to help show the effect of different school situations, and one big situational difference is likely to be between the world of the classroom and the world of the playground. Despite its distinctive character, the breaktime setting has been overlooked. For example, despite an otherwise wide (and helpful) review of the effects of different contexts on children's friendships and peer relations — including classroom, home, and social and spatial density — Erwin (1993) does not consider school playgrounds.

How are breaktime experiences and activities affected by contextual factors, such as the breaktime and playground setting itself? Are there particular characteristics affecting pupils' experiences? Do more specific social contexts, such as friendship status, sex composition of the group, a crowd at the possibility of a fight, affect behaviour and experiences?

Research Approach

Researching pupils' behaviour and experiences at breaktime can present particular difficulties. As we have seen, breaktime is a separate and very different world to that of the classroom, and researchers as well as teachers can feel like outsiders. It is not always easy to gain access to, or make sense of, children's actions at breaktime. At primary level, adults can struggle to understand the rules of a game, and may find it difficult to distinguish between playful and real fighting, and at secondary level they can feel they are intruding when they come upon a group of pupils talking.

In this book the main source of evidence comes from interviews with pupils. The research approach involved a combination of quantitative and qualitative methods. Structured questions were asked in order that precise comparisons could be made, for example in the prevalence of teasing and fighting across age levels, and associations calculated between measures, for example, in order to see if children who liked breaktime were also more popular with their class mates. But open ended questions were also asked, especially at 16 years, and a more qualitative analysis was therefore possible, in the sense that pupil accounts were examined and sections collated in terms of themes, with verbatim quotes then being extracted for illustrative purposes. The aim was not to test or support a particular theory of peer relations. The overall research strategy was exploratory and inductive in nature, with the main aim being to describe and analyse pupils' answers and accounts, in order to arrive at a better understanding of particular aspects of breaktime experiences, and where possible arrive at more general inferences and implications for schools.

There are alternative forms of data collection. Observation methods, for example, have certain advantages and have been used in studies of playground behaviour (Boulton, 1992; Ladd and Price, 1993; Pellegrini, 1995). Classroom observations of teachers and pupils were collected in the early phases of the research (Blatchford et al., 1987). But observation methods have limitations too. Ultimately research methods are best chosen in relation to the nature of the research questions. In this sense interviews were preferred, for example, as a way of getting full descriptions of activity preferences, that could be checked with pupils, and as a means of probing in order to get a full account of rules, nuances, content and social dynamics of games, attitudes to breaktime events, the nature and causes of friendships, teasing and fighting. This is not to say that other methods are not useful, and indeed in the case study of 8–9-year-olds other forms of peer rating data, for example, on social popularity, and self concept and academic attainment data, were also collected.

Clearly one needs to be cautious about the accuracy and validity of pupils' accounts. The data came from interviews within which children were asked a series of questions by an adult. Pupils may never have discussed this part of the day before, and may be surprised that an adult seems interested in it. Some of the topics, for example, fights and racist name calling, have strict sanctions attached to them, and it is inevitable that this raises questions about the honesty of the information collected. For example, even though the interviews were confidential, to what extent do pupils worry and keep back information, for fear of possible reprimand, should teachers hear about what happened? Conversely, to what extent do they exaggerate their accounts of fighting, and their role in fights, in order to appear more powerful? Sometimes the interviewers could detect exaggeration. This might be revealed in inconsistencies between, for example, a lurid account of a child's involvement in fights, whilst answers to later questions showed a pupil had in fact very little experience of fighting at all, or at least not for many years.

However, the questions we asked were designed to be as specific as possible, both to facilitate accuracy of recall, but also to avoid over-general accounts, coloured by attempts to put themselves in the best light. To take the example of fights again, a main set of questions asked of pupils was on the basis of a description of one fight in which they were involved, or failing that, one that they had witnessed. Information on the complexities of friendship networks and friendship status distinctions would be difficult to obtain without careful questioning of pupils. Overall, the detail of many of the accounts, and the expression of real emotions aroused, for example, by teasing and name calling, suggested to us that much of what we heard was near at least to a pupil's real memory of events.

Institute of Education Longitudinal Study

The main source of data came from a longitudinal study of pupils' progress from 5 to 16 years in inner London schools (see Tizard et al., 1988, for the rationale and research design of study). One part of the research involved interviews with children at 7, 11, and 16 years. Other topics covered included academic self assessment (Blatchford, 1992a; Blatchford, 1997), attitudes to school work and school (Blatchford, 1992b; Blatchford, 1996), but also views on breaktime, teasing, fighting and friendships, which are reported here. This book builds on earlier reports, for example on playground games at 11 years (Blatchford et al., 1990), and teasing and fighting at 11 years (Mooney et al., 1991). Early results from the pupil interviews when aged 7 years can be found in Tizard et al. (1988).

The original longitudinal sample consisted of children entering in September 1982 the reception classes of 33 infant schools in inner London. The schools were in multi-racial, mostly working class and relatively deprived areas. Details of the sample selection are in Blatchford (1992 a and b) and Tizard et al. (1988). In brief, to be included schools had to have two children entering whose parents were of Afro-Caribbean origin and two whose parents were white indigenous. Only children in these two groups were interviewed. At 7 years 133 children (37 white boys, 28 black boys, 38 white girls, and 30 black girls), and at 11 years 175 children (50 white boys, 46 white girls, 38 black boys, and 41 black girls) were interviewed (at 11 years the sample was expanded by the inclusion of 'reserves' who had required characteristics for each of the four ethnic/gender groups, see Blatchford, 1992a). At 16 years, 108 of the 175 pupils contacted at 11 years were re-interviewed (25 white boys, 29 white girls, 23 black boys, 31 black girls).

Interviews at all ages were conducted individually in a quiet place in the pupils' schools. Interviews were semi-structured in the sense that at each age there was a core of pre-piloted questions consistent over time but adapted to changes in age. As described above, some questions were structured and some open ended, with answers categorized after data collection. Both types of data were analysed numerically. But at each age, and especially at 16, there was flexibility in the ordering of questions and in allowing the interview to extend beyond core questions. At 7 and 11 years, answers were noted verbatim by interviewers. At 16 years, interviews were taped and later transcribed. Interviews with 7-year-old pupils were more limited in coverage than the later interviews and did not address directly activities at breaktime.

Case Study of 8–9-Year-Olds on Entry to Junior School

I also conducted a separate interview and field study of the playground experiences and development of games of one class of 32 8–9-year-old pupils over the course of one school year — their first in junior school. Children's games were studied in terms of changes over the school year, processes of initiation and decline of games, and the role of games in friendships and conflicts. The study involved qualitative analysis of semi-structured interviews, in parallel with quantitative analysis of children's views and ratings of each other, self concept and academic data. Pupils were interviewed twice, once at the beginning and once at the end of the school year. Interviews covered the basic core questions but were also adapted to examine, and explore more fully, emerging themes. Interviews were taped, transcribed, and analysed in terms of main themes. Peer rating data, for example, on social popularity, and self concept and academic attainment data, were also collected at the beginning and the end of the school year. Further details about methods used in this study are described in Chapter 5.

A note on statistical analysis: The results reported in this book are based where appropriate on statistical tests on the numerical data. In order not to interrupt the text, and in the interests of the non-technical reader, full details are not given.

Chapter 3

Pupils' Views on Breaktime at 7, 11 and 16 Years

P It's good, it's good, it's great.
I Ok and why do you feel like that?
P Because you've just got freedom, you can do what you like.

We have seen that school breaktimes are a relatively neglected part of the school day and there has been surprisingly little research or policy on it. An important part of an approach to breaktime in schools is to take seriously, and look carefully at, pupils' perspectives. Adults may not know much about pupils' experiences at breaktime, but these experiences are bound to be a major part of pupils' overall experience of school.

Some measure of the importance of breaktime to pupils' school experience comes from their answers to questions concerning the best and worst things about school. In separate analyses of data from the longitudinal study, we found that the pupils at 7, 11 and 16 years were most occupied with two things: work in school and meeting friends. At all ages they thought that the social opportunities for contacting and playing with friends were important, and these are most likely to be experienced at breaktime (Blatchford, 1996).

As we saw in Chapter 1, there is a better understanding now that school improvement needs to take account of pupils' views about school and factors influencing their motivation in school. But academic experiences are only one facet of school life and a parallel account of their views on their social lives in school and experiences during breaktime is also important. It is important, for example, in order to see the extent to which academic and social experiences are independent, complimentary or perhaps in conflict. This latter possibility could occur for example if pupils' experiences at breaktime are negative — they may be worried by disruptive behaviour or teasing — and this could adversely affect their work and relations in class. But it may be that breaktime, from pupils' points of view, has particular purpose and value, which might benefit their overall development, and even school life and relations. The point is that very little is known about pupils' views and experiences during this part of the school day.

There is some agreement that, in developing policies and approaches toward behaviour in school, staff need to be aware of pupil views and reactions, and to encourage pupil involvement in the life of school and its governance.

School breaktimes may have a particular role here, because of pupils' privileged knowledge. Calls for greater pupil involvement are easily made, but experience suggests it may, in the event, be fairly superficial, and partial (Blatchford, 1989). Close analysis of just what pupils feel about school and breaktimes can help inform policy initiatives, and facilitate more meaningful pupil involvement in school.

The longitudinal study provided the basis for a unique analysis of changes in views over the school years, and also of differences between boys and girls and ethnic groups. The interviews showed that pupils often have strong and clear views on breaktime, and their experiences then. In later chapters I look at selected aspects of breaktime activities and social relations, but in this chapter I first examine their more general views on breaktime.

We have seen that breaktime is a feature of all schools and takes up a sizeable part of the school day, but to what extent do pupils feel positive about breaktime? And does this change as they move through school, from infant to junior and on to secondary school? And why do pupils feel the way they do about breaktime? It is often said that girls can be disadvantaged at breaktime, losing out on space to boys' team games, and confined to the edge of the playground (Blatchford, 1989). Given this possibility, do girls and boys differ in how positively they view breaktime?

In the national survey we found that in most primary schools pupils have to go out to the playground, weather permitting, while there is more freedom by the end of secondary school for pupils to stay in the school or even go out of the school at lunchtime. To what extent do pupils like to go out to the playground or school grounds or would they prefer to stay in the school building? Is there a view at primary level that they would like more freedom to come into the school itself during breaktime? Again, I look at changes over the school years and whether there are differences between girls and boys, and ethnic groups.

In Chapter 2 I reviewed research relating to pupils' experience and activities at breaktime, and discussed the possible social benefits and difficulties of breaktime. But what do pupils themselves like and value about breaktime? There has been evaluation of the value of breaktime for social and educational development (Pellegrini and Smith, 1993), but this has not to date been greatly informed by study of pupils' own perspectives. It may well be that the value of breaktime for pupils changes with age; if active games and play decline with age, do pupils become less positive toward breaktime? Again, overall results may hide differences between boys and girls and ethnic groups in what they liked best about breaktime, and group differences were therefore examined.

Conversely, we were interested in what pupils did not like, and how they felt breaktime could be improved. In my earlier study of teachers' views on ways breaktime could be improved (Blatchford, 1989), suggestions included improving supervision, unacceptable behaviour, and the playground itself. But teachers often have only an indirect experience of breaktime and the school grounds, and are not users in the same way as pupils. Earlier analysis of

interviews with children when aged 11 years had indicated the often constructive way pupils could discuss possible improvements at breaktime (Blatchford
et al., 1990), and I was keen to extend this over the whole of their school careers.

How Did They Feel about Breaktime?

A first basic question was asked of the pupils at 7, 11 and 16 years, and pupils'
answers were recorded in the same way. They were asked to indicate which of
the five faces shown in Figure 3.1 best indicated how they felt about breaktime. It can be seen that the first two faces expressed degrees of liking, and the
fourth and fifth faces degrees of disliking, with the third face expressing neither liking nor disliking.

Figure 3.1: Smiley face scale

The question was asked separately for morning break, lunchtime break
and afternoon break (where this occurred), but as the answers were similar we
concentrate here on the longer lunchbreak (as far as possible we asked pupils
not to think of the period of time during lunchbreak when actually eating; this
we addressed separately). Results are shown in Table 3.1.

Table 3.1: Views at 7, 11 and 16 years on dinner breaktime (% of pupils)

	Positive		Neutral	Negative	
	v.pos	pos		neg	v.neg
7 years		69	13	18	
11 years	(58)	84	(26) 9	(4) 6	(2)
16 years	(32)	73	(41) 23	(2) 3	(1)

Notes:
1 v.pos = very positive, pos = positive, neg = negative, v.neg = very negative.
2 Numbers of pupils: 7 yrs = 133, 11 yrs = 175, 16 yrs = 107.
3 At 7 years the five point scale was converted into a three point scale, because of concerns
   about the reliability of finer categorization at this age. In order to compare the figures at
   the three ages, those at 11 and 16 years are presented as three point scales, and also five
   point scales (the numbers in parentheses).

It can be seen that there was a predominantly positive view about the dinner breaktime and this seemed to hold throughout their school lives. Over half of the pupils at 11 years and a third of those at 16 years indicated the most positive face (that is, face number 1). These results can be contrasted with their views in relation to academic subjects. Though the majority of pupils were positive toward maths and reading at both 11 and 16 years, they were less likely to choose the most positive face — for example, only 33 per cent at 11 years, and 16 per cent at 16 years, chose the happiest face.

Other studies paint a similar picture. Price (1994) asked pupils to choose their favourite from a list of subjects and parts of school day. She found that the majority (61 per cent) of year 7 pupils (11–12 years) and year 10 pupils (14–15 years) selected the lunchbreak as their favourite part of the school day, and this was far in excess of attitudes to other subjects and parts of the day at school. Sutton-Smith (1990) reports a similarly positive view.

However, there were some pupils who had worries about breaktime, even when their overall judgment was a positive one. As can be seen in Table 3.1, there were more negative judgments at 7 years, and in this sense pupils were more ambivalent about breaktime than at 11 or 16 years. But there was also a minority of pupils at 11 and 16 years who had a predominantly negative view about breaktime, and who could find the experience of breaktime distressing.

Analysis of sex and ethnic differences showed that at 7 and 11 years there was a clear sex difference in views about dinner breaktime, with boys liking it more than girls, and only girls expressing a negative judgment. There was no difference between boys and girls at 16 years in how much they liked lunch break, and no clear ethnic differences at any age.

Views about Staying In and Going Out at Breaktime

We have so far seen that pupils had a generally positive view about breaktime but we wanted to find out more directly whether they wanted to go out to the playground or school grounds, or whether they would have preferred to stay in the school. The pupils were asked at 11 and 16 years to indicate which of the following statements applied to them — see Table 3.2. They could choose more than one statement, though few did. At both ages most looked forward to going out. They were rather more likely at 16 years to indicate the milder

Table 3.2: *Views about staying in and going out at breaktime (% of pupils)*

	11 years	16 years
Really Look Forward to Going Out	32	29
Look Forward to Going Out	38	51
Prefer to Stay in and Work	31	7
Prefer to Stay in and Do Something Else	17	23

Note: more than one answer possible, so column tables can exceed 100%.

expression of enthusiasm about going out ('look forward to going out'), and were more likely to want the option of staying in at 11 years. These answers are likely to be influenced by the fact that at 11 years going out at breaktime and lunch was compulsory, and therefore being able to stay in, especially on a cold day, might appear a more attractive option, whilst at 16 years they were more likely to be able to come into the school. At 11 years pupils were much more likely to want to stay in, particularly to do work, indicating this might be considered as a particular option with pupils at this age, where this does not already take place.

Analysis of sex and ethnic differences showed that at 11 years there was a clear sex difference, with girls being much more likely to want to stay in, especially to do work, and boys more likely to look forward to going out. There were no clear differences at 16 years in preferences for going out, though more girls said they preferred to stay in school to work and do other things.

Why Pupils Liked and Disliked Breaktime

We asked the pupils what they liked and disliked about breaktime. Pupils were probed with 'anything else?' in order to get up to three answers to these questions.

What Did They Like Best about Breaktime?

The most complete analysis was possible at 11 and 16 years and main answers are given in Table 3.3.

Break from Lessons

At 7 years only four children said that they liked breaktime because it was a break or rest from lessons or school work. But by 11 years this was the main reason given (41 per cent of pupils). This was still seen as important at 16 years when over half the pupils said they liked having a break from work. At 16 years a separate and extra code was created for those answers which stressed liking breaktime because of the freedom it allowed, for example, in getting away from schools, lessons and allowing free time. These answers were a stronger expression of favouring independence of movement than the more basic break-from-work type answers, and were given by a quarter (24 per cent) of pupils at 16 years (see Table 3.3). It therefore appears that the perceived value of breaktime as a break from work has developed strongly by the end of primary school, and that at 16 years, just prior to leaving school,

Table 3.3: What did pupils like best about breaktime

11 years (% of pupils)		16 years (% of pupils)	
Break from Work	41	Break from Work	59
Playing Games	33	Talking to Friend	49
Being with Friends	32	Freedom from Lessons/School	24
Fresh Air	24	Food/Drink	18
Football	16	Playing Games + Football	5
Exercise/Run around	15		
Food/Drink	4		

Note: more than one answer possible, so column totals may exceed 100%.

pupils like breaktime for the opportunities it provides for independence from adults and the rules and control that operate during other parts of the school day.

Talking to Friends

A second reason for liking breaktime was because pupils could talk to friends. At 11 years 32 per cent of pupils gave this answer. It was mentioned more by girls than boys. By 16 years this was even more important to pupils, with a half (49 per cent) giving this answer. Again this was mentioned more by girls than boys. This then is another important function of breaktime, from pupils' points of view, which is apparent at both primary and secondary levels. Again, it is easily underestimated and not easily documented, even when asking pupils themselves to describe their activities. It was not always easy for pupils to talk about something as self evident and everyday as talking to friends, but, especially at 16 years when interviews were more extensive, and answers transcribed, it was possible to see the importance of talk with friends.

P   Dinner time, I love it, number 1.
I   And why is that?
P   No lessons, no teachers, you can come out of a lesson (in) which you've had a really horrible teacher and you just sit on it and you can slag this teacher off as much as you like . . . in a classroom another teacher can say 'I don't wish (you) to insult another member of staff in front of me'. You can sit and insult them away 'cause all your mates are going to feel exactly the same. So you get a chance to relax, you don't have to sit and think 'hang on Miss S. . . . is coming. Is my shirt tucked in?' You can just slob out, and it gives you a chance to have a chat.

We see here how breaktime talk allows the opportunity to speak openly about teachers in a way that would not be possible during lesson time. It also allows pupils to behave in ways to some extent freed from constraints expected in school, for example, with regard to appearance. In short, breaktime provides opportunities within school for a degree of independence.

P My friend will bring in a pack of cards and say 'Do you know how to pay this game? No, right, you're going to learn'. Or there'll be a magazine article . . . and we'll all sit round and discuss. Now and again, more lately now than I did last year, I'll sit and I'll have a discussion with a friend over something that we have opposing views. Like I'm a vegetarian and she thinks that I should eat meat and we'll sit and we'll have this really long conversation over it. It's not just chit-chat over like Take That or East 17. It's more serious. And we'll sit and really get into that.

This is an account of social life familiar to adults. Because of its familiarity its value is easily taken for granted, but important qualities of social life, including the value of purposeful, if non-lesson, talk, are being developed in this girl's account of her final year at school.

Playing Games

The third main reason for liking breaktime during the primary years was the opportunities it gave for playing games. At 7 years pupils liked playtime because it gave them the opportunity to run around and play games (Tizard et al., 1988). As seen in Table 3.3, by 11 years a third of pupils gave this answer, and 16 per cent mentioned football in particular, boys more than girls.

But there was a main difference by the time pupils reached 16 years. In line with pupils' activities at breaktime (see Chapter 4), very few said they liked breaktime because of games they could play (only 5 per cent — and this included football, which, because it was mentioned far less than at 11 years, was not recorded as a separate category). We will look more closely in the next chapter at this change in breaktime activities between primary and secondary years.

Other Reasons for Liking Breaktime

At 16 years, 18 per cent said they liked breaktime because it allowed them to consume food and drink (girls more than boys). This was not mentioned so much during the primary stage, though this could be partly explained by the clearer separation between the eating and non-eating parts of lunchtime break. Other reasons given at 16 years, but mentioned less often (and not shown in Table 3.3) included being able to do homework, and being able to smoke. Smoking as a breaktime activity was discussed in several interviews, and it was interesting for the matter-of-fact way it was discussed, and how this contrasted with a view of smoking in school as in some way a show of defiance. For some children smoking was a fact of life, rather than an act of rebellion.

So to summarize main reasons for liking breaktime: it provided opportunities during the primary years:

- to have a break from school work;
- to have fun and relax;

- to play games; and (later, during secondary school)
- to develop independence from school and teachers.

Throughout the school years, breaktime was seen to provide opportunities for social contact with friends.

What Did They Not Like about Breaktime?

The main reasons pupils did not like breaktime were similar throughout their school careers. The main things cited at 7 years were fear of physical or verbal aggression from other children — *'You get beaten up for nothing', 'They kick and punch and throw stones'*; dislike of the cold; and having no one to play with (Tizard et al., 1988). Main reasons given at 11 and 16 years are shown in Table 3.4.

Table 3.4: What did pupils not like about breaktime

11 years (% of pupils)		16 years (% of pupils)	
Weather	26	Too Short	32
Disruptive Behaviour	21	Nothing Disliked	32
Nothing Disliked	17	Want More Freedom	14
Having Nothing to Do	15	Nothing to Do	13
Frustrations Arising out of Games/Activities	12	Weather	11

Note: more than one answer possible, so column totals can exceed 100%.

The main things that pupils did not like at 11 years were:

- the weather, usually the cold and wet, though sometimes the heat (girls more than boys);
- disruptive behaviour, bullying, fighting, being beaten up, and people starting trouble;
- having nothing to do and no-one to play with (girls more than boys); and
- frustrations arising out of games, for example trying to play football in a confined space, being knocked over, being hit by a football, losing balls over fences or when other children messed about or cheated during games.

Some (17 per cent) said there was nothing they did not like about breaktime.

By 16 years, pupils still mentioned the weather, and having nothing to do or wanting more variety of activities. The theme of boredom during break came up a lot at 16 years. We hear it expressed in the following extracts:

> **P** Sometimes we just walk about, well it's quite a boring area as well. There's not really anything to do at lunch-time except walk about or stand about doing nothing.

I Okay and would you ever do any sort of sports?
P They don't really have any sports at lunch-time to do.
I So do most people really just hang around waiting for break to be over?
P Yeah.

P Breaktime is a bit boring 'cause all you do is either sit on the staircases or go in the library but the library gets full up . . . you walk around but you're walking around the same place every time and it gets boring, 'cause there's nothing really to do.

At first read these transcripts indicate a worrying lack of purpose, but we need to be careful about too hastily assuming this time has no value to pupils. One of the pupils just cited was then asked by the interviewer:

I Ok. On the faces scale again, how would you say you feel about dinner-time at school?
P It's good, it's good, it's great.
I Ok and why do you feel like that?
P Because you've just got freedom, you can do what you like.

From an adult's perspective it is easy to see boredom and social value as contradictory, but from a pupil's perspective both can be connected in a developing need for independence from adults and school, and a growing sense of their own freedom of action. In a sense they valued the freedom to be bored.

Pupils at 16 years also did not like breaktime because they wanted more freedom, for example, to go out of school or be allowed into school (14 per cent). They could be annoyed at rules prohibiting them access to the school buildings. And, conversely, they could resent being forced to stay in school, especially if this resulted from the misdemeanours of other pupils:

P We have to stay in school now, 'cause they say . . . that we was naughty or something. So you have to stay in school . . . I don't really think that people were doing anything bad when (we) was let out.
I Was it particular people who were thought to be doing it?
P Yeah, and going to flats, estates over there. And just making noise or something. And they didn't like it. But I think people are quite angry about the people who did it, but I suppose if it's true in a way then they're right in keeping us in, but I think they should give us a chance in a few things. I think it's a bit unfair.

P We're not allowed to go out any more . . . the year's gone a bit downhill. They don't think we're acting or behaving properly. They said that people were stealing, spitting on people in the street, it's disgusting. Just general things like behaving really badly on the street and not giving the school a good reputation.
I And do you feel cross then that you're all being punished?
P . . . The school says that you're responsible for your own actions, yet it's punishing people for other people's actions, so that is a bit bad.

So this reason is the same as that given for liking breaktime, that is, wanting the opportunity to get away from perceived restrictions of school and teachers. But here the desire is thwarted by school rules designed to keep pupils in the school.

A few expressed dislike of the food provided and the organization of dinner time.

P The reason I don't have lunch (in school) is that they serve chips every day without fail and you get really bored with chips, you feel like, I don't want to see another chip in my whole life.

P It's really disgusting, there's nowhere to sit at all. It's just nasty. They have just got it in a stupid way where its quicker, but there is nowhere to sit.

P I have to say it's disgusting. I don't have the dinner.

I So what would you normally do, would you eat at lunch-time?

P Just go out at and get some chips or something.

P They could organize it a bit better . . . it's like a stampede of cattle trying to get it, at once. They don't organize it right.

Other answers at 16 years showed a positive view about breaktime (see Table 3.4). One in three (32 per cent) said there was nothing they did not like about breaktime. And, in a similar way, the thing most disliked about breaktime at 16 years was that it was too short. In the national survey on breaktimes we did in fact find that the lunch break was shorter at secondary than at the primary stage, and so pupils may be expressing their disapproval of this trend.

So constant themes throughout their school careers for not liking breaktime are not liking the cold, not knowing what to do or who to be with, and not liking aggression expressed then. By 16 years there is if anything less dissatisfaction with breaktime, at least in terms of those who said there was nothing they did not like about it. The main changes between 11 and 16 years are the increased concern with freedom of movement, either to go out of the school site, or to come into the school buildings, and a view that breaktime is not long enough. Breaktime faces pupils with a number of difficulties, for example, concerning what is allowable, or where in the school grounds they are allowed to go.

Pupils' Views about School Grounds and School Rules Concerning Breaktime

Examination of the interview transcripts of 16-year-olds identified several themes. First, there seemed a general dissatisfaction with the outside environment available at breaktime. For many it seemed that breaktime was of interest despite, rather than because of, the environment provided. The school grounds used at breaktime, especially at secondary level, seem to be rarely considered by staff. It appears to be assumed that pupils will just get on in their own way. It is argued in this book that there are important forms of independence that are being developed at breaktime in school, and that these can come from pupils determining their own activities. But boredom arising out of an impoverished environment, and an accompanying sense of not knowing how to spend one's time, is surely not in the interests of pupil or school.

Second, there was greater disconnection, at secondary level, between activity and location. Pupils often appeared to wander from one place to another with little firm connection between activity and environment. They sometimes seemed not to have anywhere definite to go, and sometimes did not like spaces provided for them. In comparison to primary school, there was a less secure ownership of outside space.

> I   (Do you) come back into the school during lunch-time break?
> P   Oh no, there's a basement where people can sit but you're not meant to be in the building.
> I   So you can go in the basement, and what's in the basement?
> P   It's just a big area with benches, it's dark, it's horrible.
> I   So it sounds like you don't like going in there very much?
> P   No, it's noisy as well.
> I   And what do they do when they're in the basement?
> P   Just shout and run around.

During the primary years their interest in games and active pursuits attaches activity to environment. But at 16 years the predominately social activities are not mediated through games, as we shall see in the next chapter, but carried on despite the lack of provision. Staff seemed to have little notion of how older secondary spent their breaktime, as long as they kept out of trouble. It is difficult to escape the conclusion that more consideration could be given at secondary level to pupils' use of outside space.

Third, school rules concerning where to go at breaktime, and about entering the school buildings and leaving school at lunchtime could appear unclear and arbitrary to pupils. Rules seemed to be broken.

> P   They said people couldn't go to the cafe but people go there anyway ... we're not meant to be in the road but we go there anyway.

Here the school rule and the authority of supervisory staff is openly flouted.

> I   Do you ever go outside of the school grounds?
> P   Yeah.
> I   And where do people go?
> P   They normally go to the shops, some people don't like the school dinners so they go to the shops, they climb over the fence ...
> I   They're not actually supposed to go out are they?
> P   No.
> I   So the teachers don't know about it?
> P   No if you've got a home pass then you can go.
> I   OK and do the teachers not bother too much about it?
> P   Well the dinner ladies do.

I   Yes, what outside?

P   At the gates.

I   So people have to go some other way to get out do they, so they jump over walls?

P   Yeah but some people just walk straight through — they tell them 'stop' but they just ignore them.

I   If Mr K. . . . was standing on the door you wouldn't walk straight past him?

P   He can get them suspended but the dinner ladies can't.

P   We didn't used to have to get a letter . . . there didn't used to be a teacher at the back gate and we'd just walk out and go to the chip shop and all that . . . but now there's a caretaker at the back gate so I had to get a letter signed in my diary saying that I could go out. So I got that done right and now the teacher won't sign it, so I just leave before he gets there.

In these and other accounts the effort expended in leaving school did not seem to be matched by the interest of experiences once outside. Their own descriptions showed that they seemed largely to walk to the shops, chat, muck about, and walk back to school again. But the comments made above with regard to the seemingly boring nature of breaktime activities at 16 years are relevant here. For the next boy, the experience of leaving school, albeit illicitly, is accompanied by a positive view about the break.

P   I sneak out of school, go to a chip shop and play football on the field.

I   And do you ever get caught?

P   No, I've never got caught . . . I know all the short cuts out the school. How to avoid every teacher. I've had sort of teachers chase after me.

I   And then once you've had your chips you come back and play football here.

P   No. I play football just outside in the field.

I   And is that with other pupils from here?

P   Yeah.

I   So you all kind of sneak out and do the same thing.

P   We sort of meet up in a group with other people. We play with some 18-year-olds.

I   Okay. And in relation to the scale, how do you feel about dinner time then?

P   One!

I   So it's quite an enjoyable time? And why do you feel so positively about it?

P   I like playing football. I like being with friends. I don't like work that much . . . It's sort of like free period.

What Would They Like to Do at Breaktime That They Do Not?

This question was only asked at 16 years. The main response was that they would like more activities to be provided, for example, clubs, TV, video, magazines, organized activities (41 per cent of pupils) and, in line with results just presented, 18 per cent of pupils wanted more freedom to go out of school or stay in the school buildings more. A third of pupils (34 per cent) said that breaktime was fine as it was, and there was nothing they wanted to do that they did not.

How Did They Think Breaktime Could Be Improved?

This question was asked at 11 and 16 years. At 11 years the most frequently mentioned improvement (35 per cent of pupils) was for permanent equipment to be installed. Examples given were a swing, adventure playground, scramble nets and climbing frames. Another 18 per cent wanted portable equipment, like bats and balls, to take out. Other suggested improvements at 11 years were changes to playground space, for instance, separate playgrounds for boys and girls, young and old, and infants and juniors, or separate areas for football, races or skateboarding (25 per cent); alterations to the playground surface, for example, better or more game markings, like hopscotch and stepping patterns, or proper games pitches (10 per cent). Other suggestions were 'green' additions such as the development of a garden, wildlife area, planting of flowers (6 per cent), structural alterations to the playground such as shelters, sheds, walls to throw things against, and higher fences (6 per cent). Some (13 per cent) wanted to see more control of bad behaviour such as suspending bullies, stopping fights, not allowing people to play in the toilets, banning ex-pupils from school premises, and stopping rudeness to adults. And 12 per cent wanted to see more freedom of behaviour allowed, for example, being allowed to listen to personal stereos, taking out sweets, being allowed to play banned games, and bringing in toys and equipment. This last answer indicates that 11-year-olds also attached value to having the freedom at breaktime to pursue their own activities, and resented school rules that stopped them. Given the difficulties reported in schools regarding the dominant place of football (see next chapter and Blatchford et al., 1990), it was interesting to note that there was not a general desire, either of girls or boys, to see football curtailed.

The major shift by 16 years was that pupils did not think of improvements to breaktime in terms of playground equipment or play space, or even, more generally, in terms of playground use. The most common response (36 per cent) was for more activities to be provided and more things to do, and these were in-school activities such as clubs, TV, videos, magazines. In line with other comments already discussed, another 14 per cent thought breaktime would be improved by them being allowed more freedom, for example, being able to go out of school, perhaps to the shops, or, conversely, being allowed to stay in school. Ten pupils (9 per cent) would have liked the provision of a place in school, such as a year, common or leisure room, where they could go at breaktime.

These responses indicate a comparative lack of interest amongst secondary aged pupils in the school grounds as a factor in improving breaktime, and a greater interest in the provision of activities and freedom of movement. As we have seen, the impression gained was that pupils' activities at breaktime were rather marginalized from school life, and pupils were uncertain about what to do and what parts of the school grounds to inhabit. It seems unfortunate that pupils at 16 years also appear resigned to the way breaktime is in their schools, even given some negative comments. Given the opportunity, pupils could be constructive in their suggestions, though it was our impression that primary aged pupils took the question more seriously. For some 16-year-olds, the taken-for-granted nature of breaktime, as well as its dissociation from school and classroom life, seemed to make reflection on changes to breaktime as a whole difficult.

Conclusion

In this chapter we have examined pupils' views on breaktime in schools. It was clear that on the whole pupils, throughout their school careers, liked breaktime, particularly the longer lunchbreak. They liked having a break from work and they liked the opportunity to socialize with their friends. Breaktime is of value to pupils throughout school, though the nature of the value changes from primary to secondary. At primary level breaktime provided the opportunity for playing games, while by the end of secondary school they liked breaktime because of the opportunities it provided for independence from adults. Their accounts showed how valuable breaktime and lunchtime could be for talking openly about school and teachers in a way that would not be possible in lesson time, and for allowing them to behave in ways freed from the constraints expected in school.

On the other hand, there were some pupils who had worries about breaktime, even when the overall judgment was a positive one, and there were a minority of pupils who had a predominantly negative view about breaktime, and who could find the experience distressing. The main reasons for not liking breaktime were the cold, not knowing what to do, and fear of physical or verbal aggression from other children. We have also in this chapter examined the dissatisfaction some pupils felt at 16 years with the school grounds, and the way that breaktime at this age, and the environments in which pupils find themselves, appears marginalized. Older pupils at breaktime, in contrast to primary aged pupils, seemed to have little ownership of space.

There were differences between boys and girls in their views about breaktime. On average, girls were less positive about breaktime and had worries, for example, about the cold and having nothing to do. Of the minority of pupils at 11 years who did not like the dinner break all were girls. Girls were also more likely at 11 and 16 years to want to come into the school buildings.

Implications for Schools

Here, and at the end of subsequent chapters, I will draw out some implications for schools, arising from particular aspects of breaktime, discussed in each chapter. In the last chapter I will then pull main points together, and suggest features of an approach to breaktime for schools.

A consideration of pupils' views on breaktime has implications for schools, in that any proposed changes to breaktime, such as shortening it, altering its organization, or altering the playground space, would need to take account of the positive vote of confidence by pupils. We should not assume that because some problems can arise at breaktime, pupils have given us a mandate to change it. In particular, given current pressures to cut back on breaktime, results presented in this chapter show that there is no mandate to shorten or abolish breaktime.

It seems appropriate to conclude that staff in schools should consider the breaktime experiences of pupils and consider the environments used at breaktime. There are a number of difficult issues and dilemmas when considering school approaches to pupils' non curricular time in school, and these are taken up in the last chapter. Here, I draw out a few basic points, that arise out of pupils' perceptions reported in this chapter.

As described in Chapter 1, breaktime in schools changed during the 1980s, because of teachers' industrial action. One consequence was the decline in teachers' involvement at lunchtime; indeed, teachers now have a legal right to take a lunchbreak. As a result, clubs and extra curricular activities at lunchtime declined and supervision arrangements during lunchtime, at primary level in particular, changed in a substantial way. As we found in the national survey, supervision is now provided, in large part, not by teachers but by ancillary staff. At primary level, the activities of pupils, which we examine in the next two chapters, are more vigorous and playful and are more obviously appropriate to the playground environment provided. Staff need to consider approaches in relation to this interest of pupils. Possible improvements, for example, to the playground environment, are discussed in Blatchford (1989) and Blatchford et al. (1990). Pupils themselves, when aged 11 years, as we have seen in this chapter, had many constructive solutions.

By secondary level the less active and seemingly less purposeful pursuits highlighted the absence of organized activities. Schools seemed to vary greatly in the degree to which clubs and activities were provided (Blatchford and Sumpner, 1996). Pupils' suggestions for improving breaktime at 16 years mostly concerned the provision of activities, and this is certainly something that needs to be given more attention. However, this chapter (and those to follow) make the point that we should be careful not to underestimate the social value of even the most desultory activities, and that a response in terms of simply reducing or even abolishing breaktime may not be in the best interests of pupils or schools.

We have in this chapter only scratched the surface of life at breaktime. In the following chapters we look more closely at social life then and, in the next two chapters, we look at activities at breaktime.

Chapter 4

Changes in Breaktime Activities from 7 to 16 Years

Well when I was in primary school (it was) play time, it seemed like it was always time to play. It would be morning play, lunch play, last play, I just felt like I was playing all the time. But now you don't really get much time to regain your youth, you have to be an adult all the time, even when you're in school. You have to think rationally about everything, you don't get time to mess about.

They're not half as fun. When you were a little child you used to play games and go outside and you were wild, sort of thing, you know, go and play games like 'had' or skipping ropes or something — fun. You used to look forward to them and you never used to know the time, you just went in when the whistle went, you didn't know when it was or anything like that.

Having looked in the last chapter at pupils' views about breaktime, in the next two chapters I examine activities that take place. In the next chapter I look at changes over one school year in the playground games of one class of 8–9-year-olds. But in this chapter I provide a broader picture of changes in playground activities from 7 to 16 years.

Background

In Chapters 1 and 2, negative and positive views about breaktime behaviour were described. In some accounts, behaviour is seen as a problem, outside activities are seen to be low level and needlessly aggressive, and traditional games have declined, as has the quality of play more generally. We also saw that the duration of breaktime in some schools had been reduced as schools concentrated on the demands of the National Curriculum, and in response to worries about the behaviour of some pupils. In contrast, others have stressed positive aspects, identifying the subtle social skills that can be shown, and the social and educational benefits that may follow. One reason I decided to look closely at pupil breaktime activities was to examine the validity of these views.

Sutton-Smith (1982) has argued that much research and comment on peer relations has been in terms of identifying its distinctive socializing function. One assumption is that life on the playground can help in the acquisition of many subtle social skills essential to later life (Sluckin, 1981). This notion of recess play as preparation for adulthood has been called a 'socialization model' (Pellegrini, 1995). In an interesting paper, Sutton-Smith (1982) cautions against an extreme version of this view because of the way it can detract from a recognition of the value of interaction to pupils here and now. 'An approach to peer groups only in terms of their "socialisation" value is . . . mistaking an occasional consequence . . . for the central meaning of the activity. Peer interaction is not a preparation for life. It is life itself' (1982, p. 75). Sutton-Smith goes on to argue that 'the most important thing to know about peer culture is what is going on there. That is, that we might learn more of the structure and more of the function if we first studied *what the action is*. And perhaps if we begin with the performances that are central to children, our ideas of structure and function might also change considerably' (p. 68).

There has been a tendency to look at age developments in children's play in a general way, usually in terms of stages of cognitive development. Piagetian theory has been influential in seeing a transition with age from symbolic play to games with rules. But there are also important questions concerning the interplay of cognitive development and more specific environmental factors such as the playground setting. As Evans has said, '. . . too often . . . we have confined ourselves to the cognitive dimension and overlooked the importance of the social context in which play occurs' (1989, p. 20).

The purpose of this chapter is to provide a description of breaktime activities over the school years — in Sutton-Smith's term to describe 'what the action is' — from primary through to secondary school. The Institute of Education longitudinal study provided what may be a unique opportunity to gain insights into children's breaktime activities and social lives over the whole of their schooling.

So in this chapter I concentrate on pupils' activities at breaktime, and the particular focus is on change in activities over time from primary to secondary. This is approached in three ways.

1   Changes with age in breaktime activities
    I was interested in basic information on preferred activities at each age (7, 11 and 16 years) — on how these change and on gender and ethnic differences. Informal observation had suggested a major change in activities from primary to secondary school and I wished to chart the nature of the change and whether changes had taken place at or after transfer to secondary school.

2   Pupils' descriptions of changes in their breaktime activities
    I was also interested in hearing from pupils themselves, when aged 16 years, and therefore in their last year of compulsory schooling, their views on how breaktime activities had changed.

3   Pupil explanations for changes in breaktime activities
    I analyse pupils' own explanations at 16 years for why activities at breaktime had changed.

Breaktime Locations

Before we look at breaktime activities, I want to look briefly at results showing the locations of breaktime activities. During the primary years children were expected, weather permitting, to spend the morning and afternoon breaks (where the latter existed), and the time at lunchtime when not eating, outside on the playground. This impression from the interviews was supported by the national survey. The main location for breaktime in primary schools is therefore the playground itself.

But by 16 years pupils were less likely to have to stay outside. The national survey showed that in most secondary schools pupils were allowed to come into the school, though they differed in terms of whether access was allowed to most or only particular areas. Moreover, staff in only a quarter of schools (27 per cent) reported that pupils were not allowed off school site. In another quarter of schools (25 per cent), pupils were allowed off site, though there was a tendency for this to apply to the older pupils in school. In nearly a half of secondary schools, pupils were allowed off site only with parents' permission. This figure is difficult to interpret because it is unclear how many parents requested permission for their children to leave school at lunchtime, and how thoroughly schools controlled the numbers of pupils who left the school site. These results indicate that by 16 years there was a greater variety in possible locations during breaktime.

In the national survey we tried to get more precise information on just where, within the school buildings, pupils were allowed to go during break. At primary level the most common locations in school were classrooms, and also the library and the hall. As would be expected, given the increased access to school during breaktime at secondary level, there were more types of locations available then to pupils. The most popular locations in school used at breaktime (other than the canteen used for eating lunch and lunchtime) were the library, the canteen or tuck shop, computer or IT rooms, classrooms and the corridors.

I turn now to the pupil interviews at 16 years, which provided an alternative source of information about breaktime locations. At the same time as the coding of activities at breaktime, we also coded up to three locations within which activities took place. The question asked of pupils was: 'What do you do and where do you go at dinner break, when you are not eating in school?' We obtained a long list of locations — library, playground, canteen, park, street and so on. Locations could be classified into three main types: out of school, in school, and in the school grounds. The most common location for pupils was within the school building, for example, in the classroom, common room, library, or canteen (46 per cent of mentions). The other two locations — being out of school and being in the school grounds — were about equal in frequency (26 per cent and 28 per cent of mentions respectively).

As far as ethnic and sex differences are concerned, though numbers of pupils in groups were low, there was some indication that girls at 16 years were more likely to use the classrooms and the library. The clearest result was for boys to be more likely to go outside and use the school grounds during the morning and lunchtime breaks. Six girls, but only one boy, went home for dinner. Price (1994) found that the majority of the older secondary girls in her study went home during lunchbreak, and appeared to have opted out of school breaktime altogether. She also found, using a methodology involving systematic counts of pupils in chosen locations, that more boys than girls used outside areas, and dominated the larger areas of the playground.

Changes with Age in Breaktime Activities

In this section I only give data on activities during the dinner time break. Data on the morning breaktime gave a similar picture. Questions were also asked about activities at breaktime on the day of, or immediately prior to, the interview, and results were again broadly similar.

7 Years

Data from the longitudinal study at 7 years on activities were limited. The pupils clearly liked playtime and the main reasons were because of the opportunity to run around and play games (Tizard et al., 1988).

11 Years

At 11 years, pupils' first three answers were coded and classified using a scheme based on the work of the Opies (1969) and adapted by Blatchford et al. (1990). Full results on prevalences and gender differences of activities can be found in Table 4.1. In order to increase sample sizes, results for the full available sample at each age were used. (This will therefore include the smaller longitudinal sample, that is, children interviewed on all three occasions.)

Breaktime activities were dominated by active games. The most popular activities were ball games and chasing games. The most popular game of all was football (soccer) played by 60 per cent of children, boys more than girls (84 per cent of boys, 36 per cent of girls). Other ball games such as netball, basketball, cricket were played by a third of children. Chasing games were defined in the same way as the Opies, that is, games in which a player tries to touch others who are running freely in a prescribed area. The most common chasing game by far was the basic game of 'it', 'had' or 'he' (46 per cent of children). Seeking games (17 per cent), catching games (16 per cent), racing games (12 per cent) and skipping games (9 per cent with a rope, 6 per cent with elastic) were also noted. In response to a separate question concerning what else they did at breaktime, talking to friends (48 per cent), walking and hanging around (32 per cent) and just sitting down (28 per cent) were the most commonly cited activities.

Table 4.1: What games children say they play in the playground: 11-year-olds

	Boys %	Girls %	N	%
Chasing Games: Basic	46	47	80	46
• Back to base	3	8	10	6
• Touch with ball	11	1	11	6
• Chased at disadvantage	3	9	11	6
• Chased have immunity	1	5	5	3
• Chaser at disadvantage	1	2	3	2
• Caught join chaser	9	5	12	7
• Touch has noxious effect	5	6	9	5
Catching Games	19	12	27	16
Seeking Games	8	27	30	17
Racing Games	10	13	20	12
Daring Games	0	1	1	1
Guessing Games	0	2	2	1
Pretending Games	2	9	10	6
Ball Games: Football	84	36	105	60
• Other ball games	36	27	55	32
• Ball games using wall	10	7	15	9
Skipping Games:				
• With rope	5	13	15	9
• With elastic	0	13	11	6
Games Using Playground Markings	2	5	6	3
Marbles	0	0	0	0
Ring and Clapping Games and Rhymes	0	4	3	2
Toy and Pretend Fights	2	0	2	1
Others	6	7	11	6

There were differences between boys and girls at 11 years. As can be seen in Table 4.1, girls were more likely than boys to play seeking games, pretending games, and skipping games. Daring games, guessing games, pretending games, games using playground markings, ring games, rhymes and clapping games and games using marbles or other materials were rarely or never mentioned, and only by girls. Boys seemed involved but less varied in their play than girls. Football dominated their playground activities.

16 Years

At 16 years, different activities were described by the pupils and therefore different codes sometimes had to be used. Comparisons with 11-year-old data are therefore not always possible. Full data on prevalences of activities and gender differences are reported in Table 4.2. Results on activities that could be compared at 11 and 16 years are summarized in Table 4.3.

The main change is that games apart from football have all but disappeared; football is now played by only 26 per cent of pupils, and only one pupil mentioned a chasing game. As we have seen, at 11 years other ball games were mentioned by a third of pupils; at 16 years, the proportion playing netball, basket ball, patball etc was down to 11 per cent. So there are far more active games at 11 years.

Table 4.2: *Lunchtime activities: 16-year-olds*

	Boys %	Girls %	N	%
Talk to Friends/Socializing	60	82	78	72
Messing about	13	15	15	14
Smoking	4	5	5	5
Eating/Queuing for Food	2	0	1	2
Working	17	37	30	28
Reading	6	8	8	7
Football	48	8	28	26
Other Ball Sports	15	8	12	11
Cards/chess	25	15	21	20
Chasing/Catching Games	2	0	1	1
Prefect Duty	2	3	3	3
Listening to Music	0	15	9	8
Debates/discussion	0	8	5	5
Talk to Teachers	2	3	3	2
Playing Pool/Snooker/Fruit Machines	10	2	6	6
Shopping	2	0	1	1
TV	0	3	2	2
Other	0	3	4	4

Table 4.3: *Activities reported by pupils at 11 and 16 years (% of pupils)*

	11 Years			16 Years		
	Boy	**Girl**	**Total**	**Boy**	**Girl**	**Total**
Football	84	36	60	48	8	26
Other Ball Games	36	27	32	15	8	11
Basic Chasing Games*	46	47	46	2	0	1
Catching Games*	19	12	16			
Talking to Friends**	48	48	48	60	82	72
Walking Socializing**	23	39	32			
Cards/Chess	1	0	1	23	15	20
Working	0	0	0	17	17	28

Notes:
* These were combined in one code at 16 years, but were separate codes at 11 years and could not be added because they could be the same pupils.
** as above.

By 16 years, the most popular activity is talking to friends, hanging around and socializing (72 per cent of pupils).[1] Another main change by 16 years is the extent of working at lunchtime (28 per cent of pupils). None of the 11 years reported this, and in any case they would have been much less likely to have been allowed into the school.

As at 11 years, there was a significant difference between boys and girls in reported breaktime activities. As can be seen in Table 4.2, boys were more likely to report playing football, other ball games, and cards and chess. Girls were more likely to talk to friends and socialize, do school work, and listen to music. In answer to a separate question, boys at 16 years were more likely than girls to say they played games.

Pupils' Descriptions of Changes in Their Breaktime Activities

We were interested in getting from pupils themselves information on what changes they felt had taken place to breaktime activities, and why. Pupils at 16 years were asked how they viewed the change from primary to secondary breaks, and which they preferred. To the question, 'looking back, how are breaktimes different now to when you were at primary school?', the most common answer was that they played more games at primary level (46 per cent of pupils). They also said that they were more active and energetic at primary school (21 per cent), and had more fun there (21 per cent). About a quarter (28 per cent) also said that breaktimes at primary were longer. There was a perception held by around a third (32 per cent) of pupils that there was more freedom of movement at secondary school, for example, to go out of the school, though still not enough for some. Others also identified differences in organization between primary and secondary, so that, for example, there was more choice of food at secondary school, and they did not all have to sit together (21 per cent of pupils). One in 10 pupils also felt that breaktime at secondary was more grown up and less childlike than at primary.

Given these contradictions in pupils' views which did they prefer? Or rather, which did they prefer when asked at 16 years? It might appear from their answers that they would favour primary playtime, but in fact rather more favoured secondary school breaktimes (50 v 32 per cent). In addition, 17 per cent said they liked both or that it was impossible to compare. Price (1994), also found that secondary pupils preferred secondary to primary breaktimes, despite worries about aggressive behaviour at secondary level. It is possible that, despite fond memories of the primary years, there is a general tendency for present social concerns and experiences to dominate, and seem more important than the past.

Given the perception of change from primary to secondary in breaktime activities, how sudden was this change? Is the transition to secondary enough to alter the more active style of playing seen at primary school? Or is there some continuity from primary to the early years of secondary school? To pursue this we then asked pupils if the things they did at breaktime had changed over the time they had been at secondary school, that is, from 11 to 16 years. Most (73 per cent) said they had, and most commonly this was thought to be because they played more games, for example, football, in earlier years at secondary school. They also said they acted more grown-up now at 16, and had more grown-up interests. An allied response was that they had more freedom now, for example, to go out of school.

Girls more than boys said that a difference between primary and secondary was that more games were played at primary school, and that they were more active, and had more fun then. This seems to reflect an important shift in girls' breaktime culture. During primary school playtimes, games and play figured largely, but by the end of secondary school they played no games at all. Boys on the other hand to some extent keep up an involvement in active pursuits and games through football.

A look in more detail at themes arising out of examination of the interview transcripts helps illustrate answers arising from the quantitative analysis.

A main aspect of pupils' accounts was the sense that primary playtimes were *more fun, enjoyable and carefree,* for example, as in the second quote given at the beginning of this chapter. Also:

> **P** (At) Primary school everything was so exciting, everything was easier. You didn't have to think about . . . even now in your breaks you think about the class what you've just done or what you've got next, whereas in primary you didn't have nothing to worry about . . . you get out to break, you can forget about the work . . . I enjoyed that time at primary school, I suppose I miss the playtimes 'cause there was a big playground and everyone could run around and everything seemed bigger then.

At some point in their school lives the 'fun' goes out of play activities. The following extract describes how play activities stopped after a short time in secondary school. One can sense the distance from previously enjoyed activities.

> **P** Yeah we used to play football or, what's it called — 'Bulldog' and something else, what's this thing where you run forward and run back again. Basically we thought (it) was fun but not any more . . . it was just like one person in the middle and fifty of you there and you have to run by without getting touched and we thought this was fun [laughs] but not any more, that soon stopped.

A main reason why fun and excitement is seen to go out of breaktime activities is the decline in playground games and activities. As activities change so does the sense of enjoyment that pupils find in activities decline. So changes in activity are connected (probably in mutually reinforcing ways) with changes in felt enjoyment and excitement.

> **P** They're not so much fun.
> **I** Why is that?
> **P** 'Cause at breaktime in primary school the playground was packed with all people your own age having fun and playing hop-scotch or whatever. And now that you're older, you're not into all those sorts of things so, it's not such fun as it used to be.
> **I** You think primary school breaks are a better experience?
> **P** Yeah.

A second main change from primary to secondary, and from early to late secondary, clearly evident from pupils' accounts, is a *decline in activity levels,* typically from running about to a more sedentary style of behaviour, involving sitting and talking. It seems that over the secondary years comes less taste for, and more contrary forces against, activity for its own sake. Physical activity is more likely to be accepted in time periods allotted to it, e.g. in physical education, or football out of school. There was a general sense of unease expressed by the pupils about their inactivity, no doubt exacerbated by the recalling of how much things differed at primary school. They sometimes expressed a desire to have more activities, yet seemed unclear or uninterested in how this might come about, or, one suspects, whether they really wanted to change what they did currently, and return to earlier styles of behaviour.

> **P** I enjoyed the physical side of breaktimes and lunchtimes . . . But now I would seem to be, I would feel too mature to do those things what I used to do, I wouldn't mind doing it in like say, physical education or like say spare time,but I don't really feel that I could use that energy at breaktimes, I just feel too lazy, too laid back to do those things now.

This quote contains an admission found in other pupil accounts, that is, of having become lazy and idle, of not feeling they can be bothered to move vigorously.

However, some are happy with not being as active as at primary school:

> **P** Here's more enjoyable because you can sit in your classroom . . . but outside . . . it's worse because it's cold and in the summer it's too hot. I mean we don't go out at break, we would stay in the building constantly because it's easier and there's so many stairs here you have to keep going up and down and it's a waste of time. You'd rather just stay in, so here's a lot more enjoyable for me.

The main way breaktimes were seen to differ over time, based on the quantitative results, was that *less games and play activities* took place.

> **P** In primary I used to play a lot of games, but now no games, no games really.

> **P** At primary school, we'd queue up, have our dinner then go out and lunch-time just seemed so longer, and then we'd play hopscotch, football, he, had, Chinese skipping, skipping, double dutch, and different kinds of games.

> **P** Well in primary school like you used to play about more, you used to play had and football and run about and play games but in secondary school you don't do it any more, its sort of like stopped.

Also between early and late secondary:

> **P** Yeah, I used to play pat-ball more in the first, second and third year, but I hardly play it now.

For the following pupils the reduction seems to occur at the transition from the lower and upper schools at secondary, that is, between years 8 and 9 (12/13 to 13/14 years).

> **P** Yeah when I was in the lower school I used to play he-ball which is just 'had' with a ball and pat-ball you know just playing the ball against the

thing . . . and I was always running around doing sports kind of thing, but when I got up to here I just don't do that any more.

P   Well when I was in first and second year in the lower school, you know I'd run and play games, play rounders and that, run around the playground . . . Like most of my friends as we've come up through the years have changed. I suppose now, I'm probably boring now, I just sit around reading or something. I talk to someone where as then I would be up and running around.

Reasons for Changes in Breaktime Activities: Pupil Explanations

Perhaps the most important developmental question concerns *why* these changes take place. There are likely to be many reasons, maturational, cognitive and cultural that would help account for changes. But how do pupils themselves account for the changes they identified in their own behaviour over the school years? How do they account for the main developmental trend toward a reduction in play and games at breaktime over the school years? The following discussion comes from examination of their reflection on changes in activities.

The first reason is the expectations of what was appropriate for their age. This had several forms. Perhaps the main reason is to do with pupils' growing sense of *maturity*, and with what they consider is appropriate for someone of their age. So this is a process connected to pupils' attitudes about what they should be doing, sometimes with a sense of unease that the loss of activities has not been adequately replaced.

P   If I was back being 7 years old I would most probably have told you I liked it then 'cause I was out playing and having fun but now 'cause I'm older and I'm more matured I think now well I'm going to the canteen and get myself a hot drink 'cause I'm cold, so I think its better now. We used to play 'Had' and all things like that. Just run around and be silly.
I   At what point does that stop? . . .
P   You get to the second year and you think you're grown up then don't you?
I   And it's not appropriate to do those things any more?
P   Yeah.
P   I actually miss primary school because you could go outside and run around and play and it seems that as soon as you get to a certain age you don't play any more.
I   And why is that?
P   I suppose it's considered to be immature.

The following pupil is becoming more conscious of adulthood, and more work conscious.

P   Well in primary school we were like in the playground and like running up and down, and it's like totally different because in this school now, you're more like adults and like we don't have time to be running up and down and playing this and that. We're like more civilized and more grown up so we like, have discussions and play cards.

And from another pupil comes the belief that with age you have to forego playful activities and become more serious-minded at school.

I   Since you've been at secondary school, like say in your first and second year . . . would you have done different things (to) what you do now?
P   Yeah . . . we still used to run about a bit, and I was more noisier in the first and second year, now I've settled down like, 'cause there's more work to do and you have to be serious.

It was difficult to distinguish between a real development in maturity and a pupil's sense that this was the way one should behave in order to appear mature. Similarly, it was difficult to know from pupils' answers to what extent they actually *wanted* to engage in more active pursuits, as at primary school. The next pupil does suggest that it is both a sense that they should not engage in playful behaviours, but also that they are now less enjoyable.

P   We've got older I think. I mean you couldn't really see us running around playing 'Had', 'cause it's just not really done, it's not as enjoyable either.

An allied response was that they felt *silly* playing games, and would have been embarrassed to have been seen acting like this. This is part of a powerful and clearly visible peer pressure affecting behaviour during free time in school. They seemed now more self conscious about freetime activities. By comparison, what is remarkable about primary school playtimes is how un-self conscious pupils are, launching themselves into frenzied or repetitive games, and in marked contrast to the affected inactivity of the late secondary years.

P   In Primary school you, there was lots of things to do, you can have a skipping rope, play 'Had'. But you'd look silly if you run around playing 'Had' and had a skipping rope here.

Allied to maturity is more *self understanding*:

P   I suppose in primary you used to do things maybe more outrageous 'cause you didn't understand so much . . . maybe 'cause you're younger . . . you may not realize you're doing so much. But now you understand more.

So this set of responses from pupils indicates a growing sense of maturity and self understanding, which seems to go beyond maturational change, in the sense that it reflects an attitudinal change strongly influenced by peer pressure, that grows in strength over the secondary years. Primary school type activities are rather frowned upon, and an exaggerated inactivity takes hold.

The second reason, drawn from pupil accounts, for changes in breaktime activities, is a growing sense of the value of *having choice* about how to spend breaktimes, and having the *freedom to choose* to go out to the playground or stay in school, and whether to go out of the school grounds.

> **P**   I think I prefer this kind of thing where you can choose what you want to do rather than everyone has to go out.

> **P**   You weren't allowed to eat in primary . . . you had to go outside, you weren't allowed in, you had to be outside cold or hot . . . Here you can be inside or out, just go anywhere you want.

A good sense of how constrained some pupils felt at primary school comes from the next quote.

> **P**   All I can remember of primary school is basically you've got to stay in. I felt quite locked up and used to try and sneak out. They used to have a lollipop man there who guard the gate. I used to always try and get out but I never could.

The following is a good quote from a pupil who clearly shows the value she puts on being able to plan and make choices about her activities at breaktime. There is much less possibility of planning in this way at primary, both for developmental reasons in terms of cognitive factors, no doubt, but also because there is much less freedom allowed pupils over where they can go at breaktime.

> **P**   You move on, you develop more yourself, you want to branch out with other people, other friends. So that's probably the main difference and I've just got more things to do now. Like in the first year I wouldn't ever have to bother about having to do homework at lunchtime because there was no real need to do it, we didn't get that much anyway so there was no problems about that. But now I would say, 'Right I'm definitely going to do this at lunchtime, I'm going to go to the library.' I'd plan it the night before and say 'I'm going to the library and finish this off, get that out of the way, then I'll do this' or whatever. So those would be the main changes.

Pupils seemed to value the freedom at secondary level that came from going out of school, even taking risks with punishment to get out, and despite seeming not to do much more than walk to a shop, as we saw in the last chapter.

> **P**   In first year I used to stay in school and play patball, but half way through second year I sort of thought I'm not staying in no more. The school dinners got dearer and you got really small things. So I just walked out.

So a sense of having a choice is connected with the feeling of wanting to be mature described earlier, and this in turn affects the kinds of activities engaged in. It is the *having* of choice that is important — more so than the activity that follows from the choice.

One intriguing aspect to pupils' reports of the difference between breaktimes now and earlier in their school careers, is their recognition, mentioned already, of something now lost.

> **P** I wish I could actually go back to doing that. It just gets really boring (at secondary).

As we have seen, by no means all regretted changes in breaktime, and at 16 years more preferred secondary to primary breaktimes. Even so, a sense of a world now gone was heard. One detected here a regret that they no longer moved and acted with the spontaneity and engagement of earlier years. One might describe this as a sense of nostalgia, and this may well depend on a recognition of alternative courses of action, and of the consequences of change. From this point of view, asking pupils to look back on — to review — earlier stages in their schooling, gives insights into social worlds they had created for themselves and which have particular meaning for them. There is more involvement likely here than in say life in the classroom, where control is not with them but with their teachers.

There is a third and allied factor which seems to explain, from the pupil's viewpoint, changes in breaktime activities from primary to secondary. As we have seen, at primary level pupils usually have to *go out to the playground at playtime*. In consequence almost all breaktime activities are activities on a playground. But as we saw earlier in this chapter, by the end of secondary school pupils spend more time in the school buildings than in the school grounds and out of the school altogether. Even taking into account other factors discussed here, more to do with pupils changing image of themselves, they are bound to adapt their behaviour and activity to the environment they find themselves in, and pupils at primary level, finding themselves on playgrounds more often, will inevitably run and play more. This may also explain some of the difference in activities between early and late secondary, because younger pupils are much less likely to be allowed out of school, and hence are more likely to find themselves on the school playground and playing games.

> **P** Every one just went out to the playground, nobody was allowed inside the building except to go toilet, you just went out in the playground, played hopscotch or whatever, chinese skipping with your friends and basically that was it. You just stayed outside, I think they just kept you outside for that amount of time.

This pupil prefers to stay in the school.

> **I** And you said earlier that first and second years (pupils) tend to be in the playground here. Did you when you were in first and second year here, tend to go in the playground?

P   Yeah.

I   At what point then did you stop?

P   Late in the second year I found out that the craft room was open at lunchtime, so my friend and I went up and asked the teacher if we could stay in there and we made a few models and that. So, then I couldn't really be bothered to go out any more. Then, by the fourth year we already had our own common room and there were classrooms open and that, so I wasn't bothered about going out into the playground.

A fourth reason for changes in breaktime activities, that arises out of pupil accounts is to do with a growing sense of the importance of *school work*.

P   You might skip breaktime and stay in and do the homework for the next lesson whereas in primary school you could just go out and have fun.

P   Well we used to play rounders in the playground and everything, but the lower school girls usually do that now. We usually just go and sit around, talk or just get on with homework while talking to our friends or whatever. We're sitting in a classroom. Sometimes there are lunchtime classes that are on, in chemistry or biology, revision classes. Sometimes go to those if there's something we don't understand that we just couldn't ask for help in the lesson, we'd go to teacher at lunchtime.

As they progress through secondary school, and final examinations grow closer, pupils come to see breaktimes as an opportunity to study, and continue work, as well as providing a break from work.

Finally, changes in breaktime were explained in terms of *social factors*. We have seen the almost universal move from play activities to talking and chatting with friends. Talking and socializing was common at the primary stage, but through the secondary years games and play had declined to leave socializing the dominant activity.

The type of social talk had also changed. One pupil said: 'It's a bigger school so you get to know more people' and went on to draw a distinction between rather mindless interactions at primary school and those now within which they talked 'properly'.

P   We used to run around, play with the boys and just scream, shout and anything, whereas now you just walk around and talk to your mates. We don't play nothing, I do sports but we don't play nothing, and I just find it more easier because we are old enough to talk to each other properly.

There was more awareness of talking to the opposite sex:

P   No, well I'd say, (boys and girls) . . . talk more together 'cause like you're older, things start to happen, but in primary school, you're young and you're a bit wild and you don't really know what you're doing. And in secondary school you're more mature and you understand girls a bit better.

Conclusion

In the last chapter we saw that breaktime was of significance to pupils through-out their school careers, though the nature of this significance changed with pupils' age. In this chapter, pupils' own accounts have been used to chart changes with age in breaktime activities. Accounts taken from the same children at 7, 11 and 16 years show a change from active games such as football, chasing and catching at the primary stage to talking and socializing with friends by the end of the secondary stage. Of special interest was pupils' own retro-spective accounts at 16 years of changes from primary to secondary. Breaktimes during the primary stage were seen as more carefree and more enjoyable, more active, and more games and play took place. Pupils' own explanations for changes in breaktime activities between primary and secondary stages centred on a growing sense of maturity and self understanding, a greater value attached to choice about how to spend breaktime, the simple fact of not hav-ing to go out to the playground at breaktime, a greater sense of the importance of school work, and changes in the nature of social relations, in which the nature of talk is more central and not tied to games. The general dimensions of concern to adolescent pupils — a concern with personal control and the onset of self consciousness and less spontaneity — are not new, but focusing on breaktime activities — the part of the school day most obviously owned by pupils — gives changes over the school years a particular application.

In one sense the changes in breaktime activities can be perceived posit-ively in that pupils on the whole preferred secondary breaktimes to primary. But one obvious conclusion to be drawn from their accounts is to see changes in breaktime activities over the school years as a progressive loss of activities. The vitality of primary school days contrasts with the seemingly covert and unfocused activities of their last years at school. But one needs to be cautious about this conclusion, in that it may be that energies are channelled into different activities. As they move through secondary school, pupils' social lives become important in new and deeper ways, and are vital in their developing sense of who they are, and what they want to do. In consequence social concerns are not so tied to location and activity, and in contrast to primary school are not so visible to staff.

An important issue concerns the reasons for changes in breaktime activ-ities; in particular, to what extent they are the result of developmental changes within the child, or affected by outside factors. The pressure of peers is likely to be a powerful force that has much to do with the deep inhibition about playing games, and the development of a seemingly exaggerated and growing inactivity, through the secondary years. The presence of playground games during the first years of secondary indicates the potential longevity of games as a feature of unsupervised activities. Pupils who transferred from lower to upper secondary schools at 13 years seemed to show a marked change in breaktime activities, and this indicates the likely influence of peer pressure and school culture once they enter the upper school. There appears, then, to be a transition stage during the early years of secondary when play activities from primary are carried over but which, within a year or two, all but disappear. It may be that games and play are useful in the early stages of secondary as a familiar medium through which to develop new friendships, but their decline is accelerated as other ways of mediating friendships develop. This role of play-ground activities and games after the transition to secondary school deserves closer study.

Another possibility for future research could take advantage of the fact that in the English school system pupils can transfer to secondary education at 11 or at 12 years, depending on the arrangements in different LEAs. A comparison of breaktime activities of same age children, some of whom remain in middle schools (deemed primary), and some of whom transfer to secondary schools, would do much to separate effects of maturity from peer and school influences.

Sex differences in breaktime activities have been reported in several places (Pellegrini, 1995). A feature of the research presented in this chapter, was the opportunity to study sex differences over a longer time period than previous research. Consequences of changes in breaktime activities seemed different for boys and girls. Whilst both boys and girls became less active with age, boys' activities at primary level were dominated by football and active games, and there was therefore more continuity into the secondary years, where football still has a place. The change was more marked for girls because there is less obvious continuity between games preferred at primary level, and the predominantly social and non-active pursuits preferred at secondary.

The picture of changes in breaktime activities with age revealed in this study has implications for debate about the quality of outside play. It is easy to assume that changes in activities are the same as a decline in quality. It is also important to consider what is meant by 'traditional' games when considering their supposed decline (Blatchford et al., 1990). The results on 11-year-old activities indicated a wide variety of chasing, ball games and other games, and a clear involvement in them, though some types of games were not frequent, especially among boys. We return to the issue of the quality of outside play in the last chapter of this book. For the moment the point is made that debate about the quality of play in isolation may not lead us very far. Outside play is probably best considered in the context of other aspects of pupils' lives in school.

Implications for Schools

In the last chapter I made the point that throughout both primary and secondary school years that there did not appear to be a clear view about the purpose and value of breaktime. Moreover, as pupils get older and their activities change and become less overtly playful, they seem more poorly served by schools. There are certainly concerns that playtime at primary school could be improved (Blatchford and Sharp, 1994), but there is generally more awareness amongst school staff of the role of play in primary school pupils' lives. By secondary school the culture has moved from expression through play and activity to purely social forms. If, as was said in the last chapter, there is a case for more attention being paid to breaktime in schools, at both primary and secondary level, then awareness of the main activities and their meaning for pupils, for example, as detailed in this book, is a basic first step. If schools are reducing time allocated to breaktime, then staff also need to consider what opportunites for social opportunities and play are also lost.

For boys, football had an extraordinary dominance. Staff can agonize over this because of problems that arise, and in some schools football can be constrained, or at best tolerated. But there may be a positive side too, for example as a cooperative team-based outlet for enthusiastic and potentially troublesome boys. A prevalent negative view toward football may be partly dependent on an adult, and largely female staff, having little feel or direct experience of football. But whatever one's view about the game, the important thing to recognize is its main role in 11-year-old boys' playground culture. Interestingly, historians have shown how the rise of football in school playgrounds at the end of the nineteenth century was viewed positively, because it was inexpensive, adaptable and provided a degree of organization (Walvin, 1982).

Differences between schools were not examined directly, but may well be an important factor affecting breaktime behaviour. Differences in school environments, provision of recreation and play areas, and staff attitudes, policies and school rules are all likely to interact with pupil perspectives, and are all likely to affect pupil breaktime cultures and are also worthy of study.

In this chapter we have examined general changes in age, and possible explanations, and have looked at how secondary school students' activities reflect developments in their social relations and development. In the next two chapters we look more closely at primary school pupils' outside activities at breaktime, particularly their games — at how these change and originate, and their role in pupils' social relations with each other.

Note

1   These codes were combined at 16 years because of the difficulties in separating them — hanging around usually meant in a social context. It was not possible to add these codes at 11 years to arrive at a score for each child, because the codes were not mutually exclusive and the same pupil may have reported both categories.

Chapter 5

Playground Games at Junior School: Changes over the School Year

Well we didn't know what to do with ourselves when we started because we were a bit shy, and we didn't know what you could do and couldn't do . . . well things have changed on the playground. And we've learnt new games from other people that we've made friends with.

In the last chapter I provided an overall account of changes with age, which was necessarily limited as the basis for understanding the social contexts within which activities occurred, and the origins and development of activities. A different approach is needed to give a more dynamic account of breaktime activities.

In this chapter I report on the study of the development of playground games in 8-year-olds after entry to junior school (see Chapter 2). The aim was to supplement material presented in the main longitudinal study. This was also the basis of the account of friendships presented in the next chapter.

Breaktime Games

As we saw in Chapter 2, the nature and function of children's playground games has been an area of disparate research interest. The Opies' work (1969) has been influential. It documents chasing, catching, seeking, hunting, racing, duelling, exerting, daring, guessing, acting, and pretending games played by children across the country. They saw the function of the game as largely social. In a pioneering study, Sluckin (1981) extended the Opies' work, documenting school playground games, and argued that the playground offers children the opportunity for peer interaction in the context of which many lessons relevant to adult life are learned.

In the last chapter we saw the central place that playground games occupy as a focus of breaktime activities as late as 11 years. This chapter extends previous work and is founded on the view that very little is known about factors influencing the arrival of, and short term changes in, breaktime activities. These factors could include the social contexts, particularly friendship groups, within which playground games originate and develop over time in school settings, as well as the influence of individual children. It was considered that an effective way to study changes was to study children for one year after the point of entry as 8-year-olds to Junior school. This seemed an interesting age to study because games are still likely to be a prevalent part of peer interaction, yet, according to Parker and Gottman (1989), this is about the time that the dominance of play in early childhood is joined by the emergence of friendships typical of middle childhood. My own observations had also suggested that pupils around 8 years of age are particularly involved and active at breaktime, and that the main activity — games — is an important context for social relations between pupils. In keeping with the emphasis throughout this book, I was interested in the pupils' accounts of changes and influences in their activities.

Four research questions were asked:

1   What games are played by these children?
The aim was to obtain a full description of games, and to categorize these in terms of the Opies' classification scheme, and previous research by the author (Blatchford et al., 1990).

2   Where do games come from?
Given the worries commonly expressed about the quality of outside play, and the possible decline in traditional games (see Chapter 1), ways in which games are conveyed and originate need to be considered carefully. The interest here is not historical, but on social processes through which they arrive in the school playground. Games may come from other pupils, or from members of teaching or ancillary staff. They may be brought by pupils from their previous schools. But there was little available research by which to judge these possibilities.

3   How do games change over time after entry to school?

4   What processes, particularly social processes, explain these changes? Changes may well result in part from developmental changes in the children, but to what extent are changes due to changes in friendships and social relations between children, to influences within the school such as older pupils, to external environmental factors such as changes in playground equipment, or to intrinsic properties of the games themselves? Do some games come to dominate, and some decline? If so, what processes seem to explain these changes?

Research Approach

As described in Chapter 2, it was decided to study one school class from the point of entry into junior school for one school year. This was therefore a short term longitudinal study and it was exploratory in intent. The sample comprised one class of year 4 (8 years of age on entry) children who entered junior school in September 1994. This was the first year after age-of-transfer changes had been introduced within the Local Education Authority, which meant that, for this year only, both year 3 and year 4 pupils entered what had previously been a middle school (year 4 to year 7), but which had now become a junior school (year 3 to year 6). At the beginning of the school year there were 31 children, but over the course of the year three children joined the class and one left, leaving 33 by the end of the summer term.

Pupil Interviews

Pupils were interviewed twice, first during the autumn term, and then again after half term in the summer term. Questions included in the pupil interviews were based on our previous work with the longitudinal study. They included questions on playground activities and games played (who played, where games came from, how people entered them, who suggested them, how they ended), and changes in playground activities since the start of term (at first interview) and over the course of the school year (at second interview). Questions were also asked about friendships and included whether they had made friends since starting at the school and why they had become friends, who they said were their friends now, whether they would call any of these best friends, what were the differences between friends and best friends, why they were friends, and whether they played different games with friends. Results on friendships form the basis of Chapter 6.

All interviews were tape recorded and answers transcribed verbatim. All children were interviewed in a small room attached to the main classroom. Most were interviewed individually, though six were interviewed in two groups of three at the first interview. Questions were open ended in the sense that children were all asked the same basic set of questions but answers were not pre-categorized. Prompts and follow up questions were given when it was felt helpful. All interviews were conducted by the author. Transcripts were then analysed by identifying main categories from pupil answers to topic areas. Extracts from transcripts were used for illustrative purposes. Accounts from individual children were cross checked against each other (for example, to give information on who they played with and who they were friends with) and, where discrepancies were apparent, an attempt was made to feed these back to pupils for clarification. Discussions were also held throughout the year with several children to get more day to day information on changes in activities and games, and with the class teacher for further clarification.

Pupil Peer Ratings and Views on Breaktime

At the same time (that is, at the beginning of the school year and at the end) pupils completed the 'Like to Play With' (LITOP), and 'Like to Work With' (LITOW) measures, adapted by Frederickson (1994). These involved giving to each child a list of all the children in the class and asking them to indicate for every one in the class whether they liked to play with them (a smiling face), preferred not to play with them (a frowning face), did not mind playing with them (a straight mouthed face), and did not know them well enough to make a judgment (a question mark).

This was repeated for 'work with' rather than 'play with'. Other methods used by Frederickson were also used. These included asking pupils to indicate who they liked to play with best and least, and a 'Guess who?' technique which asked children to indicate with a tick which children in the class fitted six separate descriptions of behaviour, read out to the children by the author. Descriptions related to 'cooperates', 'disrupts', 'acts shy', 'starts fights', 'seeks help', and 'is a leader'.

Self Concept and Academic Measures

In the first term, children completed Marsh's Self Description Questionnaire (SDQ) 1 (Marsh, 1990). This comprises 76 statements which are directed at how confident a child feels about themselves on eight sub-scales — physical abilities, physical appearance, peer relations, parent relations, reading, mathematics, general school and general self. An example of one of the peer relations statements is: 'Other kids want to be my friend'. Children are asked to indicate on a 5 point scale the extent to which they agree with each statement.

The local authority screening scores, administered at the end of the previous school year, were also used. Measures used were the Edinburgh Reading Quotient and AH1 Perceptual Reasoning scores.

Results

The school was originally designed as a small secondary school and has a generous amount of ground. The two main locations used at playtime were the playground, and the large front field which was used during the lunchbreak, sometimes in the autumn and spring terms, weather permitting, but more in the summer term. For a trial period during the school year, access was allowed at lunchtime to the back field, as long as wellington boots and track suit trousers were worn, but this seemed not to be successful and, apart from continued access to two caravans used as playhouses, children were soon not allowed on the back field. Access was also allowed on a rota basis to a tree and shrub area between the playground and swimming pool. Access was not allowed into the school at breaktime (except during inclement weather) though some children did come in to help the teacher.

What Games Were Played?

A variety of games were played after entry and dominated these pupils' activities at breaktime. The games varied greatly in their longevity, their vigour and their inventiveness. They are listed in Figure 5.1.

Figure 5.1: Playground games (8/9-year-olds)

Games could be grouped in four sets:

- **First Set:**
Ball games (mainly football)
Racing games (in one game, if a child beat a challenger they then challenged another, and so on)
Skipping (ordinary, French skipping, double skipping — that is, two or more people, for example skipping with rope attached at one end to a bench)
Equipment games (rollerboots, rollerblades, rollerskates, climbing frame, sandpit, wooded/bush area, stilts, large plastic balls that could be bounced on, car and tractor tyres, palettes, large foam shapes and vehicle kits).

- **Second Set: Traditional games**
Catching games: basic 'it', 'Shadow it' (a variant in which the aim was to step on the chased's shadow — probably classifiable, using the Opie (1969) scheme, as 'touch conveyed by substitute for hand'), 'Sticky Glue' and 'Stuck in the Mud'. Not all explanations of these last two games were consistent, which probably reflected different versions brought from previous schools, and also incomplete consolidation of the game. These games seem classifiable as 'chased at disadvantage' according to the Opies' scheme.
Chasing games: basic catching game, British Bulldog (a person was chosen to stand in the middle of the playground and they had to catch people running across), 'Catch with dungeons' (according to the Opies — 'proliferation of chasers have to return to base'), informal chasing games.
Seeking games: 40/40 ('it' has to see others before they get to base), 'Grandmother's Footsteps' ('it' turns away from others and if someone gets to them before they are seen they would become 'it'), Kiss chase (classified by the Opies as 'seekers have claims on those caught').

- **Third Set: 'Home made' games**
For example, 'someone wraps a skipping rope round you, pull it, and spin like a top'. This was done repeatedly. Sometimes they pretended to be a ballerina. 'Surnames' — called a 'mucking around' game, people were called by their surname, for example, 'Harris, come here Harris. You naughty girl come to the headmaster'. So this was a game caricaturing school discipline. Games influenced by books: Two briefly pursued pretend games were based on Enid Blyton's *Famous Five* adventures. They are too complex to describe here but involved attempts to free the Famous Five using a key, encounters with kings and witches, and a visit to their aunt in America, who was killed by the witch. A game of 'it' which was like 'Piggy in the middle' but extended to include a. cat's cradle (a kind of string) not a ball, b. boys and girls together, c. use of boys' and girls' toilets and disguising who had the elastic. Meeting of a 'club', comprising a six girl group. The 'senior' team of three girls were the leaders 'because we thought of it'. The others were 'junior' members. Password, motto and hand signs were invented, and there was a meeting place which was near the environmental area.

- **Fourth Set: Making camps**
By the summer term camps on the front field had become a main activity.

Where Did the Games Come from? What Processes Explain Their Arrival in the Playground?

From Their Previous School

The interviews took place soon after entry into junior school, and so it was no surprise that children brought with them games played at their first school.

Two girls, for example, were credited with bringing a variety of 'it', and a boy and a girl separately said they had brought 'sticky glue' from their previous school. Others brought 'Bulldog' from their first school. A girl had done much skipping at her first school and, by bringing in her skipping rope, had given a boost to the popularity of skipping at the beginning of the school year.

From a Member of Staff

A 'dinner lady' from one of the main feeder schools seems to have been a catalyst for games remembered by the pupils who came from there. According to pupils from that school, she would play with them and get them involved in games. A girl said she would hold the skipping rope and lots of people used to skip while she sang accompanying songs and rhymes. Teachers were not credited with suggesting games.

From Another Pupil

This was a common answer, and describes an important factor linking the development of social relations and playground activities. Often the same few pupils were credited with suggesting, or, in some cases, making up the games. One boy said 'well the races they started when my friend Malcolm suggested it and then he gets a group'. This particular boy (Malcolm) often came up as the instigator of games. Another 'key player', as she might be called, was Elaine, who was credited with the introduction of several traditional games, and made up games, like those based on the *Famous Five* stories, listed in Figure 5.1. A point to arise here concerns the way key players can affect the ending of a game as well as its inception. Others appeared to lose interest when Malcolm dropped out and the game then became less viable. So key players seem important in both starting and ending games.

It is important to try and identify what characteristics such key players have in common because they seemed to play a leading role both in the formation of friendship groups and in the instigation and maintenance of games. Obviously with only one class, suggestions need to be tentative. They seem likely to be popular. At the first interview, Elaine had 15 smiling, and only 4 unhappy faces, on the 'Like to Play With' (LITOP). Malcolm had 16 smiling and 5 unhappy faces. At the second interview Malcolm had the highest number of choices for the person who you like to play with best, and Elaine had the fifth highest. Malcolm received no choices for like to play with least, and Elaine only one.

But popularity alone is unlikely to fully explain why it is that some children have a key role in suggesting games. On the peer nomination measure of who they felt was a leader, Malcolm and Elaine had the joint third highest scores. Several pointed out that these two children might have been more likely to know games because both had older sisters at the school. Having an older sibling in the school may also have given them more influence. One girl said that Elaine was the main mover in suggesting football, despite resistance from the boys, because her sister in year 6 (aged 10/11 years) played football with the boys in her year.

In other ways the two children had little in common. The girl was more obviously academically able and self confident in relations with peers than the boy (she had the third highest Edinburgh Reading Score, and the second highest SDQ peer relations score). On the other hand, the boy was considered physically fast and strong and had the joint highest SDQ physical abilities score. The present study therefore suggests that characteristics of 'key players' might be different for boys and girls, with physical prowess having more influence in the case of boys.

There were other suggestions from pupils. One boy was said to be more likely to suggest games because 'he's got a lot of imagination, and knows lots of games'. The boy was also academically able (he had the highest perceptual reasoning scores) and confident in his relations with peers (SDQ1). One girl said Elaine suggested games because she was 'imaginative'. In a similar vein, another girl said those that think games up 'have more ideas than other people'.

Reference can only be made briefly here to children who are more often left out of games. One girl claimed a role as someone who thought up a lot of games, but interviews with other pupils, and examination of the peer nomination data (LITOP etc), showed that the girl was not popular, and was left out of games. There was a tendency to find her 'bossy' and 'spiteful' and her games were confined to her and a few pliant others. She had at times an inflated sense of her own social importance, but also a recognition of her difficulties in finding friends with peers. Such children are likely to be classified as 'rejected' in studies of social status. Ladd and Price (1993), for example, report that children rejected by their peers have less consistent play partners, play with younger children, and tend not to play with their friends. More details on characteristics of unpopular children with social difficulties are explored in the next chapter.

From Older Siblings

As we have seen, some said they got games from older siblings (only older sisters were cited).

From Older Students in the School

During the second interview, questions concerning where games came from were asked again and answers revealed an important development over the school year. By the third term the origins of games had moved from factors outside the school, such as their previous experience, or adults, to *factors within the school*. Of particular significance now were games and activities of the older students in the school. The pupils still played mostly with others in their year, and, with a few exceptions, friendship groups were confined to their own year, but their activities and games were now similar to the older children.

In What Ways Did Games Change over the School Year after Entry?

Changes by the First Interviews

Many pupils described how at first they did not know others well, or what to do. 'Well we didn't know what to do with ourselves when we started because we were a bit shy, and we didn't know what you could do and couldn't do . . . well things have changed on the playground. And we've learnt new games from other people that we've made friends with'. Contacts from a previous school setting are resumed, but other acquaintances also join the group and they in turn bring along others they know, in what can be an accelerating number of contacts. This first exploratory stage did not seem for most to last very long, and contacts, quickly established, set the seal on friendship groups that in large measure, especially for girls, endured through the year.

Playground games have an important role in the early stages after entry. Gaining entry to games was important to pupils at the first interview, and this seems to be because entry to games is synonymous with entry into a social group. Approaching another child or group and asking them to play is the way that contact is first made. Entry to play or a game is therefore an opening gambit when entering into a social relationship. Also, in the early stages at least, more games are learnt as more contacts and friendships are made. So the process of making friends appears integrally connected to the process of suggesting and acquiring games.

Changes over the School Year

But by the third term the children in large measure did not have to gain entry to games and did not therefore ask to join games. This is because many of them, especially the girls, have by this time a stable friendship group, and most games are played within this group. So entering a game played by others does not arise, except under some circumstances, described here by a girl: 'if I split up or they've not been very kind to me, that would be the only time I'd want to play with somebody else'. Only a few pupils, like the girl described above who were rejected by others, and who were not a part of a stable group, seemed to face more regularly the task of seeking entry.

There was some evidence that games changed in structure over the year, though I was not able to explore game development in any detail. Questions in the interviews were directed more at identifying more general changes over the school year. One needs to be cautious. It is relatively easy at the point of analysis to arrive at conclusions about trends that may still change. As one pupil said about games at breaktime: 'Changed a lot. When we first started we only played "catch", and we went through stages where we only played one game, say "4040" — we played that for ages, and nothing else, and then we played "Grandma's footsteps" for ages and nothing else, and then we came on to football and play that and nothing else. So we don't play games at the same time, we do a different game the next playtime.'

But in general, by the third term, there appeared to be less variety of play and a clear reduction in 'traditional' games like '4040', 'Grandmother's Footsteps', 'Stuck in the Mud', 'Sticky Fingers', and even the basic 'It' and chasing. This seemed to be because they had found alternative activities, primarily football and making camps on the front field, though these two activities were not popular with all, and they did sometimes revert to older traditional games when other things were not on offer. All varieties of skipping and accompanying rhymes seemed to have gone.

What Factors Explain Changes over Time?

The children's accounts were explored to identify what might explain changes in breaktime activities.

Seasonal Changes

One prosaic but main influence that should not be underestimated is the time of year. Seasonal changes can transform playground activities. Football appears relatively impervious to the seasons, but in this school the making of camps, for example, was only possible from late spring, partly because of the warmer weather and partly because access to the field was only allowed then.

Formation of Friendship Groups

As we have seen, after entry to school first contacts with others at breaktime seemed closely tied to the playing of games. Over the course of the year, friendship groups for many were to a great degree stable and this seems to have been a major factor in the narrowing of games played. Once closely associated with a group, it is not an easy matter to take up a game played in a different group, if that means leaving your usual friends. Sometimes several members of a group could join another group, but this is likely to be a temporary event. So there is a dynamic toward game suggestion coming from within a group, and the same games therefore being played. This says nothing of course about the quality of play, as seen, for example, in the variety and richness of actions.

New Playground Equipment

The new equipment proved to be attractive to some and seems likely to explain some of the decline in traditional games. Foam shapes and palettes were used to build camps on the playground, and the vehicle kit, tractor tyres, and also the caravans on the back field, were used. The increased availability of the front field also meant making camps was possible. Taking up the opportunities provided by these settings and equipment could well lead to a reduction in games that are not mediated by equipment.

Some Games Became Less Interesting

A common view was that some games became 'boring'. This term could be used to describe why games stopped in the short term and also the long term. With regard to the former, one boy said 'if we kept playing the same game say in two years' time it would get a bit boring. So we have to play another game'. Another boy said '(we stop) just because you get bored with it'. So playing a game for too long makes it boring. But, more fundamentally, the children seemed to find some particular games — including traditional games — boring. 'It's a bit boring. No one else really plays them, they don't want to' (about 'Stuck in the mud'). A girl, in response to the questions 'Have you stopped playing any games?' said, '"What's the time Mr Wolf", because its boring . . . someone is the wolf, you say "what's the time Mr Wolf", walk three steps if 3 o'clock. Say "what's the time Mr Wolf", and has to chase you . . . It's a bit boring, a bit babyish, a bit tiring'.

At the same time, some games increased in interest. Football was played constantly but this did not seem to lead to a loss of interest. The question of relevance, therefore, is why some games become boring, and why some games become dominant.

The Emergence of Dominant Games

So why have a few activities, by the summer term, become dominant at breaktime? Why has football, in particular, become so popular with the pupils, even among some of the girls? A girl simply said 'football seems better'. A boy had this to say at the second interview: 'When we used to play "It", it's chasing around and once you've been chasing around a long time it gets boring, because there's nothing different happening. It's not like football where sometimes you win and sometimes you lose.' A girl at the second interview said she did not play 'Stuck in the mud' any more. 'It's like a game that never ends. [How *does* it end?] I don't know. People get "stuck" by somebody and somebody has to go under their legs or under their arms to free them, and once they've been freed three times they're "up" and if there's more than three they're all "up" and so. . . . it doesn't really end'. For her, football — her current main game — was more interesting, and more satisfying. One could see here a rather sceptical reflection on the purpose of older games. Another member of the same group was more blunt. She said she could not imagine ever playing 'Granny's Footsteps' and other similar games again.

The interest of some in making camps was one of the intriguing observations to come from this study. Camps were mentioned rarely at the first visit, and this no doubt owed much to the reduced access to the front field. But by the second visit the activity was very popular with some, and dominated their activities at all breaktimes, and for a good part of the term. From one boy's long and detailed account, it appeared to be of interest because it had a long term structure, with accompanying roles (second in command etc.), props (for example, a register of weapons), transactions such as trading for sticks with stone money, clear criteria about who were friends and who were the enemy, end points such as successfully defending and successfully attacking the enemy, and negotiations to increase the size of one's army, or establish allied forces and allied camps. Many of these characteristics stand in contrast to those of traditional games and could help explain the interest of camps at this age.

As has been found before (see Blatchford, 1989; Blatchford et al., 1990; Boulton, 1992) football has a special attraction particularly, though not exclusively, for boys. One reason for the popularity of football as a playground activity is that it no doubt reflects its popularity and significance out of school. But the attraction of football also seems to be because it is free moving, has a clear set of rules, has a competitive rationale and clear criteria about who wins, with a fluidity and speed of action which can change things around quickly, and can be played in most open spaces. As with making camps, football could reveal a good deal of skill and imagination.

Part of the explanation for the decline of some games appears to be that they do not have a dynamic or structure that ensures longevity. 'Home made' games (see above), for example, seem to have a limited lifespan because they are restricted to a few people and do not have a rule structure and competitive excitement that give games their interest. The social structure of the group could also affect games. From one girl's explanation of the course of a 'home made' game involving a spinning top, it appeared that the game developed not so much as the product of one leader or suggester but was the result of a group decision. All contributed and seemed to feel involved and enjoyed just seeing what happened. It was fun but not long lasting. Other games are instigated by just one person and these seemed more prone to withdrawal and collapse. These games were in turn different to established games like 'sticky glue' which have a structure understood by most and not just the individuals who created it.

Sense of Games Being Childish

As can be seen in some of the comments above, part of the explanation for change in breaktime games seems to be that some games begin to seem childish. The children begin to feel it is inappropriate for them to play games that they now feel are for younger children. One girl, like others, had stopped all games except football. [Why not 'Granny's footsteps'] 'It's a bit babyish. We played it at parties. Just didn't like it much'.

Peer Influence

The sense that some games are childish is connected to another factor. It is the influence of other children in the school that has much to do with why games are perceived in certain ways. Football and camps are played by older children and, as shown above, are picked up by the younger entrants into school.

One thing pupils quickly seem to learn after entry into school are quite complex informal rules governing games and locations, often structured by an hierarchy of power, usually based on age. For example, at the beginning of the year three locations for football were identified by the pupils: outside the classrooms, nearer the main building, and on the front field. Rules governing who played where had to be explained to the interviewer but were obviously clear to the pupils. And rules were reinforced by older boys making it clear to younger children if they were found playing in the wrong place. Only on special occasions were year 4 children allowed to play with older pupils. 'You ask them to play, and they don't let you play. [Does this happen quite a lot?] Lots. 'cause year 6 . . . don't let any year 4 . . . We can't actually suggest the games, tell them what we think. They just ignore us'.

Conclusion

This chapter has reported a study of the development of school playground games in a class of 8–9-year-olds after entry to junior school. When collated, there was a long and varied list of games. The chapter has examined factors influencing the arrival of games and the social processes affecting how games developed over time. Games came to the playground by being brought from pupils' previous schools, from a member of staff, from other pupils, from older siblings, and, later on, through the influence of factors in the school, such as games played by older children.

One way games originated was through the influence of what I call here 'key players', and some characteristics of these pupils were identified. They are credited with suggesting, maintaining and ending games, and they are a main force around which the groups and their games function. There appears on present evidence to be a particular blend of popularity, social impact, imagination, boldness, and the experience of games perhaps from an older sibling. But there were also differences between the children who might be classified as key players, and the validity and composition of the classification 'key player' needs further study, as do connections with aspects of social functioning such as leadership and popularity. Further study of the influence of certain individuals on the development of playground games is likely to help understanding of the formation and development of children's friendship groups.

In general the main change over the year in games was a decline in traditional games, and skipping and rhymes, and an accompanying narrowing of games to a few dominant ones, mainly football and camps. What could account for these changes? There are likely to be two general processes at work. Firstly, there are those that result from developmental changes in the child (see review in Smith, 1994). These probably explain why some games like football and camps become more interesting to pupils. They are more likely to adhere to rules of engagement, and fantasy and rhymes are not of such interest. As they mature socially, they are able to keep up longer conversations and socialize unaccompanied by play. Eifermann (in Sutton-Smith, 1990) found that younger children showed more variety but less duration in games, and fewer competitive games.

Secondly, analysis of pupil accounts indicated that there are changes that result from factors in the school. A main influence stems from social processes such as those involved in getting to know other people. As friendship groups stabilize, the games played become narrower in range and more stable themselves. They tend to play one game mostly by preference, e.g. football. They also talk more, unaccompanied by play, as they find out more about each other. Another set of influences in the school are external factors such as seasonal and environmental changes.

It was suggested in the last chapter, when discussing changes in breaktime activities from primary to secondary, that one influence within the school was the effect of peers on what activities were considered acceptable. In the present analysis of changes over time in games, the effect of other pupils, especially the oldest pupils in school, seemed to become stronger over the course of the first school year after entry. When the pupils first came into the school they seemed to play games particular to their own age group. But by the third term, though still playing predominantly in same age groups, their playground activities had assimilated predominant activities played within the school, especially those of older pupils. This process is rarely direct; as Boulton (1992) has found, mixed age playing is discouraged by the older pupils. Rather, the exclusion of the younger children probably serves to *increase* for them the social desirability of the activities. Through play and other activities they seem to be acquiring long established activities within the school, like making camps, and rules of engagement, that seem independent of influences from the existing school staff, and of developmental factors within the child. Apparently, camps, for example, have for many years been set up on the front field. At breaktime, the pupils were therefore acquiring a distinctive culture, particular to the school, and, in the process, acquiring a history of the school's informal life.

Another example of peer influence affecting changes in playground activities was seen in the way that traditional games come to be viewed as childish. There is pressure on pupils, albeit indirect, to see traditional games, played when younger, as not suitable. We saw in the case of one girl a rather sceptical reflection on her previous involvement in games played when younger. This attitude is similar to that evident in the accounts of 16 year pupils when asked to reflect back on their primary breaktime activities, as we saw in the last chapter. That it is evident in a 9-year-old, seems to signal that this girl at least will not again engage wholeheartedly in the younger games.

Whatever the balance of developmental and social and school influences on changes in breaktime activities, there were some indications that this year was a transition stage between a less self conscious and more active style of play characteristic of play in their first schools (5 to 8 years), and games like football and activities like camps, as well as socializing without play, characteristic of older children. As one child said, 'We're in the middle — we play games and chat.

Implications for Schools

It seemed that staff in the present school had little influence on the children's playground games, though the potential influence of staff was shown in the case of several of the children who came from the same first school, and described how one dinner supervisor there had introduced them to games and rhymes through playing with them.

The picture of a rich informal social life in school, that is largely independent of school staff, and which runs parallel to life in the classroom, raises for me questions about the appropriate role of adults, with regard to breaktime. As I mentioned in the last chapter, a first response is an awareness of breaktime activities, and their meaning to pupils, and along with this, an awareness of the consequences if changes are made to breaktime. Reduction in time at breaktime may not just affect pupils' enjoyment, but also their involvement in a separate culture. If a more direct role for adults is favoured, for example, by suggesting games and activities, and providing play equipment, then it would also be important to take notice of existing activities and use of outside space. Playground life has a structure and a history, and activities imposed on pupils are unlikely to be maintained for very long.

I look in more depth in the final chapter of this book at the difficult issue of the role of adults and school staff in breaktime activities and outside play, though here I note that the description of how one game was brought back from a visit by one pupil to another school suggests one facilitative factor. Ways might be found to bring pupils from different schools together so that they can share ideas. More generally, a forum might be provided within which breaktime activities might be discussed, while ownership of games and activities lies with pupils.

In this chapter a number of influences on playground games have been identified. We have seen the effect of social influences such as other pupils and the informal culture in the school, the influence of particular 'key players', and the influence of new equipment. Any consideration of the general quality of outside play and games would need to consider these. Perhaps the most important findings involve connections between developments over time in breaktime activities, particularly games, and friendship formation. I felt this was a main theme emerging from the study of the playground games of 8–9-year-old pupils, and I extend this in the next chapter.

Chapter 6

Friendship Formation after Entry to Junior School

We used to play with Lucy and Noreen when we first came to (the school). But not now. [Why?] We don't like the games they play. They hold hands, run round in a circle, and they twist themselves up, and that's all they play . . . So we don't play with them and aren't friends with them because of the games they play.

As Goodnow and Burns have written, *'To be at school — especially in the playground — surrounded by peers but without friends is awful'* (1985, p. 119). One of the most important achievements during the first uncertain days in a new school is forming friendships. As described in Chapter 1, children's friendships have been found to be supportive at a time of adjustment to a new school. We saw earlier that pupils' positive attitudes toward school are much affected by the social opportunities it provides for meeting friends.

For primary aged children another main interest at breaktime, apart from making and meeting friends, is playing games. Making friends and playing are likely to be linked. Davies (1982) has argued that much of the building of shared understandings that lies at the heart of friendships is developed through play. She describes how the compulsive dynamic of the game can draw children in, and aid friendship formation. It is only when children make friends that they can participate in a shared children's culture.

In this chapter I extend the analysis in the last chapter by looking more closely at the formation and development of friendships in the same class of children over their first year at junior school. As we saw in Chapter 2, the study of children's friendships has been the subject of much research, but in this chapter I focus on friendships as expressed during breaktime, which is the main setting in school when pupils, especially those not in the same class, get a chance to meet. Hirsch and Dubois (1989) have analysed settings in which friends and best friends develop in early adolescence but this has not been addressed in younger children in playground settings. We saw in Chapter 1 that there are signs that children of primary school age have less independence, and spend less time out of school playing with peers. Breaktime in schools may therefore be an increasingly important forum for the development of friendships. Better understanding of how friendships develop and are maintained during this time may increase understanding of pupils' adjustment into school.

Research Questions

I was interested in finding answers to five research questions:

   1   How can the nature and composition of friendship groups of children after entry to junior school be best described?

Furman (1989) concludes that the nature of group development in the primary school years has not been carefully studied. The well known research of Berndt (Berndt, Hawkins and Hoyle, 1986), like many others (Furman, 1989), have at their centre the assumption that childhood friendships are dyadic in nature. Bukowski and Hoza (1989) in fact define friendships as 'the experience of having a close, mutual, dyadic relation'. But should it be assumed that the dyad is the basic unit of friendships? The experience of my own children indicated that this was too narrow a view, and I wanted to look closely at the nature of friendship groups in this class.

     Whom do pupils see as their friends on a day to day basis? How can their social networks in school, especially on the playground, be described? Who do they play with on the playground? Do they mostly involve children of the same age and sex? There is evidence that boys' and girls' friendships differ, with boys being more extensive and less exclusive (Eder and Hallinan, 1978, in Hartup, 1989). There is also evidence that friendships in schools predominantly involve pupils of the same sex (Hartup, 1992). Hartup (1996) has summed up the research evidence by quoting Aristotle: 'birds of a feather flock together'; that is, friends tend to be similar on important dimensions. To what extent was this true of the friendships of this class of children?

   2   What distinctions do pupils make about friendships? Do they distinguish between 'friends' and 'best friends'?

A second aim was to find out how best to describe, from the pupils' viewpoint, differences in friendship status. Existing research has tended to look at whether or not children have friends, but, as Hartup (1996) has said, there are likely to be important differences between companions. Is a distinction between friends and best friends adequate, or are finer distinctions required? Do these distinctions change over time after entry to school? It was felt that an exploratory approach was appropriate in order to seek answers to these questions. As Belle (1989) has said, there is a scarcity of research using children's descriptions of their social networks, and I hoped that the study of networks during breaktime might contribute to a more general understanding.

   3   What factors are important in explaining why children are friends?

A main aim was to obtain better understanding of reasons *why* pupils of this age became friends at school. This was studied on the basis of pupils' own accounts of their friendships, with a focus on the playground. Research has recognized relatively 'surface' factors such as age and proximity, and also the degree of similarity between friends (Epstein, 1989; Erwin, 1993). There is some agreement that 'deeper' factors such as personal characteristics of pupils become more important in adolescence, though my own observations had suggested that friendship choices in younger children can be based on personal characteristics as well. I felt that these factors could benefit from further exploration in a British school context. In a more applied way, interest was also on ways friendship formation is affected by previous school contacts and contacts out of school. What role do they play, and under what conditions do new friendships overcome them? The overall attempt was to get more bearing on the balance of surface and deep factors.

4   How do friendships and social status change over the year?

Recent research has pointed to the importance of friends in adjusting to a new school (Ladd et al., 1996), and also to the importance of understanding more about the quality of friendships, as well as whether or not children have friends (Hartup, 1996). Understanding the 'quality' of friendships is likely to be aided by examining how they form and develop over time. This is perhaps best done by studying pupils on entry into a new school, when many will not already know each other. This strategy was adopted in the present study, and interest was in how friendship groups were formed in the days after entry to school, which children were popular and which unpopular, and how stable these characteristics were over the course of the first year.

5   What factors are associated with individual differences in friendship formation and social popularity? Do some pupils have difficulties in making friendships, and if so why?

Children are likely to vary in the success with which they form friendships and are perceived by peers. Children with friends tend to be more socially competent than children without friends, and are seen as more sociable, cooperative, self confident and less lonely (Hartup, 1992, 1996). Children with more stable friendships are more popular and judged by peers as more sociable (Berndt, 1989).

What factors help to explain why pupils are more or less popular and have more or less friends? Associations between social popularity and other factors were explored, in quantitative analyses, by collecting information on how much pupils liked to play and work with each other — as well as peer 'nominations' on dimensions such as who cooperates, starts fights, disrupts, leads, and is shy — dimensions identified as important in previous research.

Associations with academic abilities were also explored, as were links between success in forming friendships and self esteem. Sullivan (in Bukowski and Hoza, 1989) believed that adequate peer relationships during the school years were required for the formation of a healthy self concept. Markus and Nurius (in Parker and Gottman, 1989) conclude that by middle childhood the reactions of peers has come to rival parents in terms of their importance in children's self esteem. Empirical support for the connection between friendships and self worth is presented in Bukowski and Hoza (1989) and Berndt

(1996). At the same time, recognition of the multifaceted nature of self concept has led to advances in the development of measures of self concept. Marsh's Self Description Questionnaire (1990) has been particularly influential, and allows the analysis of relationships with different facets of self concept, including physical and academic, as well as general self esteem, to be calculated.

Children who are not part of a friendship group can suffer greatly. Do they recognize and how do they explain the situation? There has been a tendency in research to label all children who have difficulties as 'rejected' or 'neglected' — but it might be important to consider differences between children within this group. Case studies of individual children were conducted to help understand more about why they have difficulties.

Research Approach

The research method and data are the same as that described in the last chapter. A short term longitudinal study of friendship and social networks after entry to junior school was considered to be a useful way to study processes involved in the formation and development of friendships, and stability over time after entry. As there seemed little descriptive information available on friendship formation in the British school context, the approach was inductive, in the sense of moving toward overriding themes on the basis of careful analysis of data.

Nature and Composition of Friendships Groups

The girls had formed two main groups of five and six children. There was also one pair of girls, which was rather isolated socially. These girl groups were different in kind to boys' groups. In line with other studies they were more exclusive and less extensive (Eder and Hallinan, 1978 in Hartup, 1989). The boys were more free ranging, formed larger groups, and were less exclusive in their alliances.

Girls were similar academically to others in their group. Katherine, Elaine, and Celia had three of the four highest scores in the class on the Edinburgh Reading Test, and two others in the group — Gillian and Janet — were ranked nineth and twelfth. But in the other girl group, Helen, Candy, Ruth and Sandra had lower scores that did not overlap at all with Katherine's group. As for the boys, Tim and John were friends throughout the year (see below) and were both high scorers, academically, with Tim having the sixth and John the eighth highest Edinburgh scores. They had the two highest scores on the AH Perceptual Reasoning Test.

Friendships, as others (Hartup, 1992) have found, were mostly same age choices from within their own class, and to some extent the parallel (i.e. same age) year 4 class. Some were friends with a few children from year 3 and this appeared to be because they were known from their previous school. It was interesting that younger boys who were mentioned were also game suggesters and appeared, from pupil reports, to be popular. A few children played with older friends. In Martin's case this was his best friend, and this appeared to be because they lived near each other. Malcolm had gained access to year 6 (10/11 year old) boys' games, seemingly because of his physical prowess. So the few cases of mixed aged friendships appeared to result from the social success of the younger children.

Boulton (1992) has reported, on the basis of observations in English schools, that same sex and same age groups are not inevitable on the playground. But Ladd's findings (in Epstein, 1989) of considerable grade level mixing do not seem applicable here. If this reflects a more general difference between England and the US, it may stem from the greater likelihood of mixed aged contact in US schools, resulting from pupils having to repeat a grade on academic grounds. But in this, and probably other English schools, there was also strong peer pressure against interacting with children from different years. I was at a weekend event at the school and witnessed one of the year 4 girls — Katherine — watch as one of her best friends in the class — Elaine — played with her older sister and other year 6 girls. It was suggested that Katherine go and join Elaine but she was aghast at the suggestion and was adamant that the year 6 girls would not want her to play.

Distinctions Made about Friendships. Do They Distinguish between 'Friends' and 'Best Friends'?

Friendships are often defined in terms of whether two children independently say they are friends — what is termed 'reciprocal nominations'. However, this tends to presuppose a particular view of dyadic friendships, as we have seen, and I was keen to obtain the children's own descriptions of friendship status.

Some children, especially in the first term, said they did not have 'best' friends. For some this was because they felt their friends were equal in status. Katherine had a group of friends but though she referred to them as 'best friends' she did not want to discriminate between them in terms of status. In answer to the question 'Who are your best friends?' Matthew said, 'I don't know, all my friends really'. [So you wouldn't say you've got best friends, but you've got a lot of friends?] 'They're just good friends'. For one boy there was a reluctance to admit or develop best friends because of consequences for other social relations. 'Because in my last school when I said I had best friends, my other friends got a bit upset'. Similarly Gillian: 'Molly [girl in parallel class] wanted to sit next to me all the time but I didn't want to always be with her, I wanted to meet others'. So Gillian does not want to be committed to a dyadic and exclusive relationship.

So there appeared to be three categories of children without best friends: first, those who had equal friends and did not recognize the concept of 'best friend' in their social network; second, those who preferred not to have best friends; and, third, those who appeared to lack friends overall. Some, though, at the first interview said they did have best friends. Hannah and Edna were the best friends, already referred to, who formed a pair at the first interview. They were also best friends at the second interview, at the end of the school year. These two girls were the only case in this class of a dyadic relationship, not connected to a wider group.

More typically, Tim said he had friends and within that group there were two — Graham and John — who were his best friends. The same embedding of best friends within a group of friends was seen in Ruth's first interview: [Who would you say was your best friend?] 'Well there's Harriet in year 5 and she's my best best friend . . . And then I've got like lots of friends. Noreen, Katherine, and Helen, Cindy . . .' (These come from her own year cohort.) There was a further distinction for Ruth between her small group of Katherine, Gillian, Noreen, Helen and a larger group with whom she was friendly. So for Ruth there were three levels of friendship group embedded within each other, the highest level of which is, as she puts it, her 'best best friend' (Harriet). By the end of the year her friendship network had changed. Ruth now chose Helen and Cindy as her best friends, and Lara (not chosen at the first interview) as her friend only ('because she is sometimes silly, and falls on me'). So the older child (Harriet) is not now chosen, and two children from within the same age, second level group, have been promoted as best friends. Ruth had fallen out with Noreen (see below). So there is in some senses stability over time in friendship choice, but instability in other ways. Tests of stability involving a purely dyadic definition of best friends would have missed this.

For the class overall, by the second interview the distinction between best and other friends seemed easier to make. Katherine and Elaine now chose each other and Celia as their other best friend, and Gillian and Janet as their friends. Janet appeared to have lost a degree of popularity in her group, but was still accepted. Tim at the second interview now had no doubts about choosing just John as his best friend.

The distinction between best friends, friends, and non friends may in some cases not be fine enough to capture pupils' friendship networks. Tim expressed his friendship choices in terms of an hierarchy of friendships, this time involving four levels — best friend John, then Graham, then Sean (in parallel class), and then Simon, George, and William.

There was an extension to the connection between playground activities and friendships described in the last chapter: activities could be connected to friendship status, in that different games could be played with best friends, friends and non friends. Ruth early in the year skipped with Gillian, Janet, Kathcrine and Noreen, but she played 'Sticky glue' and 'Stuck in the mud' with a larger group comprising some in her class and some other girls in the parallel same-age class. So the degree of intimacy in social relations was connected here with different games; that is, skipping (perhaps because it involves a shared knowledge necessary in order to sing accompanying rhymes) is with best friends, but bigger and less intimate groups are needed in games like 'Sticky glue'.

What Factors Are Important in Explaining Why Children Are Friends?

The following reasons were identified from pupils' interview transcripts.

Age

We have already seen that the great majority of friendships were with pupils of the same age — that is, others in year 4.

Known the Longest

Elaine still chose Celia at the second interview as one of her two best friends because she had known her the longest. This reason usually overlapped with the previous one.

Known from Previous School

Friendships could stem from friendships or contacts carried over from attending the same previous school. This seemed an important factor, at least in the early weeks at the new school. It offers support to children at a time of uncertainty, but could also help to facilitate wider social networks, even when they were superseded by new friendships they had helped bring about.

There can be difficulties for those who have no connections with others from a previous school. As Katherine explained, there was nobody from her old school (except Grant who was not popular — discussed later in Individual Studies), though she knew Gillian and Janet from her swimming club. 'I wasn't very well off, because I came from a completely different school'. At first Katherine was worried about not knowing anyone and being left out of groups based on old school acquaintances.

Known outside School

Pupils were also friends at school because they knew each other out of school, usually because they lived in the same neighbourhood. Martin: 'Jamie is my best friend because he lives in the nearby estate, it's like close . . . we like fly our kites and that . . . sometimes Jamie's cousin comes out and Jake McGurk and we normally play a game of football'.

Out of school contacts can affect distinctions between best friends and other friends. Martin drew a distinction between his best friend — Jamie — who he played with out of school, and his school friends George and Colin.

Moreover, his best friend was two years older than him, which would ordinarily be expected to be too wide a gulf to bridge. After the first interview a note was made to see at the second interview if the out of school friendship had withstood school pressures against cross age friendships. There were signs that they were beginning to fall out, but Martin and Jamie still collaborated most lunchtimes on an elaborate game of making and defending camps on the field.

Out of school contact that begins *after* school entry can signify a shift in friendship status. Inviting a child around to one's house, which can grow out of friendships developed in school, is recognized as a marker of, or a bid for, status as someone more than an ordinary friend.

Having Interests and Views in Common

This lay at the heart of many comments on why children were friends. Elaine and Katherine chose each other because they 'thought the same things' and liked the same TV programmes. A particular interest in common was liking the same games and, as we saw in the last chapter, this could help friendships develop at breaktime. Conversely, changes in friendship status could also occur because of not liking the same games, though this probably reflects other and more fundamental differences. Elaine 'We used to play with Lucy and Noreen when we first came to (the school). But not now. [Why?] We don't like the games they play. They hold hands, run round in a circle, and they twist themselves up, and that's all they play . . . So we don't play with them and aren't friends with them because of the games they play.'

They Always Play with You

This extends the previous reason. '[What about you John — what is a friend?] Someone who plays with you most of the time.' As we have seen, Tim was his best friend. 'Best friends *always* play with you and are there when you need them. So sometimes Graham doesn't play with me and sometimes Shawn doesn't but Tim always does though we play different games'. So this is another way in which playground activities help to define friendship status. Best friends are friends you play with, in a sense independently of the game, whereas friends can be people more specific to a particular game or activity.

Personal Characteristics of Friends

Other reasons given for being friends were because they helped you (Simon: 'My friends believe me and help me if I'm in trouble'); they had a sense of humour (Tim: 'John, he has a massive sense of humour, and he sometimes asks, "Are you a boy?" That's quite funny. Graham I like because his laugh is quite funny and he goes red in the face and tears start coming out of his eyes. Most of (my friends) have got a sense of humour.'); they were not 'bossy'; and because they worked together in class (Ruth: 'cause I play with them and I eat with them . . . and quite a few sit on my table').

With regard to this last reason, sitting at the same table often meant children worked together, and, in this class, this also meant they were of similar ability. Interestingly, Katherine started off the year at the same table as Ruth and they played together, as described above. But by the second interview they were on separate tables, and did not play together very often. Causal direction here seems to work both ways in that mid way through the year the teacher allowed friendship choices to affect where children sat. So Katherine sat with Elaine, Celia and Gillian, and they also happened to be of similar ability.

It is worth noting here that some accounts revealed how hurtful losing a friend could be, and the importance of maintaining friendships. Simon: 'Well Malcolm, I used to be his very best friend, and now he just goes off with other people. [Why is that?] because he's so big, he thinks he's so strong . . . I'm not saying I'm so strong, but he thinks he's so strong . . . he just agrees with the others. He doesn't agree with me.' Simon's social relations at the first interview were much affected by his loss of friendship with Malcolm and resentment toward his social success, for example with older boys.

How Do Friendships Change over the Year?

How Friendship Groups Are Formed

Katherine described the process by which she got to know other children after entry. She knew several girls who attended the same swimming club, but who had gone to a different first school. Through them she met other girls who had gone to their previous school. She also knew another girl who had lived in the same village but went to a different school. On entry she then also met children who were friendly with this old acquaintance who had gone to her previous school. Her social network therefore expanded in a way she was quite aware of, and the process might with justification be called 'networking'.

So for many at the beginning of the year there was a myriad of social contacts forming, at first tentatively, on the foundations of previous out of school and previous school contacts, and then progressing to new combinations of contacts. It was not possible to assess exactly the speed with which contacts were made but judging by accounts at the first interview much of the early rather frantic and formative networking had occurred in the first week or so, and a degree of stability in friendship groups had already been attained.

As we saw in the last chapter, the means through which contact was made was very often the playground game. If peers offer social support at a time of uncertainty on entry to a new school, then it is the game that often provides the means for that support.

Changes and Stability of Popularity and Friendship Groups over the School Year

I look first at the quantitative analysis of peer rating and nomination data. Measures calculated for each child were:

- from the LITOP (Like to Play With)
    - — popularity in play (number of smiles),
    - — rejection in play (number of frowns),
    - — neglect in play (number of straight mouths),
    - — child not known in play (number of question marks);
- from the LITOW (Like to Work With)
    popularity, rejection, neglect, and not known in work (calculated in the same way as for LITOP);
- and peer nominations of (i.e. numbers of ticks against each child): who they like to play with best, like to play with least, who cooperates, disrupts, is shy, starts fights, seeks help, and is a leader.

There was evidence of considerable stability in ratings of popularity in play from the beginning to the end of the school year. Children who were popular in the first term (that is, had the most smiley face ratings) were also more popular in the third term. However, there was no sign of stability in the other LITOP measures, that is rejected, neglected and not known at play. Children who were more popular as someone to work with at the beginning of the year were still likely to be popular at the end of the year. Stability was also found in the case of those who others did not like to work with, but there was no sign of stability in the case of those who were 'neglected' or 'not known' as workmates.

There was clear evidence of stability in other aspects of social functioning. Correlations between the first and third term nominations of: play best, play least, cooperates, disrupts, starts fights, is shy, is a leader were all highly significant. Only 'seeks help' was not significantly stable over time. It thus appeared that children who were popular at play and at work, who others liked to play with most and least, and who were seen as cooperative, disruptive, shy, likely to start fights, and a leader at the beginning of the school year, were also likely to be viewed by peers in the same way at the end of the school year.

The analysis so far in this section has been concerned with peer nomination measures, including popularity. However, when it comes to friendship groups, capturing the extent and nature of stability over time is not as straightforward as these correlational data might suggest. We have already seen how some children's friendships networks were complex, involving, for example, an hierarchical, embedding of levels. Information taken from pupil accounts indicated that changes over time could involve changes in the positioning of pupils in levels of the network; for example, the 'promotion' to the status of best friend from that of ordinary friend, the reordering of the hierarchy, or children dropping out of the network altogether.

For some girls, there was stability in friendship groups over the course of the school year. The group of Katherine, Elaine, Celia, Gillian and Janet came together over the first few days in their new school and by the end of the school year were still together, with the addition of Noreen who had just joined the group through a recently formed friendship with Gillian. It is noteworthy that they played all their games together, and it was the games they played that over time, in part at least, defined them as a group, different to others.

One consequence of this stability over time, as mentioned in the last chapter, is the progressively fewer opportunities for meeting others outside the group, and it becomes difficult for outsiders to be included once a group has formed. In comparison to the initial, exploratory stage after entry, by the end of the year the possibilities of changing friendship groups are much more constrained. In this class at least, this was much clearer in the case of girls. The way Noreen was assimilated into the group was informative. Gillian said at the second interview: 'I liked her, then she asked me to go round to play . . . then I became friendly with her, and I really like her. And everybody else liked her, so we let her play with us. [And who did she used to play with?] Ruth . . . then Helen had Ruth to play with and they wouldn't let Noreen play and (now) Helen has Ruth as best friend and Ruth has Helen . . . so Ruth and Noreen aren't best friends any more.'

This description of the assimilation of a newcomer to an established group indicates several processes that allow it to occur: Gillian likes Noreen, Noreen has lost status in her own group, and the existing group do not mind her joining. So as Ruth made friends with Helen, Noreen made friends with Gillian. This kind of symmetry in children's social relations is unlikely to be accidental. The loss of a best friend is likely to be a strong force in seeking friendship elsewhere.

We have already seen how games are a main medium through which groups come together and friendships are formed. But games are important later in the year, after friendship groups have become more stable, because they are a main medium through which friendships are then enacted. Processes of change in friendships and social relations over time can also be expressed through changes in play. In the spring term, for the first time after entry to school, Katherine and other girls began to play with boys. A freeing up of social relations between boys and girls seemed here reflected in more interesting hybrid games, so that creativity in games (for example the 'piggy in the middle' game with cat's cradle, described above) reflected developments and exploration in social relations. A cheekiness, and checking boundaries of what was permissible with the opposite sex, was expressed in the game, for example, by hiding and daring entry into the prohibited area of the opposite sex toilets. Thorne (1993) has described cross-gender playground chasing games in which girls often create safety zones, for example, toilets adjoining the playground, to which they can retreat.

What Factors Are Associated with Individual Differences in Friendship Formation and Social Popularity? Do Some Pupils Have Difficulties in Making Friendships, and If So Why?

Numerical Analyses

Again I look first at numerical analyses of the peer nomination data. These showed that children who others liked to play with by the end of the school year (number of smiles on the LITOP scale) were also likely to be popular at work, to be seen as more cooperative, to be seen as a leader, less likely to be seen as seeking help, less likely to be disruptive, less likely to start fights, and to receive more nominations as someone others liked to play with most and less nominations as someone others liked to play with least (all at both the beginning and end of the year), and to have higher perceptual reasoning ability. All of these correlations were statistically significant.

Interestingly, the situation with regard to children who received the highest 'reject' scores at the end of the year, that is, more frowns on the LITOP scale, was not simply the converse. Children who were less popular had lower SDQ peer relations scores, that is, they had a less positive view of their relations with peers, and were less positive about the lunchtime break at the end of the year.

We can sum up these results by saying that children with whom others liked to play were seen as cooperative and leaders, but not aggressive and disruptive, and were likely to have better powers of reasoning, whilst children with whom others do not like to play had a low opinion of their own relations with peers, and did not like the long dinner breaktime. Social popularity and rejection seem, then, not to be inversely related, and they have different associations with other social academic and self concept data. Popularity is associated with other social and academic factors, whilst rejection is associated more with a pupils' own awareness of their poor relations with other children and with a less positive attitude to the part of the school day within which, presumably, their lack of social success is most apparent to them.

Individual Studies

During the course of interviews with pupils, and informal observation in the playground and class, it became clear that several of them had difficulties in forming friends, and upset others. Here I briefly describe the comments of other pupils about them, and try, by examining other social, academic and self concept data, to expand on reasons why the pupils were less successful.

Robert

Robert was often cited in the interviews as someone who was aggressive and caused others problems. This was reinforced by the 'guess who' data. At the beginning of the school year 10 pupils, and by the second interview 23 pupils, indicated that Robert was 'disruptive' according to the behavioural description read to them. At the first interview, 6 pupils, and by the second interview 18 pupils, indicated that Robert 'caused fights'. The 'play best' and 'play least' data were clear. At the first and second interview, none of the other pupils in the class nominated Robert as someone they liked to play with best, while 8 at the first, and 22 at the second, interview nominated him as someone they liked to play with least. At the second interview only 1 pupil nominated him as some-one who 'cooperates'. At the first interview, Robert chose David (who left the class mid way through the term), Grant and Josh as those he liked to play with best, but none of these chose him. At the second interview he chose Malcolm, Grant, and Martin, but again none of these chose him as one of the three people they liked to play with best. Robert was therefore a very unpopular boy and this had much to do with the perceived way he disrupted things and caused fights. To some extent he seemed aware of others' views of him; he had the fifth lowest peer relation self concept score on the Marsh SDQ1.

Robert's social difficulties were accompanied by academic difficulties. He had the second lowest Edinburgh Reading Quotient (89). He seemed aware of his academic difficulties, having the third lowest reading self concept, the second lowest maths self concept, and the lowest general school self concept scores. Others also saw him as someone needing help; he had the highest number of nominations at the second interview as someone who 'seeks help' in class. He also had the third lowest general self concept scores and so his poor self esteem was not only related to school progress. He had a high view of relations with his parents.

Grant
There were a number of similarities between Robert and Grant. At the first interview 10 pupils, and at the second interview 21, thought Grant was disrupt-ive, and at the first interview 14, and at the second 24, said he caused fights. Only 2 children at both interview points chose Grant as someone they liked to play with best, but 4 at the first, and 17 at the second, chose Grant as someone they liked to play with least.

Grant was cited by many pupils in their interviews as aggressive and not pleasant to be with. Unlike Robert, there was little sense that he was aware of how others perceived him. In his first interview he said he did not have many fights and then only because the other person caused trouble. He gave the least coherent answers. He spoke dispassionately of breaking someone's nose at his last school. There was no sign at all that he saw his own behaviour as a problem. This lack of social self awareness was shown in the SDQ scores, in that his peer relations score was above average. In contrast to Robert, Grant had high general self esteem. Like Robert, Grant's social difficulties were accompanied by academic difficulties. Grant was absent when the Edinburgh test was conducted, but had much the lowest AH1 perceptual reasoning score in the class. Here he was more self aware; he had the second lowest reading self concept.

Linda

Linda was the least popular of the girls. Only 1 pupil at the first, and none at the second, nominated her as someone they liked to play with best, whilst 4 at the first, and 7 at the second, nominated her as someone they liked to play with least. She had low scores on 'cooperates' (0 and 3 at the two interview points), but high nominations on 'disrupts' (9 and 16 — the third highest after Grant and Robert). She was seen by others as 'spiteful' and 'bossy'. In her own interviews she seemed confused when describing her relations with others. At the first interview she said she played with Helen, Gillian, Katherine, and Ruth, and said that these were her friends, but these children did not cite her as a friend or playmate; indeed, none of these four ticked her as someone they liked to play with best, and on the LITOP (Like to Play With) two indicated that they preferred not to play with her and one did not mind either way. At the second interview, Linda chose Malcolm, Tim and Gillian, but none of these three chose her as someone they liked to play with, and Tim actually chose her as someone he liked to play with least.

She also had exaggerated views on her own social influence and what she saw as a leading role in suggesting games. When asked 'why are they friends with you?' she said 'because they respect, they like me and they don't just stomp off, and start getting angry'. Elsewhere she gave an unusual answer to a question concerning why she was friends with others: she said others asked her to be their friend.

Unlike Grant she was troubled by her social difficulties. She had the lowest peer relations self concept score. In her interviews she said bluntly that others did not want to play with her, and this affected her liking of playtime. But her explanations for falling out were alternatively honest and self deceiving: 'Because they were being horrible to me, and they've got new friends. And I've been with them for ages . . . I've fallen out because they're just getting too old, been with them for ages'. Linda had a high physical abilities self concept, but the third lowest physical appearance self concept, and third lowest general self esteem.

These case studies show ways in which measures of social preference, social functioning, self concept, and academic ability interconnect in particular ways for individual children. Although there were similarities between the three children, which would probably lead to them being classified as 're-jected' in studies of social status, there were also differences between them, that warn against the use of over-inclusive categories of social functioning, and which would need to be taken into account in any school intervention.

Conclusion

This chapter has reported results from an exploratory study of friendship formation during the first year at junior school of a class of 8–9-year-olds. The study is limited in terms of the size of sample, and generalizations to other schools are clearly not justified. But the careful analysis of accounts from pupils, supplemented by quantitative analysis of social preference, self concept and academic data, has allowed a picture to emerge of some processes involved in friendship formation in this particular class of children.

Here, I pick up several main themes emerging in this chapter. Firstly, it would be wrong, on the basis of this study, to see the development of friendships as only or principally occurring in dyads. The girls had formed unisex 'cliques' of between four to five friends. It has been said (Selman, 1980 in Furman, 1989) that it is not until adolescence that peer groups share common interests and a consensus of norms. However, in a number of ways, revealed particularly in playground behaviour, one could see the groups in this study sharing a common interest, purpose and identity. Awareness of this may be rudimentary at first. As Furman (1989) has said, it may be that children experience groups as a cohesive unit before being conscious of shared norms and beliefs.

Examination of pupil accounts has also showed that categorization of friendship distinctions in terms of best friend, friends, and non-friends would not be fine enough. Some children described an hierarchy of friendships, with one or perhaps two children at the apex and groups of varying size at lower levels. Some, as we have seen, did not have or want to have best friends, preferring to be in a larger group of friends. Furthermore, changes over time in friendship groups could involve shifts in friendship status within groups, as well as movement between groups. These distinctions could benefit from further exploration.

It was possible to identify a number of factors that, from the pupils' point of view, explained why they became friends. These were: age, length of acquaintance, contact made at a previous school, shared interests, and personal characteristics like giving help, sharing a sense of humour, not being bossy, and working together. Many of these explanations involve variations of 'similarities' (Epstein, 1989). Some show the important role of environmental factors, such as neighbourhood influences. Some factors, like age, are the 'surface of selection' (Epstein, 1989). Others, showing more 'depth of selection', involving appreciation of, and grounds for, friendship in qualities such as not being bossy, having a sense of humour, and, most commonly, giving help. These results indicate the advantage of building a categorization of reasons for friendship on pupils' freely given accounts.

The different reasons given for being friends needs further exploration and teasing out. For example, it is difficult on the evidence here to judge to what extent these deeper factors govern or merely justify friendships already struck up on the basis of other characteristics. There is also an allied question concerning the interconnections between the factors, for example, the relative force of within, and out of school, factors. The suggestion here is that out of school, and previous school factors play a part in, and help support, early friendships, but within school and 'deeper' characteristics then become the dominant factors.

One can conceive of the likelihood of friendships occurring in terms of a cluster of factors, some environmental/situational and some personal. Probably the balance between the situational and the personal shifts toward the latter as the child develops with age, but the balance of personal and situational characteristics may well need to be considered more on an individual basis, in order to understand the processes involved, and build effective models of factors influencing friendship choice.

The early formation of friendship groups was examined. Furman and Childs (in Hartup, 1989) call these early interactions, which involve questions to determine common interests, 'coorientation', which is followed by shared actions. This term does not perhaps do justice to the dynamic and socially creative nature of these first weeks when, often on the basis of existing contacts, and through the medium of playground games, new networks are created. There is a flexibility and experimentation about this stage which the interview methodology could only partially capture. Given the speed with which friendship networks appeared to be established, and as we have seen, the ensuing stability over the school year in friendship groups, these early contacts seem to be important in creating influential impressions of each other and setting in place many of the components of pupils' subsequent social networks. They therefore deserve more detailed study than has been possible here.

Implications for Schools

In the last chapter we saw a rich informal life and varied activities at breaktime. In this chapter we have seen the rich social life that accompanies them. Breaktime is an important forum for friendship formation, and the learning of many social skills and adjustments that support this process. Again, any changes to breaktime should be made with an eye on the likely effects on the informal social life of school. Of course, as many parents will know, and research is beginning to explore (Hartup, 1996), friendships can be destructive as well as positive. Children can be made upset by the attitudes of their friends, and, especially after a while in school, it can be a terrifying prospect to have to find new friends, when a friendship or friendship group has broken down. But these problems are unlikely to be improved by reducing the opportunities for working them out. Rather, it implies the value of a sensitivity by staff to breaktime experience and friendship groups. The fact that teachers are not now the main supervisors at breaktime, suggests much could be gained from discussion between teachers and supervisory staff about friendship groups. This can happen in schools, but supervisors can find there is little time, or encouragement, for meaningful discussion about individual children at breaktime (Sharp, 1994).

    The early days in a new school are a time of considerable uncertainty for children, especially those without support from previous school,

---

or neighbourhood, contacts. It seems likely that developing new friend-ships can help reduce uncertainty and thus help adjustment to school. This may be affected by wider educational policy changes within which parents, under a more market-led system, are encouraged to search out schools, not always the local school, which offer the best possibilities of academic success. In travelling further afield, the child may have less connection with the surrounding community, and may accordingly experi-ence more difficulties in building up networks of contacts, leading to secure friendships.

A main theme of the last two chapters has been the connections between friendship formation and playground activities and games. I would like now to draw out some main conclusions. When asked about friendships at school, pupils' accounts were often couched in terms of life on the playground. Play-ground games seem to have a role that changes with time after entry to school. The game supports and gives a justification for first contacts, and this seems to be an important social function of games at this age, and stage in the year. They provide the means by which children can first make contact — they are a means toward a form of social networking — and through which shared activities can then develop and friendships begin. This is one process at work during 'first encounters' in friendship formation, about which Hartup (1992) concludes little is known. During this early stage, expansion of social networks is likely to be related to an expansion of game repertoire. It seems likely that those with the richest repertoire of games have the more extensive social network, though this possibility needs to be tested.

At a later point after entry into school, the social function of games ap-pears to change to one of supporting and maintaining friendship groups, and is perhaps best described as a stage of 'consolidation'. Games are a main medium through which friendships are enacted and they also help to define a group as distinct. There was some evidence that over time stability in friend-ship groups leads to a narrower variety of games. So, as friendships develop, so games develop, as suggestions are made and taken up. There was evidence that different friendship status levels were defined by different games. Games played within a group serve to define and give identity to that group, and show how it differs from others. Friends tend to like the same games. Games can buffer and support the progress through school or friendship groups. Games can also be a way of exploring aspects of relations between groups ('borderwork', is the term used by Thorne, 1993), for example, chasing games involving boys and girls.

Games and friendship are interconnected because of the way that friend-ship and social relations are expressed through what 8-year-olds *do* together — that is, games and play. So an examination of games — their content, their development, the social dynamics involved, gives important insights into the formation and development of friendships. The connections are intriguing but on present evidence can only be tentative. They could profit from further research, for example by using other forms of data such as systematic observation, as well as pupil report. If it is the case that children have less opportunity out of school for developing friendships away from adult supervision, then this makes more important the understanding of processes in friendship formation in school settings, and of the facilitative role of games.

In the main longitudinal study, pupils were interviewed at 16 years about friendships in school. These interviews showed that breaktime was still a main forum for friendships and social contact but these were not now mediated through games. It is to the accounts of older pupils that I now turn.

Chapter 7

The Experience of Friendship at Breaktime at 16 Years

It all depends . . . if I'm in a class like maths, I've got my best mate what I've grown up with since nursery and I just sit with him all the time. But when it comes to breaktime, I hang around with all my mates, all my different mates.

In the last two chapters I explored the development of games and friendships in one class of 8–9-year-olds. In the next three chapters I return to the main longitudinal study, and the interviews conducted with the same pupils, when aged 7, 11 and 16 years. In this chapter I extend the analysis of friendships by analysing the nature of friendships among the children when aged 16 years, and therefore during their last year of secondary school. In a similar way to the last chapter, I examine the nature of friendship groups and factors influencing choice of friends, but, because of the larger number of children, and the way the sample was set up (see Chapter 2), it was also possible to look at the influence of ethnic and gender differences.

The first two research questions addressed in this chapter are therefore similar to the last chapter:

1   What are the characteristics and composition of friendship groups? How do pupils themselves define friendship relationships? What distinctions do they make about friendship categories, such as best and other friends? Are these distinctions affected by ethnic and sex differences? Brown (1989) identified three types of peer group in adolescence: dyads, cliques and crowds. Cliques are defined as a small group of say 5–10 adolescents who 'hang around' together, and which are seen by members as the primary base of interaction with others. Brown's review suggests the literature is unclear about structural developments in the nature of cliques over adolescence, though the change from the rather small same-class based cliques of the primary stage, as described in the last chapter, to the complex arrangements of cliques and crowds at the secondary school is more noticeable.

Many researchers have commented on a developmental change in friendship expectations — from an interest in friends as activity partners, as we saw in the last chapter, to expectations of loyalty and trust in friendships. Many have followed Sullivan in identifying the importance of 'chum' friendships during adolescence, for example, for support and enhancing self esteem, and the move toward more stable and intimate relationships with peers (Savin-Williams and Berndt, 1990). This change is accompanied by distancing from parents and adults in school and a developing sense of self identity. Brown (1990) argues that the importance of belonging to a peer group diminishes steadily by the end of secondary school, though some research suggests that by the last year of secondary school there is more cohesiveness between class members, perhaps as they are confronted with shared concerns about impending exams and life outside school. As with younger pupils, peer groups and friendships can support social adjustment in school (Berndt and Hawkins in Savin-Williams and Berndt, 1990), and adolescents who have a positive view of their friendship group develop a positive view of all classmates.

Savin-Williams and Berndt (1990) show that the number of best friends peaks in early adolescence, at about four to six, and then declines thereafter until adulthood, when typically there is one best friend, a few close friends, some good friends, and a number of colleagues or acquaintances. But research has seldom made the distinctions between terms like best friend, close friendships and friends which we saw in the last chapter were needed to adequately portray friendships even in younger children.

2   What factors affect friendship choices?

To what extent are the factors identified in the last chapter, with regard to younger children, still applicable? For example, are contacts from primary school still influencing current friendships? What is the role of situational factors, in particular, the breaktime context?

The next two research questions are additional to those in the last chapter.

3   To what extent did pupils from different ethnic groups form friendships? What factors influenced mixed and separate friendship groups?

Denscombe (1983) pointed out that teachers' perception of their pupils as unprejudiced in terms of choice of friends, conflicts with the common finding that pupils show ethnic bias in their choice of friends. Davey (1987) reports on the pervasiveness of within ethnic group friendship choices, and how these are well established by age 7, and become more noticeable with age. He found that Asian children showed more ethnocentricity in friendship choices, than white and Afro-Caribbean children. He makes the point that within ethnic group friendship choices were more obvious in the playground than in the classroom and this might be one reason why teachers tend to perceive more mixed ethnic group friendships than pupils. These points highlight the likely significance of breaktime as a setting for studying within and inter ethnic group friendship relations.

Brown (1989), on the basis of US studies, has shown that a main influence on friendship choice and peer relations in adolescence is the ethnic composition of the school. In schools with a variety of ethnic groups, this may be a main defining variable in cliques that are formed. Yet he also concludes that we know very little about the degree to which adolescent peer groups are ethnically mixed, and under what conditions ethnic group membership supersedes other influences on secondary school peer group relations. What do the results from the pupil interviews tell us?

4 To what extent did boys and girls form friendships? What factors influenced mixed and separate sex friendships?

Davey (1987) concludes that gender differences as well as ethnic differences are obstacles to friendship choices. There is some consensus in the research literature that girls and boys differ in friendship choices and behaviour. Girls place more emphasis on affiliation and intimacy, while boys place more emphasis on status. Epstein (1989) concludes that research has shown considerable sex segregation in friendships, from nursery to early adolescence, but that by adolescence the situation is complicated by the appearance of both mixed-aged and same-sex groups.

We saw in the last chapter how at breaktime separation between boys and girls could be at its most clear, but also how it could be tested and explored in games and activities together. What did the pupils' accounts at 16 years reveal about sex differences in friendships at school, particularly during breaktime?

Nature and Composition of Friendship Groups

Let us look first at the quantitative results. Most of the pupils (80 per cent) said they hung around with a group of other pupils; only 1 in 5 did not. As for the size of friendship group, a third (29 per cent) said 5 or less, another third (31 per cent) said 6–10 people and 20 per cent said more than 10. In contrast to the 8–9-year-olds, these friendship groups are larger in size, and there did not appear to be any sex differences in their size. Friends were by no means restricted to their own class. Only 18 per cent said that their friends were from their own tutor or registration class. But, in the same way as the 8–9-year-old pupils, friends were mostly (76 per cent) from the same year group. Boys, particularly black boys, were more likely than girls to have friends in other year groups. Most (80 per cent) saw their friends out of school, and there was a tendency for this to be more likely in the case of girls than boys.

We then asked them if they had a best friend or best friends. (As with the 8/9-year-olds we left it to the children themselves to define 'best friends'.) As many said they had best friends (46 per cent), as did not (49 per cent). Girls were much more likely to say they had a best friend. But again, as in the last chapter, an analysis of friendships only in terms of best friends, and on the basis of numerical analysis, does not do justice to their social networks. We now turn to the accounts of friendships given in the interviews, in order to understand something of the complexities involved. Five main distinctions were identified.

Just One Best Friend

P I just have one specific friend . . . I just talk to him about certain things that I don't want other people to know, 'cause I know who the people are that will go back and tell everybody else, so I don't really tell them, I keep it to myself unless I'm telling the person that I specifically talk to.

Friends within a Larger Friendship Group

As with the 8–9-year-olds, some of the 16-year-olds had a small group of 'best friends' in the context of a wider set of contacts. Here is a white girl:

P I'm part of the group . . . there are best friends within it, like two of my friends are best friends, and there are people I won't get on so well with in the group . . . it's like . . . two groups stuck together.

The following girl also had a small group of one or two best friends, within a larger group of about 12, though here there is another, additional friendship group.

P Well that depends, there is one or two people that . . . are with me, but then we can go into another group that are in my class as well and we all just stand there and talk and that . . . I do speak to a lot of people, but we don't always hang around with each other, we do go off to talk to other people or go to other people's places, but mainly I am with my two friends.

No Best Friends

There were a number of distinctions under this general heading. The following girl had a fragmented friendship network because, rather than one close friend, she had close friends who were not themselves a part of the same group, and she therefore divided her time between them.

P I've got a few close friends who don't hang around together themselves so I'm like between a few groups. I don't just hang around with one person, I like divide my time round all my friends. I don't suppose I've really got one special friend.

Similarly, the following boy spent time with a group rather than with 'best' friends:

P I don't really have best friends. I hang round with a group.

Feeling Uncomfortable about Being Part of a Friendship Group

P I don't like to walk with big groups 'cause that's when the friction happens. I prefer to move with people that I'm closer with. I find it very hard
to trust people, so that's why.

A common observation about adolescents is their strong need for affiliation, bound up with a search for identity and a growing independence from
adults. But the interviews indicated tensions underlying any general developmental process. Some spoke of concerns about developing close friendships
and of worries about being let down. The peer group can be supportive and
aid adjustment, as we have discussed, but for some, like the next girl, there
were reservations about getting too close to others.

P I think now I'm more of a person who doesn't need to hang around in
groups . . . other people see (it) as a necessity, they see it as if you're on
your own, you're like a loner or nobody wants to talk to you . . . But I just
choose not to because when I look to specific groups of people who I see
like in the year room I don't see myself as wanting to be a real part of any
of that. Even though I may be good friends with some of the people . . .
I won't just exclude them, I'll just go up and talk to them lightly.

Others expressed more fundamental difficulties with having best friends.

P No, I don't like to have a best friend, we just argue. I'm friends with
everyone in my year, I speak to everyone and I'm not always with the
same person. It's better to be with other people.

This reservation about particular friendships is similar to that offered
by some of the junior aged pupils in the last chapter. Some did not want to
commit themselves to being friends because they could be let down. This is
the negative side of a concern with loyalty and intimacy.

P I don't really describe anyone as a friend because everyone lets you down
now and again . . . just people you hang around with.

All Friends in the Group

But, for others, like the following two girls, not having close or best friends
could result from a positive appreciation of equal affiliation within a larger
group.

P Well with my friends, we're all in a big group, there's 10, 15 of us. No one
(has) a best friend, like we're all each other's best friends, we can always
tell each other anything. That's the way it is in our group, you know
everybody is like equal, each and every single one of us. We're just really
good friends. Not like some people, we don't have one particular best
friend, we just speak to everyone.

P   I used to have a best friend but now he's gone off to work. There's a whole load of us who hang round, we're all like really good friends like, stick by each other. I've been mates with them since I started . . . I know most of the people in this school now, everyone knows me, it's a good atmosphere, between friends it's good.

These observations appear consistent with Brown's (1989) observation that pupils near the end of school can become cohesive and draw together, as a future out of school beckons.

What Factors Affect Friendship Choices?

Affected by Situation: Importance of Breaktime

P   There's one group who's like my tutor group, and that's fairly big and I'll hang around with them in lessons, and then there's another group who I hang around with at break and in the summer we all sit out on the grass together. So it's like massive by that time.

P   It all depends . . . if I'm in a class like maths, I've got my best mate I've grown up with since nursery and I just sit with him all the time. But when it comes to breaktime, I hang around with all my mates, all my different mates.

Different people can be encountered, and therefore different kinds of social contact occur, in different parts of the school day and in different settings within the school. In the first extract, friendship categorization is connected to breaktime, in that the pupil 'hangs around' with her best friends, and spends time with them at break, while her other friends are those she meets in her tutor group and in lessons. One role of breaktime is to provide a forum within which close friends, perhaps not in the same class, can meet; without breaktime there would be little opportunity for this, at least within school.

Again:

P   Mainly three of us, but it depends where we are, like in the library . . . certain people sit on our table, and in the dinner hall certain people sit on our table, and for that time, they're like the group. They're not the group of friends. When we're walking about that's just me, Karen and the other friend.

As we have seen elsewhere, dinner time is an important setting for seeing friends in school.

P   Yeah, like we usually all hang about together, or we just like go off like and do our own thing . . . I usually hang about with Kelly . . . say I'm going up dinner or I'm going to have a jacket potato . . . we meet each other.

The reference to 'hanging around' as a description of what one did with friends came up again and again. And 'hanging around' is usually done, during the school day, at breaktime.

Out of School

We saw in the last chapter that friendship status in younger pupils could be denoted by contact out of school. This was also evident in the older pupils. One girl said of her best friend in a group: 'I've got one that I think of more and we do more things outside the school.'

For the next pupil, friendship status is closely tied to degree of contact out of school:

> **P**   Yeah, I would see them outside school, but I wouldn't make it like on a regular basis, only if they're like my good friends . . . I don't really talk to them as good as I would talk to my good friends. I would just leave it at that, outside school. I wouldn't phone them or like socialise with them.

For some of the pupils, though, friends in school were different to friends out of school. For the following boy, this appeared to stem from a deliberate effort to keep the two worlds separate.

> **P**   I just like to stick to school friends in school and my own friends at home.

For a girl:

> **I**   And would you see many of them outside school?
> **P**   I used to see them nearly every day, like all of them, but now I just go round my girlfriend's house. They've all got girlfriends or boyfriends. We split up outside school but when we're in school we're together.

Here, the development of friendships with the opposite sex had reduced the amount of larger group and same-sex contacts out of school. But, in other cases, the separation between home and school friendships had much to do with the practical problem of not living close to each other. These secondary schools could draw pupils from a wide area of London, and pupils could have long journeys to and from school. As a result, although 16-year-olds are more independent than younger pupils, meeting friends out of school was in some cases impractical and expensive.

Some Friendships Were Long-standing, Originating in Primary School

> **I**   And do you see them outside school as well?
> **P**   I see a few of them, it's not like I go to see them, 'cause I have friends like from primary school who I still see when I'm home . . . I don't really see

them 'cause they like live quite far. I live in Earlsfield, one lives in like West Ken, one lives in Brixton . . .

This quote shows how friendships out of school can endure from previous primary school attendance. In the last chapter we saw ways in which social relations on entry to junior school were affected by having been together at an earlier school. Pupils at the end of their secondary schooling can look back over a longer period of friendships developed at school, yet some said that present friendship choices were still affected by knowing people from primary school, and sometimes these had endured more than friendships developed in secondary school.

But friendships from primary school days were not always viewed positively, as one girl explained:

P When we come here from primary school I asked to be taken away from all my friends from primary school so I could get on. Like my mum said to me the other day, 'maybe it's better that you was taken and put in a different class 'cause you can get on with your work, and like if you was in a class with them you would be talking to them half the time'. It's just like hanging around with all the same people since nursery, and my primary schools.

But, by their final year in school, pupils could see the value in longstanding friendships.

P I have two close friends with me in this school who like I've known for ages from primary and we all live in the same area and they are in the same class.

Common Lifestyles and Music

The importance at 16 years of shared views and taste in music was apparent in affecting friendship choices, and defining who was in the friendship group. Here is a white girl:

I What is it that you think keeps you all together, what do you all have in common?

P The way we dress . . . we can get a lot of stick from the other pupils . . . about the way we dress and what we do . . . I suppose we're the people that have been taken the mickey out of for what we've been dressed like or done, and we've just come together . . . it's a bit Indi I suppose.

Age of Friend

As with the 8-year-old pupils, the age of friends could be important. Mixed age contacts were facilitated by having relations in school.

> **I** So you have friends in every year, how come you manage that?
>
> **P** I've got cousins in every year so their friends are like my friends, 'cause I mess around with them.

But as with younger children, peer pressure could be exerted in order to stop mixed age friendships. A white girl explained:

> **P** We did have this one girl who . . . tried . . . she comes to school with me 'cause we live near each other . . . I made a big mistake of introducing her to my friends. She suddenly got this idea 'cause she knew them that she could hang round with them, she's only, what, year 9. I mean, in the end my friends are saying 'Tell her to go' and I said 'I won't tell her 'cause you're paying her attention'. So in the end she was told like 'We don't mean to be horrible or anything but, like, you're just a little too young to hang around with us and what we discuss, so why don't you go and find some of your own friends'. She kind of went away after that.

To What Extent Did Pupils from Different Ethnic Groups Form Friendships?

Pupils were encouraged to give fully their views on, and descriptions about, whether they had mixed friendship groups, in terms of ethnic background, whether pupils from different ethnic groups were as fully a part of the friendship group as other friends, and why (if appropriate) they felt they did not have friends from different ethnic backgrounds. Were friendship groups ethnically mixed?

Almost all (85 per cent) said the group they hung around with was ethnically mixed, comprising both black and white pupils; only seven pupils said they hung around with people who were white only and only seven pupils said black only. As would be expected, it was whites who were in all-white groups and blacks in all-black groups. To get a better picture of whether ethnicity and friendship were connected, we next asked them if the people they hung around with, who came from a different ethnic group, were part of their group of friends. The proportion now dropped to 66 per cent, but, even so, we can see that a majority still said their friends were from different ethnic backgrounds.

When asked to explain why they had friends from different ethnic groups, the main answers were that they were tolerant, non racist and open minded (nine pupils) and that they never really thought about it or got along with everyone (10 pupils). Four pupils thought it was a non-issue and that they did not notice colour. As to why they did not have friends from a different background, eight said they had never thought about it or it was just the way it is, and five said that they tended to hang around with people with the same interests as themselves, and people from different ethnic groups had different interests.

In common with the view emerging from the numerical results, it is important to say that the general impression obtained from many pupils was of a lack of hostility between ethnic groups. This is apparent in answers in which they stressed that they did not like sticking to people who happened to come from their own ethnic background, or view people in terms of colour or ethnic origin, but were more inclined to view others in terms of what they were like as people.

A white girl:

> P I'm not the kind of person that will only mix with my own kind because I don't believe in that . . . I don't think that's right . . . if there's someone that's Asian and I can get on with them, they'll be my friend, and I'll like them, and I have Asian friends and white friends.

And a black girl:

> P Yeah, it's mixed . . . I think in primary school it was more just black friends but now I've come here it's mixed . . . Like there's something of each of those people that I feel comfortable with as friends and they've all got their different personalities that I like and that I can fit in with.

And black boy:

> P Probably 'cause I'm an open person I can mix with really anybody and, because the school's actually got mixed community, really you just make friends through the years. You don't really look at a person and see white, black, half-caste, Turkish, you just see them as a friend and as a person.

Some pupils were, therefore, at pains to say they viewed other pupils not in terms of their ethnic origin but in terms of what they are like as people. They were, in other words, stressing the individual rather than the group basis for friendship choice. To some extent, this was evident with the younger children discussed in the last chapter, but in the case of the older children it was expressed more clearly.

Some were very clear about their dislike of racism. Here is a white girl:

> P I know quite a lot of white people my age, not in this school, that are racist towards black people. But I don't think that there is any in this school because it is a really mixed school. I don't think people think that way . . . I don't like racism at all, I hate it.

Clearly, one needs to be cautious about accepting too easily a positive view about relations between pupils from different ethnic groups. It is possible that some pupils in the interview situation would feel obliged to present their school experiences in a positive way. It is also likely that they would be aware of school policies and views on racism and this could affect their account of relations between ethnic groups. In the last extract we can see that the school context has an effect on the pupil's view, and I return to this later.

Pupils' accounts indicated that there were also limits to the degree of inter-group relations. As we saw with the numerical data, although pupils could say they hung around with mixed groups, further questioning showed that children from other groups were less likely to be part of their friendship group. Here is a black boy:

> **P** They're mostly black but I've got a couple of good white friends in school.
> **I** And are they, the white kids, in that smaller group?
> **P** Out of six?
> **I** Yeah
> **P** No.

Some, like the following black girl, were clear that groups did tend to comprise pupils from a similar ethnic background, and that there was separation between the groups.

> **P** If you was to go to any tutor group, and especially our one, you can more or less call our table the black table 'cause everyone on our table is black, the next table . . . it's all white and the other table it's all Asian . . . And like a couple of mixed race sort of hangs between both, that's quite funny.

And a white girl:

> **P** I'm not being racist or nothing, but all the black kids hang around to-gether, the white kids hang around together, all the Asian kids hang around together, you know I don't really make friends with them because they are not really around to make friends with . . .

Some pupils agreed there was a separation between groups, on the basis of ethnic origin, but were quick to say that this did not mean there was hostility between the groups. This is well captured in the following quote from a white girl:

> **P** If you walked into my form now you'd say our class was completely racist because all the blacks sit on this side and all the whites sit on this side, but it's not — we are the best class going, we stick together we have a laugh . . . we stick together as in friend-wise but we're all good with each other. It's not because 'oh we hate blacks' or 'they hate whites' . . . we're all good friends still.

This is supported by a black boy:

> **P** The black kids will go to the chip shop, white kids will stay, go to the park. Like the Indians, Chinese, they will play football. It's like always

been like that . . . we all get on . . . My friends and the white boys in my year, we're all good friends as well. When we're in class we sit next to each other and talk and that.

From this perspective, the explanation of the separation between pupils of different ethnic backgrounds is relatively prosaic, and due to such factors as a shared history of having known each other for a long time. At this age, shared interests give substance to a common identification with the group. Some white pupils, for example, had quite distinct tastes in music, for example, 'Indi' music, that was unlikely to be shared by other ethnic groups. Separation between the groups is likely to increase in proportion to the overtness with which musical preferences are seen to be making a statement about the group. The relevance of breaktime is that expressions of shared interests are more likely then, and the basis of group separation therefore more apparent. Even so, the impression gained was that members of different groups could be convivial with each other, if rather indifferent.

For some, like this black boy, the differences between ethnic groups was more fundamental still, and located in a common ancestry and history of immigration:

I   Ok, why do you think that whites and Asians don't belong to your group?

P   We can probably relate to each other . . . our parents are from the same country and we know about each other's cultures more.

So, just like the younger children, described in the last chapter, one import-ant basis of friendship is similarity, though in the case of the older children, commonalities are more sophisticated, and include common interests, like music, as well as more broadly a shared culture, and a shared lifestyle.

So far I have looked at the more positive side of relations between ethnic groups. We have seen how some disliked racism, and how some said they based friendship choices not on colour or ethnic group but on personal qual-ities of individual pupils. We have also seen how some recognized a separation of ethnic groups but that this reflected differences in shared interests rather than any hostility or antipathy. But some answers did indicate difficulties be-tween groups. One white girl analysed the way that relations between the ethnic groups could sour and the way that the school could provide a malign context for relations between groups:

P   Well in this school — this school's got to be the worst school for racist remarks.

I   Really?

P   Yeah, 'cause this school, there's a lot of black boys in this school and they all stick together, they pick on you.

I   So in this school basically white boys hang around with white boys and black boys only hang around with black kids?

P   Yeah, all the time, all the time . . . You never see like all the black boys hanging around with all the white boys, never, not in this school.

I And why do you think it's happened like that, what do you think has caused that?

P I don't know, you get some white boys what really don't like the blacks and they've been racist and it's gone all round the school, and gradually all the blacks don't want to know us and like we don't want to know them.

To What Extent Did Boys and Girls form Friendships? What Factors Influenced Mixed and Separate Sex Friendships?

The pupils were asked similar questions, as in the last section, but this time with regard to friendships involving boys and girls. Again, I look at the numerical results first. We need to bear in mind that about half of the pupils interviewed at 16 years (53 pupils) were in single sex schools. Of the rest, in mixed sex schools, there was more indication of sex of pupil as a factor affecting friendship groups, in comparison to ethnic group, though even here there were reports of mixed gender friendship groups. Altogether, 26 pupils said they had as many girls as boys as friends, 15 said mainly boys or boys only, and 8 said mainly girls or girls only. As would be expected, girls were more likely to be in mainly or all girl groups, and boys in mainly or all boy groups. White boys were more likely than the other three groups to be friends only with others of the same ethnic group and sex.

When girls were asked if boys were in their friendship group, and boys were asked if girls were in their friendship group, overall 20 per cent said yes, and 30 per cent said no (as we have seen, 50 per cent were in single sex schools). Although these results are not directly comparable with those reported in the last two chapters, the indication is that mixed gender friendship groups are more likely in the case of older children.

When asked to explain why they mixed with the opposite sex, their answers were that they just did and that they never thought about it, that they liked the company of the opposite sex, and that they had things in common. Reasons why they did not have friends of the opposite sex were that they had different interests, for example, they did not like football; that their presence was inhibiting, for example, it was not possible to talk freely in their company; or that they tended to be immature.

The 16-year interviews showed that 'hanging around' and socializing (see Chapter 4) were main activities. In contrast to the preoccupation with active games, favoured by pupils during the primary years, the more sedentary activities of the older pupils provide a different context for relations between boys and girls. For the younger children, games can separate and draw together girls and boys, while, for the older pupils, hanging around can provide the context for talk that can separate or draw them together.

Pupils' views about mixed sex friendships ranged from positive to negative. Some, like the following boy, considered they mixed easily with the opposite sex.

P Maybe 'cause we're all basically the same, we all like the same things, do the same things, so, even the girls will challenge us to a game of football or something like that.

And a black girl:

P Well most of the time there's a couple of boys with us, but sometimes there's more. 'Cause we're not like immature — see a boy walking with a girl and start going 'eeer' and stuff like that, no. Friends.
I So things get more mixed, boys and girls as you get older?
P Yeah, it does.
I Ok, and you think that's a good thing?
P Yeah I think it's a good thing. Get to understand them and you find out they're more like you and you're more like them.

Some described peer pressure against cross sex contact, for example, in the form of teasing about a supposed romantic interest.

P I don't think boys really want to be seen hanging round with — like friends — with girls, 'cause they may get taken the mick out of. Like 'how's your girlfriend', and being stupid.

But the following girls thought that this was less likely now.

P When we were a bit younger we (used to say) 'oh no, you can't like have boys', but we're just like the same (as boys), and we like talking to each other and things.

P In this particular year you hang around with boys, you're not bothered, but when you're younger you hang around with . . . like female, but it's changed.

Another explanation offered for an increase in contact between boys and girls by 16 years was the reduction in the amount of time boys spent playing football, and therefore the more time available for contacting girls. This contrasts with the primary stage when the different activities of girls and boys, and, in particular, boys' overriding interest in playing football, could lead to separation between the sexes. This is another way that breaktime activities are implicated in developments in social relations in school.

I So why do you think boys have their groups and girls have their groups?
P I think it's from primary school really because like the boys would be going out and playing football and stuff and the girls would be there but now in the fifth year quite a few boys just walk about as well . . . people you hang around with.

Separate Sex Friendships

Others felt that boys and girls were not, by and large, friends in school. Some reasons for this were:

1   Different interests/breaktime activities

As we have seen, changes in breaktime activities could be one reason why boys and girls now had more contact, but some felt they could still have different pursuits, and these could still separate them. As one boy put it:

> **P**   Like we do things they don't like and they do things we don't like. Sometimes at lunchtime they'd go to Mere Street. We don't really like going there so we stay in. Or they have a girl chat and we have our boy chat . . .

Here a change in boys' activity at lunchtime brings about a separation of girls and boys. Previously, boys and girls seemed to have gone out together at lunchtime. Here is another boy:

> **P**   It's all boys (in my) group. There used to be some girls . . . we weren't playing pool then, when the girls used to come with us, we just used to go out to lunch, like we used to go down Dalston Cross Shopping Centre and hang around there for a while . . .

Even though, as we have seen, football had declined overall, it could still be the cause of separation between boys and girls. This point was made by boys:

> **P**   Where we play football there's a few benches just by the side and nearly all the girls . . . all sit there and chat and everything like that. We're just getting on with the football . . . I don't think girls really like football . . . But they like a good old chat.

and girls:

> **I**   And why do you think that boys aren't in your group?
> **P**   Because they've got different interests — at lunch the boys will be playing football and the girls will be just talking.

In the following quote, we see that the breaktime context can affect the degree of mixed sex contact. When walking around, girls and boys mix, but when football is played at breaktime, girls tend to be on the edge of the group, or leave it.

> **I**   Are there any girls in this big group you belong to?
> **P**   Some of them come but they won't play football. They sit on the side, sort of jeering on.
> **I**   Would you say that your friends are mainly boys or as many boys as girls?
> **P**   In this group there's not a lot of girls but when I go to my friends we meet up with loads of girls and we walk around. If we're in a group that plays football and girls don't like football — I've never met a girl that does — so it's mainly the girls go with other groups because we mainly play football.

I   But outside school when you're not playing football, you'd mix with girls more?

P   Yes.

2   Girls show more understanding

In some answers, girls preferred other girls because they were seen as more understanding of each other.

> **P**   The majority of boys are doing other things like playing football or stuff like that and you just tend to hang around with girls because they're more understanding . . . to women's problems.

3   More negative view

Sometimes not mixing with the opposite sex was explained in a more overtly negative way. One girl said of boys:

> **P**   They tend to be a bit irritating and immature . . . they're just really stupid in class, just say stupid things and act really stupid. I always end up arguing, I'm not really good friends with boys, with many boys . . . there's boys you talk to but I don't really consider them to be friends, more like acquaintances . . .

As we saw, when examining the numerical results, another explanation given for not mixing is that the opposite sex could inhibit talk.

I   Why is there not more mixed groups?

P   Due to the things that boys and girls like to do, because girls like to talk about the boys and then again the boys would like to talk about the girls. You really wouldn't want the girls involved in the boys' talk . . . if they were there, you wouldn't be able to talk about them.

Conclusion

In this chapter, I have examined the pupils' perspectives at 16 years on friendships in school. There were some differences to the friendships of 8–9-year-olds, described in the last chapter. Though exact comparisons are not possible, there is some suggestion that friendship groups of the older pupils were larger and there was little difference between boys and girls in the size of friendship groups. Girls, though, were more likely to say they had best friends and to meet friends out of school.

As with the younger children, analysis of friendship networks simply in terms of numbers of friends fails to capture their complexities. Some pupils had a few friends or one best friend, some had hierarchical networks, as with the younger children, with perhaps a few or one best friend in the context of a larger group, and some preferred to maintain a more equal degree of friendship with a number of people.

One new development in friendship relations was the emergence, for some pupils, of a mistrust of close friendships, because of negative experiences of previous friendships in school. More positively, and again different to the accounts from primary aged pupils, other pupils spoke by the end of their school days of the cohesion and closeness of large friendship groups. This indicated one important benefit of friendship groups at this age. It provided a valuable support as they moved toward their final exams and a life beyond school.

As with the younger pupils, I was interested in factors influencing friendships in school. We saw in Chapter 3 that pupils throughout their school lives feel that one of the main things they value about school is the opportunity for meeting friends. Breaktime is implicated in the development of friendships in school because it is the main setting within which pupils, possibly not in the same class, have the opportunity to meet. The pupils' accounts highlighted this situational effect on their social relations. The importance of breaktime in the development of friendships in school is likely to be constant throughout school, but the nature of the importance will change. As we saw in Chapters 5 and 6, 8–9-year-old friendships were often manifested in, and supported by, active breaktime activities and, in particular, playground games. But, by the end of school, friendships are furthered in the context of — in a sense — an *absence* of activity. As discussed in Chapter 4, it is relatively easy for adults to underestimate the value of 'hanging around' to pupils' social relations.

In this chapter I have examined the influence of ethnic origin and gender on friendships in school. Breaktime offered a context within which girls and boys could form separate groups, but also be drawn together. The context provided changed from primary to secondary. At primary level, different activities and games could separate boys and girls, with boys preferring football. By 16 years, football, active pursuits and games were less common, as we saw in Chapter 4, and 'hanging around' was now the context within which boys and girls could meet, at least in mixed sex schools. They could still have different interests at breaktime, of course, and these did result in same sex groups. There were also negative views expressed about the opposite sex, and some boys and girls were clearly unsure about their relations with each other. But there were opportunities for meeting and developing friendships with the opposite sex, in a relatively safe but thinly unsupervised setting. This is easily taken for granted, and its value not appreciated. Reductions in the duration of breaktimes might make it less likely.

Most pupils said they spent time, often at breaktime, in ethnically mixed groups, and some were keen to say that their choice of friendships was on the basis of individual characteristics of others rather than on the basis of their ethnic group. Where there was a perception that children mixed with others from within their ethnic group, this could result from having shared interests and tastes, for example in music, rather than because of any hostility toward other groups.

The study was based on pupil interviews and it is difficult to know how exactly the views expressed matched actual behaviour. This obviously raises issues regarding the validity of pupil accounts, which I addressed in Chapter 2. In some accounts, there were descriptions of conflict and negative views experienced about other ethnic groups, but, for the most part, there was a portrayal of a degree of separation between groups, but an absence of hostility and overt conflict. This is important, given that social psychological accounts of relations between groups have tended to emphasize conflict as a natural outcome of within group affiliation. There is likely to be a situational effect here, because pupils are likely to pursue their shared interests during breaktime more than during time in classrooms and so separation between groups is more likely to be apparent at breaktime.

Implications for Schools

Brown (1990) has observed that adolescent peer groups differ from primary aged peer groups in being more based in school buildings and desiring independence from adult attention and supervision. This suggests a special role for breaktime, because it is the main school setting within which a degree of privacy and freedom from adults is possible. This needs to be born in mind when considering changes to the duration and management of breaktime. It is relatively easy for teachers to see the role of breaktime during the primary years — running around and games are more visible and their purpose more obvious. In contrast, the social life and friendships of older children in school are much more easily taken for granted, but can be affected when changes to breaktime are being made.

With regard to the extent to which friendship groups were ethnically mixed, it must be said that the situation is likely to reflect the particular nature of London schools which the pupils attended. Most schools were ethnically diverse and since the days of the Inner London Education Authority (ILEA), inner London schools have had a long tradition of awareness of multicultural issues. This might help explain the positive impression concerning inter-ethnic group relations gained from some of the interviews. This is not meant to imply that all was successful, or that there is not a need to continue working to improve relations, but, at very least, pupils' discourse about social relations in school had been affected by school policies. Here is the account of one girl, stressing the way a mixed group can encourage learning about other's culture and background, which in turn strengthens and gives character to friendships.

> **P** We got Indian, white people, black people, half-caste people. We got all sorts of people in our group. And that's what I think is quite good because we learnt about each other's backgrounds and where we come from and each other's country, and where you originated from. It's really good, it makes our friendship better, I really think so.

I Sometimes I've been in schools, and white girls only seemed to
have white friends and black girls only seem to have black friends.
Why do you think your group is more mixed?

P We feel that, we want to know more about everyone. You know we
just don't want to hang around with black, or just hang around with
white people, we like it to be mixed. It kind of gives our group
character . . . it's really better when it's mixed, we like it that way.

To some extent getting on with pupils from different ethnic groups
is expedient — if there is no choice about which groups come into
school it makes sense to minimize conflict between those groups, in
order to make social life tolerable. But, in the final quote of this chapter,
we see more obviously the effect of school policy on relations between
different groups.

P The tutor groups are really mixed and when you're sat down, if
you're sitting on the table with just white people, my teacher will
note that down and she'll say 'Right I want you, you and you to
move.' So you sit on very mixed tables and if you have to work
together in very mixed groups you get to know other people's ideas,
what they're like and once you know what the person's like and
you can see beyond the colour, then you really mix in together
. . . because they know that once you leave school you're going
to be mixing with all sorts of people and if you haven't learnt how
to then it's going to be even more difficult.

These extracts indicate the potential schools have for setting a context for relations between different ethnic groups, and the extent to which
this will need to connect with social relations as expressed at breaktime.
We return to the school influence on inter-ethnic group relations in the
next two chapters, and arrive at conclusions in the last chapter.

Chapter 8

Pupils' Views on Teasing and Name Calling at 7, 11 and 16 Years

'If they mean it, it won't be a friend'.

As most of us will be able to testify, a common feature of school playground life is the teasing and name calling that takes place. Teasing to a large extent depends on an audience to witness it and give it effect, and the playground can provide a ready and attentive crowd and an ideal forum. The pervasive nature of teasing may be one reason why adults often perceive school playgrounds as settings for conflict and squabbling. It is also easily taken for granted, and this might explain why there has been little research on a number of aspects of teasing and name calling. In this chapter, I look closely at the pupils' experience of teasing and name calling from 7 to 16 years.

Though there has been little direct research on teasing between children, it has been covered as part of a broader interest. This has tended to have been of two kinds. Firstly, there have been more qualitative studies. The Opies (1959) recorded the inventive names by which children can insult and deride each other. Other studies have included Morgan, O'Neill and Harre (1979, in Cohn 1988), Davies (1982), and Sluckin (1981). It has also been considered as part of a study of racism in mostly white primary schools (Troyna and Hatcher, 1992). A second approach has involved more quantitative surveys of teasing and name calling, for example, studies by Kelly (1988), Cohn (1988) and Mooney, Creeser and Blatchford (1991).

One aim of this chapter is to extend previous research by combining aspects of a quantitative survey approach with more detailed analysis of individual pupils' experiences of teasing. In earlier reports we have presented results on pupils' views on teasing and name calling at 7 years (Tizard et al., 1988), and at 11 years (Mooney et al., 1991). This chapter extends this work, and provides a longer term perspective, by considering developments in teasing at the end of the three stages of education in England, that is, at 7, 11 and 16 years.

As we have argued before (Mooney et al., 1991), the distinctions between teasing and bullying are not always clear and they are often considered together. One consequence is the tendency to view teasing and name calling as a negative influence on peer relations, and for schools to consider actions and school policy to stop them. Some teasing and name calling is obviously distressing and hurtful. But some teasing may involve different behaviours and different intentions to bullying, and the nature and impact of teasing, as opposed to bullying, needs much more careful study. Much is now understood about changes with age in bullying. Whitney and Smith (1993) found a steady decrease from 7/8 to 16 years in the incidence of being bullied, though less in bullying others. Olweus also found a decline in being bullied with age (Olweus, 1993). But despite being far more frequent than bullying, there has been less research on developments with age in teasing and name calling.

Better understanding of teasing is likely to come from viewing it as a part of relations between peers more generally. As Knapp and Knapp have said 'jeers are not always shouted as a part of a quarrel, but are part of the verbal texture of everyday relationships' (in Evans, 1989). It may be that some teasing is not always meant to hurt others but may vary in its purpose and effect according to the social context, for example, whether with friends, acquaintances and non-friends. The school playground is likely to be a main setting for teasing because it is a main setting for peer interaction in schools, and also because of the relatively playful and unsupervised behaviours that occur there.

Labrell (1994) has argued that the teasing by fathers of their young children may have a positive impact on the child's cognitive and social development, because it introduces novelty and ambiguity, as well as negotiation. If this is true with regard to adult–child relations, could it also be true of child–child interactions? This is suggested by sociolinguistic research (Kwo, 1994) in which female friends have been found to repeatedly mock themselves and put others down. In African-American groups, teasing can take the form of 'verbal duels' which may be in a sense aggressive, but also a contest of verbal facility (Pellegrini, personal communication). In informal conversation, friends who share a common history tend to share the same 'interactive frame'. Teasing that may seem threatening to an outsider, may be experienced by participants as playful. Teasing should therefore be seen in the context of the relationship between participants, rather than in terms of external, absolute judgments.

It is therefore at least worth considering whether teasing, which to adult ears may sound cruel and hurtful, may to pupils be perceived as an acceptable part of everyday banter. In this respect, we know that adults, particularly playground supervisors, can over-estimate the aggressive nature of playground play (Boulton, 1996). It is very difficult to get a bearing on this without engaging with pupils themselves. Playground observations, for example, have limited use in exploring the intentions, context and effects of teasing.

This chapter explores five research questions:

1   What is the prevalence of teasing and name calling in school?
Does it decline with age, as in the case of bullying (Whitney and Smith, 1993)? As has been argued, previous research has not studied age changes over the school years.

2   What is the significance of teasing to pupils?
An important part of understanding the nature and course of teasing is better information on its significance to pupils. How seriously do they take it? Is it

possible to identify when teasing is taken seriously and when it is not? Can distinctions between different levels of seriousness of teasing be identified? Much has been learned, on the basis of careful study, about the distinction between playful and aggressive fighting (Boulton, 1994), and it may be that there are particular features that distinguish playful from hurtful teasing or cussing. The usefulness of Troyna and Hatcher's (1992) distinction between 'hot' (hurtful) and 'cold' (playful) teasing was examined here.

3   Why are pupils teased?

What explanations do pupils offer about why children are teased at school? In research on bullying, a main concern has been with identifying characteristics of the bullies and victims (Olweus, 1993). To what extent are children seen to be teased because of personal characteristics of the teaser and teased? But bullying, as well as teasing, is likely to result not just from personal characteristics of children but from situational and peer group factors as well. Pupils' social lives in school are often in the context of groups; what processes, both within and between groups, affect whether or not pupils are teased?

4   How are pupils teased?

What are the most prevalent types of teasing, and do these change with age of child? Kelly (1988), in a questionnaire survey of nearly 1000 first and fourth year (year 7 and year 10) pupils in three Manchester secondary schools, conducted for the Macdonald Committee of Inquiry into racial violence, found that being teased and bullied was common: 'at least two-thirds' of the pupils stated they had been teased or bullied at school. The pupils said name calling was the single most common form of teasing and bullying. More pupils in the black/Asian groups recorded name calling than did white pupils. But one difficulty in interpreting these figures is the apparent conflation of teasing and bullying.

Are particular forms of teasing understood by pupils to be unacceptable? Cohn (1988) found that name calling fell into four categories: physical attributes, mental attributes, sex and gender, and race and ethnicity. Cohn reports that the greatest variety of names were found in the race and ethnicity category, and that racist name calling, unlike other categories, increased with age from 10 to 17 years. Boys were more likely than girls to mention the occurence of racist name calling. Cohn found only one instance of teasing involving reference to the teased's mother, but Kelly (1988), in classroom discussions with pupils aged 11 and 14 years, found that the single worst form of name calling was insults directed at another's family (1988).

Racist name calling has, with good reason, received much attention. As noted in the Swann report: 'We believe the essential difference between racist name calling and . . . other forms of name calling is that whereas the latter may be related only to the individual characteristics of the child, the former is a reference not only to the child but also by extension to their family and indeed more broadly their ethnic community as a whole' (DES, 1985). Great care is required in interpreting racist name calling. Troyna and Hatcher (1992) draw attention to some important complexities, for example, by showing how erstwhile friends can racially insult each other. They show that teasing and racist name calling need to be understood in the wider context of peer relations and how a desire for domination can support racial teasing, even when children themselves are not racist.

Another category of teasing and name calling is that involving relations between boys and girls. Everyday experience and observation suggests that such teasing can involve taunts about being a 'cissy' or a 'tomboy' (Thorne, 1993), and about sexual activity. Cohn (1988) found that girls are far more likely to complain of being called sexist names, and to complain that name calling mattered and was hurtful.

5   How do pupils react to teasing?

What do they do about it? If teasing is a main feature of playground life, and if pupils can be deeply affected by some forms of teasing, then it is important to understand how they react to it. Cohn (1988) found that the most commonly cited reaction of secondary pupils was to ignore being teased, followed closely by verbal retaliation and, to a lesser extent, physical retaliation. But actual numbers are not given in this report, and reactions to teasing may well change with age. Boulton (1993) found that teasing on the playground was one cause of fights. Troyna and Hatcher (1992) comment on how pupils respond to racist incidents. Again, they do not provide a quantitative analysis, but mention ignoring and drawing on the support of others from the same ethnic group. But the main response, according to Troyna and Hatcher, appears to be sticking up for yourself. There is therefore an apparent disagreement about the main form of reaction, with some studies suggesting pupils tend to retaliate, while others claiming that pupils tend to ignore teasing.

An allied question concerns pupils' perceptions of how teasing and name calling is dealt with in their schools. As Kelly (1988) has said: 'Teachers' responses to pupils' complaints about teasing and bullying can become an effective commentary on the school ethos — who is valued, and supported, who is taken seriously, who is regarded as a nuisance and troublemaker' (p. 11). Yet Kelly found few pupils complained about name calling and fighting to their teachers, and when they did they were not aware of an effective response, suggesting 'communication between pupils and teachers is not good when it comes to these forms of behaviour' (1988, p. 26).

What Is the Prevalence of Teasing and Name Calling in School and Does This Vary with Age?

In order to obtain basic information on the prevalence of teasing, we asked pupils at 7, 11 and 16 years whether teasing happened at school, whether it had happened to them, and whether they teased others. As with breaktime activities (see Chapter 4), we also explored pupil explanations for changes with age.

Results concerning the prevalence of teasing and racial teasing at 7, 11 and 16 years were based on closed questions in the interviews. Almost all the children at both 7 and 11 years said that teasing occurred. Two-thirds, at both ages, said that it happened to them. By 16 years, the vast majority still said that teasing occurred, and half said it happened to them. The quantitative results therefore show that teasing is a prevalent part of school life, throughout primary and secondary education, though there are signs that it has declined by 16 years.

Accounts given during the interviews, confirmed the pervasive place of teasing in school life. These extracts are from 16-year-old pupils.

P   I suppose it happens everywhere really, there's no getting away from it. There's always someone who takes the mick . . . it has to be really bad when it goes into fights and what not, but people always snigger and the rest of it.

P   A lot of people shrug it off and just put up with it and you'll get some people who will tell their parents about it and try and get it sorted out. I say 'try' because the parents or teachers can never really sort it out. It will happen no matter what, I mean the teachers . . . can never really stop it . . .

There was a commonly expressed view that there is nothing that can be done to stop teasing, and that it is part of the fabric of relations between pupils.

Pupils' accounts at 16 years were examined for explanations for the apparent decline in teasing with age. One reason for a decline, expressed in the next extract, is similar to that expressed in Chapter 4, concerning changes to breaktime activities; that is, over time certain behaviours — in this case teasing — are seen as immature and not appropriate at this age.

P   Not so much in our year or the year below. Maybe in the first year or second year. I remember in primary school, a lot of cussing used to go on, but when you mature and you get older you basically grow out of that. Just that it don't go on a lot in our years.

Pupils' comments indicated that a decline may also be the product of working and playing together over the five years of secondary school:

P   You tend to find that (teasing) in the first and second years . . . But in the older years, we can tell each other anything in our group. Like if we don't like what we're wearing or your hairstyle is horrible, we can tell each other without offending each other, and like also we can have arguments with each other, we won't have to say sorry to each other, we'll all still be talking after it.

This quote also suggests that there may be differences between groups and schools in the kinds of relations between pupils, and thus the extent to which teasing is seen as unacceptable.

Analysis of ethnic and sex differences in whether teased showed that overall, there was not a clear picture concerning gender and ethnic differences in teasing, though there was some suggestion that at 11 and 16 years boys, and especially white boys, were most involved in teasing, both as recipients and as protagonists.

What Is the Significance of Teasing to Pupils?

The numerical results on the prevalence of teasing can be used to map out age and group differences, but we also wanted to learn more about the significance of teasing for pupils. Analysis of pupils' accounts highlighted several distinctions that should be made when considering the nature and effect of teasing.

Pupils were keen to say at 11 and at 16 years that much teasing was understood not to be hurtful, but more a part of everyday banter, often between friends. As we shall see soon, more than a third of pupils at 16 years said that teasing was just fun.

> **P** I don't think it's in a vicious way. Sometimes it's just as a joke . . . sometimes just friends muck about. It's not really in a way that you would want to hurt them by saying something.

But on other occasions, teasing could really upset people. The following extended quote from a 16-year-old girl shows the unsettling effect teasing was having on her.

> **P** I was always on the receiving end . . . a lot of things would be said about me . . . I'd just generally be teased because of my surname, anything they could find. I was teased about my coat. Like I never liked it myself because my Mum got it . . . I had to wear it.
>
> **I** So why do you think people would pick on you like?
>
> **P** Because I was the easiest one in the class to pick on.
>
> **I** Did you fight back?
>
> **P** I never used to say anything back 'cause I used to be too scared that there would be a fight out of it or a big argument. So I never really got into arguments in school. I was a very passive person, too passive. I used to like just get the mickey taken out of me because of it. I was too easy . . . I could always hear titbits coming out, like if I'm supposed to have done something, they'll bring it up in drama . . . like they're talking to the teacher and they'll say a little thing but I know it's directed at me or about me.
>
> **I** Do you feel what . . . happened to you at school . . . is that a factor in maybe not going to school so much?

P   That was a factor . . . like I used to be physically ill before school. I couldn't get off the toilet before school, my stomach was upset, every morning before school. My Mum used to have to force me to get out off the toilet to go to school.

Here are two more quotes:

P   I certainly think it affects someone because they could be like too scared — in not coming to school, but people don't realize that. They are killing their education while they are teasing them for fun, but they don't realize . . . if someone is really quiet and then one of the loud ones starts picking on them they might not go to school, and they will miss out on their course work and everything.

P   I dreaded coming to school, going to certain lessons. 'Cause at that time we weren't mixed up so I had to face them every lesson . . . there was about three main ones in my class . . . it would happen all the time, every lesson. I'd have to avoid it, . . . find different transportation going home and try to get home as quickly as possible and just sort of stay out of view.

We see in these accounts how the effects of teasing may be harmful emotionally, and may adversely affect school progress. We also see that this may not be appreciated by the teaser, for whom it may be just an act of harmless fun. The type of teasing described in these accounts is probably indicative of bullying behaviour, in the sense that pupils were being singled out and picked on by others, who were not friends, over a period of time. This is a very different form of teasing to the banter described earlier. The actual taunts may be similar but are used and understood in a very different way.

One point to emerge from accounts at 16 years was the difficulty pupils faced at times in distinguishing between harmless and hurtful teasing.

P   There's a boy in my year who's a bit fat and people take the mick out of him. But it's not like spiteful, it's like having a laugh, he knows that.
I   So you feel that he doesn't get particularly hurt by it?
P   Well he does, he understands that it's messing around but it still annoys him.
I   So you think the people that do that then, they're not really being vicious?
P   No they're just having a laugh with him. 'Cause he likes having a laugh about them but he don't like getting it back.
I   Right, so does he retaliate then?
P   Yeah.
I   So would you say then that it affects him or upsets him?
P   Yeah it does upset him.
I   It does. And in what ways does it, how does he show that?
P   I don't know, I think he's had a couple of fights in school 'cause of that. He just gets mad I suppose.

This quote indicates that the speaker is uncertain about how the teased boy feels about being teased. On the one hand, the teased boy is supposed to know that teasing is not spiteful, while, on the other hand, there is recognition that he does get upset and this has led to retaliation. The line between hurtful and harmless teasing is in this case a very thin one.

But the pupils were able to articulate some criteria which defined the transition from everyday banter to hurtful teasing. One criterion, well understood as a signal of spiteful intent, was reference to a person's family, usually their mother. This is seen in the following quote from a boy, and we return to this below, when considering types of teasing.

> **I** So what happens the times you feel angry about it, what makes you angry then?
>
> **P** Sometimes if they get too personal, something that would make me angry like if I'm having an argument with someone and they brought up my mother, that would make me angry.

Another criterion was repetition of a derogatory comment about a particular, personal characteristic.

> **P** If they carry on about one certain thing about you, that they keep repeating.

These are relatively overt criteria. In practice, children are unlikely to be able to articulate much of what is likely to be, in practice, a sophisticated, but largely unconscious, social repertoire and set of understandings. As recent accounts of social perception have indicated, children's reactions to social behaviour are complex and likely to involve a sequence of steps between perception and response (Crick and Dodge, 1994).

As Sluckin (1981) has shown, there is a good deal of skill involved in knowing how far to go with others.

> **P** If I'm having a joke with a friend we'll muck around and we'll tease each other then but that's like joking and you know that it's a joke. You have to be very careful who you tease and how you do it — that it is a friend, and they do know it's only a joke.

But children no doubt vary in how skilful they are in this area of social relations, and this can have consequences for the reactions of others to their teasing.

Perhaps of most importance, judgment on how far to go when teasing someone is affected by the relationship between the teased and teaser. In particular, friends can tease each other, sometimes in ways that can seem merciless to an observer, but which are interpreted by pupils as acceptable. The same comments from a non-friend would cause offence and invite retaliation. Here are three quotes from 16-year-olds, the first two from girls, the third from a boy.

P   If they mean it, it won't be a friend.

P   It all depends, like my mate, he's got big ears and like we all call him 'ear oles' and things like that. In a way he likes us calling him it, he don't mind it, 'cause we're his mates. Any other person he just flips, he goes for them, he doesn't like it at all.

P   If one of my friends said it I would . . . know that they're joking, but if someone else said it to me then it would be different.

Why Pupils Were Teased

We asked the pupils at 11 and at 16 years why they felt they were teased. At 11 years the most common answer was that the teaser was being provocative, wanting a fight or confrontation (21 per cent of those teased), the teaser enjoyed it (14 per cent), the teaser was envious of the teased (10 per cent) or the teaser's prestige was enhanced. At 16 years, 39 per cent of those teased said it did not mean anything and was just fun, 14 per cent said the reason was accuracy (e.g. because they did have the physical characteristic, such as shortness, on which teasing was based), and 11 per cent said it boosted the teaser's prestige.

Analysis of the interview transcripts helped amplify quantitative results on why pupils felt teasing took place.

Characteristics of the Teased

Some people were seen as easier to tease than others. One example is given by a girl:

P   There's a boy in my friend's class . . . I don't know that's wrong with him . . . like he's . . . very dopey and he just sits around and his eyebrows like meet and . . . they just like tease him . . . I suppose that is horrible but they wouldn't like hit him and say 'oh, look at you you're . . .', 'cause in a way they feel sorry for him. They sit next to him and everything, like tell him what class he's meant to be in but they sometimes say things about his eyebrows.

We see here an ambivalence about teasing a particular child, apparently with learning difficulties, and a sense that this recognition tempers the teasing that takes place.

Some pupils were seen to bring teasing upon themselves.

P   Some people like bring it on to themself, like a boy he came down and said that he could read people's palms, and he used to get bullied for that. Like 'read my palm now' or 'something is going to happen' and all that. Like some people do bring it on themselves.

Sometimes the teased had become the particular subject of dislike by the teaser:

P Just didn't like me, and orchestrated teasing.

Individual Characteristics of the Teaser

Some were seen to tease because they were insensitive to others' feelings.

P Some people just ain't got no feelings, they don't think it could be them, they just think 'oh that person's not like us', when they're exactly the same . . . if it was them they wouldn't like it.

Interestingly, by pointing out the insensitivity of the teaser, this girl shows, as did others, an empathy with the teased. This reveals another aspect of a growing social sensitivity, driven, to some extent, by anticipation of how they would feel if they were teased in a similar way.

The following is a compelling account, from a white boy, of the power wielded by one provocative teaser.

P There's this boy in our form, he's like a right piss-taker all the time, to anyone . . . he goes round and he says 'I'm fat' and all that. He goes 'bleurghh bleurghh', acting really stupid and making everyone laugh, and it makes you feel horrible.

I And how do you deal with that, like what do you say to him or do? Do you do anything?

P I just walk away from him and laugh in his face. Don't take any notice. Well I try to, but it doesn't always work. He's always doing it.

I And does he manage to get off scott free, does nobody give him a hard time about anything?

P Oh yes, some people do, but hardly ever, not as much as he gives to others.

I And would you get that in this year, or is this like in earlier years at secondary school?

P All years, all years. He does it to everyone.

I It sounds weird that this guy is saying so many things to so many people, you'd imagine he'd be very unpopular and he would get kind of . . .

P He's not really, 'cause he's more of a comic, he tries to make everyone laugh. But it's really insulting the way he says it and when everyone laughs it makes it worse. It annoys you all the time, and he hangs round with this other boy who's exactly the same. They're really funny but when they have a go at you they make sure everyone know about it, and you feel really stupid.

Readers may have sympathy, perhaps based on their own experience, with this description of powerlessness in the face of a socially skilful and confident teaser. In this case, one boy has the skill to make others laugh with him, when teasing someone in the class, and thereby has control over classmates, who fear his taunts, and are nervous about not joining in, for fear of being themselves picked on and exposed in front of others. They know his teasing upsets people, but seem powerless to stop it.

Group Processes: Within Group

We have already seen that teasing between friends appeared different in intent and effect to that between non-friends. We see, in the description of the next boy, that one reason for teasing was an attempt to impress others and gain prestige within their friendship group.

I Why do you think they did it to you?
P Maybe 'cause they thought they were big and hard. You know, they just wanted to be noticed. I think people mainly do it because of their friends, if their friends are not there, you notice they're all quiet.

A different kind of within group process involved the influence that one member of a group had on encouraging others to tease someone who is perceived as weaker in the group:

P One main perpetrator — because she is admired, she's liked and if you're not with her then you will get teased. So she victimizes this one person and then everyone else will follow her so she initiates it all. She'll get some other girls to beat her up.

Group Processes: Between Groups

At 16 years, at least, teasing can occur between groups. In the following case, one group see themselves as daring and cool, and tease those outside the group for not partaking in the daring/illicit actions, in this instance, smoking 'substances', presumably cannabis.

P Well a lot of people in the school smoke like substances . . . they are sort of the big people, and there's a group of people who sort of don't, and they're the people who get teased, like me — I don't care really, ignore the idiots, but like if you sort of sit down and they go 'oh you don't smoke' and all that crap, then they just start off taking the micky. What can you do really? You hit them you get expelled, you don't hit and you get teased at.
I So why do you think people do this to you then?
P Oh just to make themselves feel bigger.

The girl's anger toward the 'big people' group can only be sensed from actually hearing the tape of the interview. Teasing here stems from differences between groups, possibly reflecting sub-cultural differences within school. We return to between group relations, when considering racist teasing and teasing between boys and girls.

How Pupils Are Teased

Information on how pupils were teased was based on two questions asked at 11 and 16 years: How are children teased and how are you teased? (The question was not asked at 7 years.)

In answer to the question concerning how children are teased, by far the main type of teasing at 11 years was reported to be individualized around someone's appearance — mostly their physical features (42 per cent of children teased) but also their clothes (36 per cent) — followed by insults directed at someone's family (23 per cent), and non-specific comments such as swearing (21 per cent). By 16 years, teasing on the basis of someone's appearance is still the most common form, with teasing of physical features now even more dominant (52 per cent). By 16 years more teasing is now seen as not serious and just fun (20 per cent), and insults based on someone's ability — whether poor or good — are evident (11 per cent). Family insults are still used (10 per cent). Insults where girls are teased as 'cows' or 'tarts' are coded for the first time at this age (10 per cent). Results concerning how *they* (as opposed to children in general) were teased were similar.

There were no obvious ethnic or sex differences in how children were teased.

The pupils' accounts at 11, and especially 16 years allowed a more detailed description of the ways they felt children, and they, were teased.

Appearance

Appearance: Body

As we have seen, this was the single most frequent way that pupils were teased at both 11 and 16 years.

At 11 years:

> **P** Has bad teeth, so call him bugs bunny.

> **P** They take the micky out of your eyes, the way they speak . . . take the micky out of their teeth when they have gaps like me and say you have big ears.

> **P** I have red hair and they say 'carrot head'.

At 16 years:

Children said they were teased in a variety of ways. One pupil was called 'frog' because he had big eyes. Others said they were teased because of their size — either large or small — because of their nose ('I got a model out of clay made of my nose [shaped like the child's nose] and I hated it'), because they had spots, because they were fat ('like when someone's fat they go, 'oi, you need a bra'), because of their hair, and because they were unclean or smelt.

Appearance: Clothes

Here is the description of a 16-year-old boy:

> **P** Mainly what you look like, what you wear. You've got to have fashionable trainers. If you don't have 60 quid trainers then you're a tramp, you live in a doss.

We see, in the next quote from a white girl, ways in which clothing and musical tastes are connected to sub-cultural affiliations, that in turn affect teasing between groups.

> **P** The way music goes today like there's a lot of like hippy and grunge and the way people dress differently — dress like in clothes that don't really match . . . And people think that they look like a tramp or something . . . People get teased about that kind of thing. 'Cause the majority of people in this school I think are more ragga and hip-hop.

This extract is taken from a longer account which describes two main sub-cultures in the school, each focused on different preferences for music and clothes. Elsewhere, the girl described how this was a backdrop against which her long term friendship with her school friend had begun to struggle, because they were in separate groups. Though they still saw each other, the girl was clearly bemused and uncomfortable at her friend's affiliation with grunge music and the wearing of (to her) strange clothes.

Ability

Children were teased at 11 and 16 years on the basis of academic ability. Sometimes this could be because a child was seen as clever:

11 years:

> **P** Smarty pants or big head or smart alec.

16 years:

> **P** There's one boy who is about 15, in my year. He's done his 'A'levels and got an A in them. He's done all his maths exam, he's passed. If you give

him a sum to do he can work it out, anything, he just, he don't play
football or anything, like excluded.

I Right, and people just don't like him because he wants to be on his own
and he's quite clever?

P Yeah. 'Cause like he's different.

One would need to be cautious about concluding in this case that it was
just ability which was the cause of teasing; other characteristics may have
marked this boy as different, and an easy target for others to tease. But ability,
and a willingness to work, and a negative reaction to it, is implicated in this
child being excluded.

Others were teased because they were slow academically:

P One boy — they used to tease him 'cause he was slow and he didn't do
any work. And he got annoyed at it.

P They can't read . . . some people will tease them about that.

Family Insults

We have already discussed this in relation to signals indicating when teasing is
meant to be hurtful. It is interesting to note that at 7 years there were no
reports of insults directed at one's family, a result explicable either in terms of
an historical change over the duration of the study in kinds of teasing, or else
in terms of developments with age. If the latter, then, somewhere over the
junior years, comments about one's close family take on a powerful message.
As we argued in Mooney et al. (1991), insults directed at another's family are
regarded as a particularly serious form of teasing, which can lead to confrontation. The simple expression 'your mum' could be enough to provoke a retali-
atory attack.

Sometimes other members of the family, apart from parents, are involved.

P He started coating off my grandad. He died, I think it was about a month
after he started saying it, and it did hurt a bit, and we wound up in a fight.

In the following account from a 16-year-old boy, we see that this form of
teasing has its effect because it is a provocation, used in a public context, and
the teased is forced to choose between backing down or retaliating.

P Yeah, that's all you ever hear, like your mum's this, your mum's that. It's
immature, it's stupid.

I Why do people get so wound up by somebody who doesn't even know
your mum?

P It's not 'cause they're saying something about your mother like, (but)
'cause your mates are there and you look stupid to this boy . . . you either
say something back or do something about it. It's not just because he's

cussing your mum, that's not half of it, it's only because you don't want to look stupid.

This type of insult appears to be well understood by pupils as an abbreviated social bid for dominance, with well understood social consequences. The pupil, just quoted, well understands that the actual words used are 'not half of it'.

Girls Teased As 'Slags'

Again, this carried a message well beyond the actual meaning of the words used. The term is commonly understood to denote a girl who is considered too easy in her relations with boys, but its impact goes well beyond the accuracy or not of the description. There does not, from these accounts, appear to be a female to male equivalent (see also Kelly, 1994), so it was always directed at girls by boys but, as we shall see, also by girls to each other.

This is from a white girl:

P There was a girl in the fourth year, and she was a little hard person. She thought she could even pick on fifth years, and she was in the break queue and she was calling me and everyone — my mates — slags. She didn't know us, and we just left it, 'cause we thought, we're in the fifth year, we can't get in trouble. But it went on and on and she ended up getting badly beaten up . . . she was shouting that I was a slag and slept around. And I was the centre of attention and everyone was looking at me. I've never had a fight, I'm not the type to fight. If it had just been me and her, I would have just walked away. I did walk away in the first place, 'cause I knew I didn't want to fight . . . But . . . blaring it all out, and everyone was looking at me, I just got a bit aggravated, just had to take it out on her.

This is an extreme example. As a consequence of the younger girl's insults, there was a major disturbance in the school and one expulsion and other suspensions followed. But it serves to show how — just as with family insults — it is the publicly understood nature of the insult — braving others to respond if they dare — that is critical.

Teasing Concerning Colour/race

The pupil interview transcripts showed examples of racist name calling and teasing:

11 years:

tell them to go back

you paki

call you 'black' this, 'black' that, more whites than blacks . . . Paul goes over the limit, cusses Hannah's colour, and then families get involved.

call you 'blacky', 'chocolate face'

call me 'funny breed' because I'm half caste

The closer analysis of pupil accounts, possible at 16 years, showed that pupils varied in their views about the amount and severity of racist teasing and name calling. At one extreme, some seemed to feel racist teasing did not occur and was not a problem. Others felt teasing on the basis of another's colour or ethnic origin was a fact of school life and not meant to be, and not responded to, as if it was serious. Yet others felt racist teasing was common, and was a serious issue.

Sometimes racist teasing was seen in terms of particular individuals, that is, it resulted from a few racist pupils.

white boy:

P There are some racist people in this school . . . he was meant to have said one thing about a black boy, so now there's a lot of them that don't talk to him, black and white they don't talk to him, and they just slag him down.
I So this one boy who's racist, he's kind of isolated by blacks and whites?
P For being racist.

Here the pupils themselves appear to deal with racist actions by isolating the offender, and we return to this strategy later.

But other accounts indicated that teasing between ethnic groups could lead to tension and resentment which came to underpin an everyday sense of getting on with each other, and appears to have been a main factor behind a degree of suspicion between ethnic groups in the school.

black girl:

P It was white people being racist to Asian people, but I don't really think they meant it in that way, you know, sometimes how things are said, people interpret it differently.
I What kind of things would they . . . ?
P There's too many immigrants in this country or something like that.
I And did that 'cause a row at the time or offence?
P Yeah, it caused offence, a lot of confliction between certain people and they didn't talk to each other for like a while and they came to their senses and like spoke it out and they said they didn't mean it how it was said, and (yet) they still don't really talk . . .

Teasing that may have been meant as fairly innocuous could escalate into open conflict between ethnic groups, because of pupils' sensitivities about racism.

white girl:

> **P** Someone will say something, maybe didn't mean it to be racist, but the
> other person has got so defensive because society has been racist to them
> that they take it the wrong way, and then they'll make a racist remark to
> get their own back, and it starts snowballing, and in the end you have
> fights over race, and it's kind of 'Where did this all come from?' So it does
> happen, it's the main cause of the fight I'd say — colour in this school.

We shall look more closely at how fights start in school in the next
chapter.

Boys Teasing Girls and Girls Teasing Boys

We asked, at 16 years, a number of separate questions about teasing between
boys and girls. When asked whether girls were teased much by boys, 39 per
cent said they were, and 6 per cent said were not. (For half (51 per cent) of the
children this question was not relevant because they were not teased or data
were missing, for example, because they were in a single sex school.) There
were no overall sex differences in answers to this question, so girls were no
more likely than boys to say they were teased by boys.

We asked pupils if they had been teased by the opposite sex; 12 per cent
said they had, and 23 per cent said they had not. There was some suggestion
that girls, more than boys, felt they were teased more by the opposite sex, but
numbers of children were low.

Boys Teasing Girls

When asked how boys teased girls, pupils said (in order of frequency of mention) in terms of physical appearance (body), physical appearance (clothes),
comments like 'cows' or 'tarts' and ability, and references to teasing as 'just fun'.

In the following quote from a white girl, girls were teased because they
were seen to be more work orientated than boys.

> **P** Girls get a hard time from boys . . . they think they're boffins, they say,
> 'you're boffins, you're boffins' and things like that. I think it's just 'cause
> they're jealous. But girls tend to get a hard time for doing all their work
> when boys don't.

Conversely, girls were also teased because they were having difficulties
with work.

> **P** The boys have always got something to say, it could be the slightest thing,
> like you could say something wrong in a lesson and they'll bring it up,

whereas the girls they'll just think well it was a mistake, get on with it . . .
I don't really like reading and sometimes if I'm nervous, I say quite a few
words wrong, and they'll tease me over that.

We have already seen the way that girls were teased as 'slags' or 'tarts', or
by use of an equivalent term. The following boy recognizes this, and feels it is
wrong and sexist. He also recognizes the unfairness of it, in that the equivalent
behaviour by boys goes without comment.

P Girls do get a hard time from boys. There's a couple of girls I know,
they've been out — it's not 'cause they're like tarts or nothing — they've
been out with a few boys and they just get called slags just 'cause of that.
I think it's really wrong. I've been out with a few girls, and no one says
nothing to me. It's all sexist views. It's like me, I ain't sexist but some of
my mates are. But it's stupid.

A similar picture is painted by this girl.

I And when girls get teased then, what sorts of things do boys say to them?
P That they're slags and everything else. 'Cause they seem to think if you do
something, or if you go out with a certain person, you're a slag.
I How do you define it, what is a slag to them?
P To them it's someone that goes with everyone. Just stupid.

Girls Teasing Boys

Girls were less likely to be seen to tease boys. Only 23 per cent of pupils said
that boys were teased much by girls. Girls were seen as teasing boys on the
basis of physical appearance (body), appearance (clothes), and because they
were immature. Overall, girls were no more likely than boys to say they teased
boys more.

Girls Teasing Each Other

Girls were reported to tease each other or 'slag' each other — that is, tease
each other because of supposed promiscuity. If boys' taunts can be dismissed
as confirmation of immaturity, teasing by other girls could be seen as far more
provocative, and was taken seriously. Girls' accounts showed how they had to
manoeuvre a fine line between being seen to be too easy with boys, and yet
attaining credibility by the nature of their affiliations with boys. Their comments showed links between girl to girl teasing and a growing awareness of
sexuality.
black girl:

P Especially in the girls' schools, girls are always slagging off each other,
that they're slags and stuff, and they don't have no proof or anything, they
just say it, because they'll see a girl and boy and they just think that.

The following offers insights into the criteria used to make judgments about girls' sexual conduct, and when they are teased.

black girl:

> As you get older, it's mainly the girls . . . they're more interested if you have a sex life with your boyfriend and if you do, then everybody knows about it and you become a slag or a whore etc, because you're involved in sex . . . If you're not having sex, then that's alright, you're safe, you're a virgin, you're pure etc, but if you've been going out with somebody, with them for a week or a couple of days, and you've had sex with him then, and everybody finds out, then you'll get called a name, that you're too easy. But maybe if you was going into a relationship and maybe you was going out with someone for eight months, and then maybe you decided to sleep with him, you thought the time was right, and you thought he loved you, and you loved him, and you felt the need was there, then that will be classed as ok. But if you just go into a relationship and you just jump into bed, like say within say two weeks or less, then you'll be classed as easy.

I   Ok, so girls can be quite harsh on each other?

P   Yeah, that's the thing about this school here, they're very, very harsh.

The following quote also offers criteria against which girls' behaviour is judged. Here the importance for girls of the type of affiliation with boys is stressed. Being seen with certain boys helps credibility; seeing 'lots of boys' has the opposite effect.

> **P**   There are some boys which if you get to go out with them, you know, that's commendable because you know 'so and so got to go out with . . . wow'. If you see lots of boys that's not a good thing. If you get to go with a certain boy, a particular boy, then yeah everyone admires you.
>
> **I**   Then your kind of value increases by being associated with him, but if you go out with too many it's really not on?
>
> **P**   Yeah, you're a slut!

In some descriptions, girls in all girls' schools were seen as treating each other appallingly.

> **P**   I find that seems to be quite particular to girls' schools — that there seems to be a lot of aggression . . . perhaps it's played down because we're only girls but it does happen and I know of at least three girls who have been driven out of this school, and their homes, because of other girls, until their families had to leave. There was one girl who — she goes to boarding school now — and her family have moved far, far away.
>
> **I**   Why?
>
> **P**   Because she was different — she seemed to have a lot of boyfriends and in this school, well in girl schools, girls bitch 'She's a whore, she's this, she's that' and it started at verbal abuse, and it escalated and eventually they turned one of her boyfriends against her, and she was dragged outside school and beaten by at least ten girls and her boyfriend.

And this kind of aggression in teasing, which can progress to bullying, is seen to be different for girls and boys:

> **P** You tend to find that when boys fight, they will fight and then that's the end of it, they'll get on with life etc. But girls will hold grudges for years. There's a few that's been going on from the first year that are still going on now and some of the girls have left but some of them are still here.

What Do Pupils Do about Teasing and Name Calling?

Role of Pupils

At 11 and 16 years, pupils were asked how they responded when they were teased. There were three main answers at both ages. At 11 years more than half (53 per cent) of the pupils said they retaliated. This is in keeping with a strong sense we had of the centrality to playground life at this age of a revenge or reciprocity norm. Pupils seemed in their social exchanges to have a clear sense of what was unacceptable and what needed a response. Even so, nearly as many (44 per cent) said they ignored teasing. About a quarter (27 per cent) said they would tell the teacher. (Pupils could give more than one answer, so total number of responses could exceed 100 per cent.)

By 16 years, numbers of children answering this question were low (only 36). Of these, 29 said they ignored teasing, 9 said they retaliated, and 6 said they told the teacher (again more than one answer was possible). There is therefore some indication that by 16 years pupils are less inclined to retaliate.

The interview transcripts showed that some pupils at 16 years stepped in to stop teasing if they felt it was excessive. Here a girl takes direct action, and threatens to tell the teacher.

> **P** There's a girl in the second year and I'm not quite sure what's wrong with her, but her face is disfigured, it's like her eyes are bigger than they should be, and they would call her 'goggle-eyes' or something like that. When they first started doing it I went mad, then I found out two weeks ago that they were doing it again, and I said 'I heard yous were doing that thing to that girl' and they went 'no', and I said 'if you do I will go straight to Miss Richardson and I will tell her'. And I says 'I don't care, yous can call me what you like but don't do it, how would you like it?', and I did lay into them hard . . .

For the next pupil, peer regulation, combined with a fear of getting into fights, is seen to reduce racist teasing, rather than school sanctions on racism.

> **I** In the past there has been racist teasing — and why do you think that doesn't happen anymore?
> **P** Well if that happens then like all of that culture they get together and a big fight just erupts and I don't think they want that.

I   So it's not because the school is educating people to try and understand different cultures?

P   Yeah the school tries to stop that kind of thing happening but . . .

I   You think it's mainly a fear of getting into fights that stops it — like people know what the consequences will be?

P   Yeah.

Role of Teachers

So if pupils themselves can play a role in regulating teasing and bullying, how do they see the teachers' and schools' contribution? In some cases, teachers were not seen to act constructively. In the following acount, this extended to collusion in the teasing of a boy.

P   Once a teacher joined in as well . . . then it got out of hand, then the boy ran out of the room, that had been teased . . . It was about his hair — got like plaits in his hair, and he got teased.

Some felt that teachers did not take notice of teasing. In the following extract the consequence is that a pupil loses confidence.

P   If they hear it then they'll turn round and say something. But otherwise . . . if someone who's getting teased goes and finally reports it, they'll turn round and say 'don't take no notice, don't take no notice'. But it's still battering on the person who gets teased's conscience, and their confidence is still getting battered down. Some of the higher teachers do take it seriously and they do do something about it, so that's good.

The next two 16-year-old girls felt teachers could do more:

P   They don't do nothing, they tell you, like if you have a class discussion, that if someone calls you a name to tell the teacher and they'll sort it out. (But) if you tell the teacher what can they do? They don't do nothing. They might say 'oh that's not nice, don't hurt people's feelings'.

P   Well it's about my weight really. I was upset and I just didn't want to stay at school basically. I told the teachers but that just generally made it worse and didn't really help.

In the next extract, from an interview with a black girl at 16 years, teachers are thought not to want to believe racist teasing is happening in the school.

P   The school preaches that it's mixed school, multi-race and things like that, but I said to one of the teachers for my sociology course, are you aware about the level of racism that goes on between teenagers, and he told me no. But I find that hard to believe that the teachers aren't aware.

I   Why is it they are not aware of it?

P It's not that they're not aware of it, it's just they want to believe it's not happening.

But sometimes teachers and the school were seen to be a positive influence and to deal effectively with teasing and bullying. Here name calling is dealt with in assembly.

I How do teachers deal with name calling, if they thought it was serious and it was going on?

P Well, the other day we had an assembly 'cause some younger girls was teasing a girl that lives nearby the school, and the teacher was very angry about it and saying if it continues some pupils could be excluded, like suspended, because the girl was sick and they was teasing her about her hair.

There was recognition of, and support for, a strong school policy on racist comments.

I So you haven't really heard any racist comments in this school?

P No, no definitely not in school, because our school doesn't tolerate that stuff anyway because if you are showing racism to someone then you're usually cautioned, and told that if you don't control it then you'll be out of the school.

The next quote shows how a strong and clear school policy can show that it is important and, what is more, effective to approach staff.

P Because this school's got a good policy . . . if you tell the teacher something will be done, it's not like they'll say, oh forget it, it's only this, it's only that. Something will be done.

In the next extract, from an interview with a white boy, prompt action by the form teacher, showing the effect on the teased pupil, is cited as the reason why teasing of one boy ended.

P There's not any racist teasing but if you're ugly you get called ugly every day. There was one boy in our group, in our form, 'cause he was really brainy and his name was Gitton, they always used to call him 'Oh Gitton' like that, and 'git' and all that sort of thing, and he went and saw our form tutor, and she stopped all that . . . when the people in our form came back for registration she made them stay behind and had a little chat with them. Told them it was getting (the boy) down.

Conclusion

This study of teasing in schools, taken from interviews with the same pupils at 7, 11 and 16 years, has shown that teasing is a common feature of life at both primary and secondary level. At all three ages the great majority said teasing occurred and two-thirds at primary level and a half at 16 years said it happened to them. By far the main form of teasing was based on someone's physical appearance, mostly their physical features but also their clothes, as well as teasing centred on other pupils' ethnic origin, ability, their family, and insults involving supposed sexual behaviour. There were some signs that teasing had declined by 16 years and this seemed to be because of a growing maturity, and also in some schools the outcome of relations between pupils within groups, who have worked and played together over the five years of secondary school.

Teasing can be seen to have both a negative and positive aspect. As described at the beginning of this chapter, teasing can be perceived in a negative way, partly because it can be viewed in a similar light to bullying. It is important to note that pupils' accounts indicated ways in which teasing could upset and humiliate people, and could in some cases adversely affect their academic and social lives in school. Some descriptions of teasing, in which pupils were picked on persistently by others, can correctly be called bullying, in terms of definitions used by Olweus (1993) and Smith and Sharp (1994), and it is important that this is dealt with by school staff. However, pupils could use the term 'bullying' in a loose way, as a general term to describe confrontation between pupils and relatively trivial forms of name calling.

Importantly, pupils' accounts also indicated ways in which teasing and name calling could be viewed less negatively. Teasing is a part of the everyday verbal banter and jostling between pupils, that is the stuff of social life. Evans (1989) has reviewed a number of studies to show that these experiences, often centred on the playground, can contribute to the development of language skills and the assimilation of pupils into playground life. Evans focuses on primary education; the present study indicates that teasing is a feature of breaktime life throughout the school years.

Pupils' accounts of teasing indicated the sophisticated but informal skills used, for example, in judging intent and acceptability. Pupils routinely make difficult decisions about when teasing is harmless and when it is hurtful. They have to learn when to adjust teasing according to the social context, in terms of situation, audience and, most importantly, recipient. Considerable skill is required in the correct reading of another's behaviour, and breaktime in school, and the playground environment, are an important site for the development of these skills. The importance of skills in this area should not be underestimated but is little understood. Children are skilful, not least because the social costs of getting teasing wrong can be serious. A misjudged taunt can lead to a fight, or a falling out with a friend. This threat no doubt adds to the excitement and bite of pupils' banter. Teasing is often meant to be provocative, sometimes mock-serious and sometimes serious, and there is in the very nature of the act the possibility of misunderstanding the intention behind it. Some pupils appear not to be very accomplished in either teasing or reacting to teasing, and problems can ensue. But all pupils face difficulties, for example, in reacting to teasing, and all can overreact, or feel guilty because they underreact.

It is therefore possible that some teasing serves a useful social purpose, helping to denote limits and show off sharpness in social discourse. Accounts also revealed a developing empathy and social sensitivity, driven by anticipation of how they would feel if they were teased in a similar way. Pupils are learning boundaries of what is socially acceptable.

Teasing could also be used to impress others within a group, perhaps as a bid for status, or as a way of consolidating power over others in a class, or perhaps sometimes just for the thrill of throwing someone off balance. Examination of two types of teasing — teasing another's family and calling girls 'slags' or a similar term — indicated aspects of their role in peer relations. Their effect depended on a context of shared social knowledge about what was acceptable. It was not the nature of the insult in itself that was primary, so much as the way it was used to test out others, braving them to respond, in a striving for dominance. There were clearly unwritten, but well understood, rules concerning points beyond which one should not go, unless the intention was to hurt, and provoke.

A theme running through this chapter has been the connection between teasing and the nature of the social relationships between pupils. We have seen that friends could say things to each other that would be unacceptable between non-friends. Teasing appeared to vary from friendly teasing, which was actually supportive and which could serve to consolidate friendships, to hurtful or aggressive teasing that was socially destructive.

There were some signs of a decline in teasing by the final years of secondary school, and this may be because teasing has been tempered by consolidated relations between pupils, as well as the imminence of final examinations and the prospect of life beyond school. In contrast, teasing in the primary years is, as Evans (1989) has described, more playful and physical. In the primary stage, and the earlier years of secondary school, teasing may be a part of the process of getting to know each other, and testing each other out. Teasing at the beginning of secondary school may reflect more clearly a jostling for domination and status. But the present study could only hint at the complexities involved, when considering the role of teasing at different stages of schooling, and further research on this would also be helpful.

As well as a general sense in which teasing has a role in peer relations, analysis of the interviews with 16-year-olds showed ways in which group affiliations structured and affected everyday relations, including teasing. Although we do not have the same depth of data on the children at 7 and 11 years by which to test age differences, it seemed that by 16 years inter-group differences were more obvious and more the context for breaktime activities. Teasing, like other facets of peer relations explored in this book (especially fighting, as we shall see in the next chapter), are bound to reflect these group affiliations and conflicts.

The two types of inter-group relations explored throughout this book are those involving different ethnic groups and boys and girls. Earlier in this chapter we showed survey evidence on the extent of racist teasing. It is clearly difficult to estimate the extent of racist teasing, but there was some evidence that teasing based on colour or ethnic origin had actually increased by the last year of secondary school. But frequency of occurrence may not necessarily be a good guide to inter-group relations; a single serious occurrence can, for example, set the tone of relations between groups that can endure over time. Conversely, some of the descriptions of particular conflicts between groups may not have been typical. There has to be, of course, uncertainty about the validity of pupils' accounts about a topic that they will know is controversial and about which the school will have a strong view. However, there was by no means a common view; pupil accounts indicated differences in the perceived importance and significance of such teasing. Some felt it was not a problem and not an issue, others recognized it occurred but saw it as an inevitable part of social life, while others considered it was serious and a part of hostility between groups that adversely affected everyday life in school. Sometimes there were a few openly racist individuals, but again it is important to consider the context of more general relations between pupils. Troyna and Hatcher (1992) agree that racist name calling may reflect racist ideologies of individual children, but also argue that it is an interactional device, particularly in order to achieve domination, which Troyna and Hatcher see as primary in peer culture. 'The . . . goal is . . . to achieve offence and hurt by using racist terms' (p. 75). In this sense racist name calling is similar in intent to family and 'slag' insults. We return to the issue of between group relations at breaktime, in the next chapter on fighting.

One purpose of teasing and name calling between ethnic groups is regulation of differences between groups. This also applies to teasing between boys and girls. Boys and girls could taunt each other, for example about supposed sexual activity, as well as academic performance in lessons. If anything a more powerful form of teasing was that between girls. For girls, 'slagging' each other seemed a main form of regulation and comment, and could be more provocative coming from other girls than boys. Teasing could reflect a growing awareness of sexuality, and the setting down and maintenance of rules of conduct.

One function of such teasing is likely to be regulation of the amount of contact with the opposite sex. As Thorne has said, 'Teasing makes cross-gender interaction risky, increases social distance between girls and boys, and has the effect of marking and policing gender boundaries. The risk of being teased may dissuade kids from publically choosing to be with someone of the other gender' (1993, p. 54). Thorne's study involved primary aged children. There was evidence of more mixed sex contact in the case of the 16-year-old pupils interviewed in the present study, but Thorne's general point is still likely to apply.

Implications for Schools

Pupils indicated, especially at 11 years, that they reacted to teasing by retaliating in kind or physically. In some schools, pupils felt able themselves to regulate each other's behaviour. Some pupils showed that they saw the futility of some teasing, and rejected its use in service of proving dominance. Though this study was not set up to look at school differences, the indication was that different schools varied in the degree to which to pupils felt their worries about teasing and bullying were dealt with by staff. In some schools they had the view that staff were not responding appropriately or effectively, while in others they seemed clear about the school view on, for example, racist name calling. We gained the impression that in some schools, more than others, teasing, for example about work and ability, could be a part of a peer culture that was opposed to school and work, and, if not dealt with, this could take an insidious hold of pupils' experiences of school. School staff need to be aware of peer relations, of which teasing and name calling are one part, in order to provide a lead that is couched in the realities of social life in school. There are difficulties. In contrast to fights (see next chapter), it is not always easy for school staff, let alone pupils, to judge how seriously to take teasing. Judgments are in some ways easier in the case of racist teasing and name calling because the sensitivities and criteria are clearer. Teachers were also able to deal forcibly with teasing and name calling employed in the context of a child being bullied by other pupils. But staff may face more difficulties with everyday cases of teasing, for example, in the case of teasing between boy and girls, and teasing about physical appearance, because these kinds of teasing can be so taken for granted.

It is not that the two worlds of peer group and school need to be brought together — they can exist relatively independently of each other. But it is important that peer culture, including such manifestations as teasing, is informed by, and given a moral lead by, the school. This does, however, raise difficult issues about the freedom allowable to peer culture in a quest toward school improvement and improved behaviour. I take up this dilemma in the last chapter.

Breaktime has been only indirectly covered in this chapter, but its relevance needs to be stressed now. Breaktime is important because it is the main forum within which pupils contact each other, and where teasing takes place. If teasing is a part of the developing social relations between children, then breaktime is the main setting within which these relations develop. The negative and also the positive features of teasing, identified in this chapter, are therefore closely linked to the breaktime context. A negative view about teasing and name calling is part of a negative view about breaktime behaviour, which we have seen is one reason why the duration of breaktime has been cut back in schools. But this chapter indicates that sophisticated, though informal, social skills are also required in judging how to tease and how to react to teasing. Teasing is one part of playground lore and culture. Breaktime can be a setting for social difficulties and teasing. Reducing it may be expedient in the short term, but may make things worse by also reducing opportunities to develop skills important in managing social relations with peers.

This may also be true of another, and more obviously negative, form of breaktime behaviour — fighting — and I turn to this in the next chapter.

Chapter 9

Fighting in School

It's like someone will suddenly scream out the word 'fight!', and like the year room is emptied in like two seconds flat. Everyone's at the windows, 'Where, where is it?' You've never seen people move so fast. But it doesn't happen often because once the teachers see there's a huge group of people around someone, they're there like a shot.

There is something particularly compelling about fights in school. Pupils are drawn to them like moths to a light. To change the metaphor, there can be a gripping sense of theatre around a fight and the playground usually provides the stage on which the performance takes place. For those involved there is much at stake — not just in terms of their physical well being, but, perhaps more importantly, their self esteem. Fights can occur because pupils do not want to lose face in the eyes of others. Fights can be the end point of a social process that may have been fermenting for some time — a desperate bid to settle a felt injustice, perhaps — or they can arise more spontaneously, perhaps out of a trivial incident, or the misreading of an accident, for example, in the course of a game. As we shall see, fights often seem to arise out of a sense of being upset by what people say — of being insulted. There is often a fine line between the hurly-burly of everyday teasing and banter, which we saw in the last chapter is a main part of social and breaktime life in school, and teasing which goes too far and produces a reaction which goes beyond the everyday.

Psychological theories have varied in their general conceptualizaton of the origins of aggression and violence. Some have seen aggression as a response to frustration, some the result of social learning and modelling, and some the result of social and cultural identifications of the participants (Howitt, 1989). There has been research on differences between people in levels of aggression, and factors predictive of violent and aggressive behaviour and bullying. But, as Boulton (1993) has pointed out, few studies have focused on what he calls 'proximate causes' of hostile interactions on the playground. There have been very few studies of fighting on school playgrounds.

In this chapter the aim is to explore the pupils' perceptions of fights in school, and this is mostly based on the interviews with the 16-year-olds in the main longitudinal study, when the most detailed questions were asked, and the most detailed accounts were obtained. But reference is also made to interviews with the 8–9-year-olds described in Chapters 5 and 6.

The chapter addresses five questions.

1   How often do fights in school occur?

Evans (1989), following Savin-Williams, suggests that fights are rare, and this is because of well established social hierarchies, operating on the playground, which children are unwilling to challenge. Teachers, on the other hand, can feel that physical squabbling and fighting are common events on school playgrounds. We saw in the last chapter that teasing is a feature throughout school life, though, like bullying (Olweus, 1993), there were signs that it had declined through the secondary years. Does the prevalence of fights change with age?

2   What is the significance of fights for pupils?

How do they feel about fighting? One would assume that they would not generally like fighting, but what is the strength of this feeling, are there differences between pupils, and what reasons do they give for their view? Do feelings about fighting change with age, perhaps as pupils grow stronger, and school sanctions become more severe?

3   Why do fights begin?

What do pupils feel are the causes of fights in school? It was felt that pupils' explanations could be valuable here, because, as with so much of breaktime life, while adults may have only a hazy idea of what goes on, pupils are often direct witnesses. In the case of fights, staff are usually faced, after the event, with the task of trying to recreate what happened from the reluctant pupils involved. Boulton (1993) found in the case of 9-year-olds that the most common causes of fights were disputes over some aspect of a rule governed game, teasing, and to a lesser extent disputes over their possession of toys and equipment, and disputes over space. In this chapter, I explore on the basis of pupils' accounts, causes of fights throughout the school years.

4   Individual and social factors involved in fighting.

To what extent are personal characteristics of children a factor in the onset of fights? Are some children, more than others, involved in fights, and if so why is this? But, as with teasing, social and situational factors are likely to be important. To what extent is fighting affected by the immediate social context. In particular, what is the role of other pupils in a fight? Boulton (1993) found that children intervened to stop in less than one in 10 fights; conversely, children generally did not escalate fights by joining in, except to defend friends. But playground fights are often likely to be in the context of a crowd on the playground. What is the role and effect of other children, including a watching crowd, on the course of fights? More widely, to what extent is fighting, like teasing, affected by within group affiliation and between group hostilities, for example, between ethnic groups?

5   The role of parents and teachers in fights.

Teachers can feel that policies on aggressive behaviour in school are not made easy because parents, contrary to school policy, can encourage their children to retaliate and fight back (Blatchford, 1989). But pupils may sometimes feel that they do not get the support they would like from teachers. In the interviews we were interested in how pupils perceived the attitudes of parents and teachers with regard to fighting.

How Often Do Fights in School Occur?

7 years
Involvement in fights was at its height at 7 years, with two thirds (67 per cent) saying they had been involved in fights. Boys were more likely to be involved than girls.

11 years
Involvement in fights had dropped by 11 years (see also Mooney, Creeser and Blatchford, 1991), by which age just over half of the pupils (59 per cent) said they were involved in fights, and again boys were involved more than girls. Of the 104 pupils involved in fighting, about a third (34 per cent) said they sometimes started them.

16 years
By 16 years, as at 11 years, about a half of the pupils said they were involved in fights at school or outside the school grounds (56 per cent). Once again boys were more involved than girls. White girls were the least involved in fights. At 16 years, one in 10 (9 per cent) said they started fights, but white girls not at all. At 16 years the vast majority of pupils (96 per cent) said there were fights at school, and 62 per cent said there had been fights this school year (interviews took place in the spring term). It was clear from pupils' accounts, that many fights at all ages took place at breaktime and in the playground or school grounds. A third (35 per cent) said there had been fights outside the school grounds.

What Is the Significance of Fights for Pupils?
How Did Pupils Feel about Fighting?

Pupils were asked at each age, using the Smiley Face scale (see Figure 3.1), how they felt about fighting.

We need to be cautious about taking these results as a necessary guide to pupils' true feelings, though allied information from pupil interviews suggested that they were a measured and independent response, and not simply affected by the negative view likely to be expressed by teachers.

7 years
When asked to indicate how they felt about fighting, 14 per cent pointed to a smiling face, that is, they reacted positively. Boys were more positive than

girls (20 per cent boys, 7 per cent girls). Nearly a half of the children indicated the most unhappy face.

11 years

The great majority of pupils (83 per cent) said they disliked fighting that is, they indicated a scowling face. Children at 11 years were particularly likely to view fights in a negative way compared to when they were younger or older. Over one half pointed to the most unhappy face. They disliked fighting because they felt fighting caused distress and pain (41 per cent of responses — girls more than boys felt this).

> **P** Because it's horrible — sometimes you end up in tears. I'd rather be their friends than fight them. Sometimes it goes on for days.

Other reasons for disliking fighting were that they could get into further trouble (22 per cent — boys more than girls felt this), that fighting was pointless and did not solve anything (15 per cent), and that they just disliked violence (15 per cent).

> **P** Because it's stupid. There's no reason for it. When somebody hits you your parents say hit them back and it usually ends by fighting.

Sometimes, though, they felt fighting was justified.

> **P** I don't like it very much but if someone hits me I will hit them back.

16 years

The majority of pupils (69 per cent) at this age disliked fighting, though more pupils than in previous years (27 per cent) said they did not feel one way or the other, and less expressed the most negative view about teasing. There is then some indication that they were less concerned by fighting at the end of their school careers.

The main reasons for feeling the way they did at 16 years about fighting were that it was pointless (26 per cent of responses) and it could cause injury and pain (13 per cent of responses). Other reasons given less frequently were that it could lead to punishment and further trouble, it could lead to escalation and get out of control, and it could lead to loss of face. In a quarter of responses (23 per cent), fighting was sometimes seen as necessary.

At 16 years pupils were clearly conscious of the sanctions involved if caught fighting in school. They knew they stood to risk notification of parents, suspensions and even exclusions. For these 16-year-olds, the importance of GCSEs was very clear, and they are unwilling to jeopardize their chances by punishment stemming from involvement in fights.

> **I** Have there been any fights this year in school?
> **P** This year, not that I know of, this year's been good. Everyone's been so concentrated on their studies like GCSEs. No-one's had time to get angry with anyone.

It is important to stress that what often was conveyed, even after a description of a particular fight, was a recognition that fighting solved nothing, was an unusual event, and that in the normal course of things efforts would be taken to avoid them. Here is a 16-year-old girl.

> **P** It's really stupid, especially over a boy, you don't solve nothing, it just makes the situation worse. You know you're better off, not even shouting about it, just talking about it. That's what I believe. I've been tempted before, but I ain't going to fight you 'cause you're not worth it, so go away from me. Fighting — you get hurt in the process and you don't solve nothing.

So, to sum up this section, at each age pupils felt for the most part unhappy about fighting, though some age differences were evident. There was a more ambivalent attitude at 7 years, with more children saying they liked fighting, but with half of them feeling very negative about fights. Children at 11 years were most negative about fights, and at 16 years more indifferent.

Why Do Fights Begin? What Do Pupils Feel Are the Causes of Fights in School?

Looking first at the numerical results, at 7 years those children who said they got into fights, but did not enjoy fighting, said they fought in self defence ('They put gangs on me', 'they beat me up', 'they kick me in the neck') or that they fought because they had become angry.

The main reason they got into fights at 11 years was provocation (75 per cent of pupils), for example, in response to insults directed at family members, being physically pushed or hit, and in response to teasing and name calling, being picked on and arguments. Also mentioned were protecting siblings or friends (12 per cent) and misunderstandings about wrongful accusations (6 per cent).

At 16 years the main cause of fights was provocation in the face of name calling, teasing, and cussing (cited by 36 per cent of pupils). Fights were also seen to start because of rumours being spread around, people stirring up trouble, and talking behind other's backs (18 per cent), and as a result of arguments (18 per cent). Other less frequent reasons given were: because of racism, as a result of mucking about getting out of control, disputes over a boy or girl, dislike of a particular person, over football, as a result of group conflict, the influence of a crowd, and because of bullying. Girls were more likely to mention people stirring and rumours as a reason why fights occurred.

I now look more closely at the causes of fights, by examining the pupils' interview transcripts.

Provocation by Name Calling, Teasing and Cussing

With younger children, the affront caused by a verbal insult can be immediate, and a fight can easily develop. This is evident in the following account from a boy in the 8–9-year-old case study.

> **P** There was two people, one's in my class and one's in 4L. They keep coming over and calling me 'monkey' and I started to get really annoyed, and had a fight with them.

A main feature of the 16-year-old pupils' accounts of how fights started, was the powerful role of things said, or rather, understandings of what has been said about a pupil.

> **I** And what happened, what caused it?
> **P** Somebody told me that a girl had said something about me and I confronted her, and then we started arguing in the corridor about it, and so she hit me, and I fell on the floor, and all my friends went mad 'cause I was on the floor, and then we started fighting, and then it got really ridiculous, and then it broke up and we both got suspended. Now we speak, so there was really no point in it in the first place.

There is a clear connection here between the onset of a fight and teasing and name calling, as analysed in the last chapter. On a continuum of negative contacts between pupils, fighting is the expression of the greatest degree of confrontation. But as we saw in the last chapter, there is often a very fine line between everyday banter, and teasing that leads to hurt feelings and sometimes physical retaliation.

Fights can occur because of misunderstanding over whether teasing is intended to be hurtful or not.

> **P** Well it started as name calling and it was a girl in my class, then we got into a really bad argument, and then the girl hit me, then I hit her back. Then it generally started as a fight and then the teachers came along and stopped it.

As we saw in the last chapter, it is intriguing how some forms of name calling — particularly cussing family members and, in the case of girls, being called a 'slag' — seemed to act as triggers which went beyond the everyday sense of the term used, or objective facts about the person being insulted. If all understand that some terms are particularly insulting, then the mere use of the words signifies a willingness to upset, and take on, the person being insulted.

If it is possible for adults to underestimate the possible positive role of teasing and name calling, it is, conversely, also easy for adults to underestimate the effect that insults of this sort can have on young people. The insults and reactions can seem ritualized and exaggerated, but a question one might ask is: how would we feel if others insulted us in the same way? The girl in the quote in the extract on p. 123 was called a slag in front of a lot of people who knew her. She appeared genuinely upset.

Stirring and Spreading Rumours

Fights could come about because of deliberately misrepresenting what some-one had said, or at least putting what they had said or done in a bad light, in order to turn someone against them. It is worth looking more closely at what was often called 'stirring' by the pupils. Here are descriptions by three pupils:

> **P** He got the impression that I'd been making remarks about his mum, but I hadn't. Somebody had been stirring, and so he got a little bit uptight about it, and somebody told me that he wanted to fight me. So I didn't really feel in the mood to back down, and I didn't really see that it was going to get vicious, so he was waiting down in the corner of the playground and we had a little fight. Then somebody told him I hadn't been making remarks about his mum, so he felt a little bit apologetic, so a few days later he apologized.

> **P** She told one of her friends — because one of her friends was still talking to me — she told her that I was supposed to have said things about her when I didn't, and she came downstairs, and we were arguing, and she said I needed a slap and she went to hit me in my face, so I just went for her.

> **P** In this school there's a lot of trouble makers, you know rumours, it's all about rumours in this school. Someone called you this, or someone called you that. You've really got to ignore it. I've had it in this school many times. I've just got over an incident just before Christmas and I've been suspended for two days.

In the last quote, deliberately stirring up trouble for others is seen as com-mon in school life, at least in this particular school. But why do pupils stir up trouble for others by spreading rumours, and deliberately misrepresenting some-one? What function does it serve?

In the following extract the motive behind stirring is specifically to drive a wedge between people, perhaps to further the pupil's own social ends.

> **P** I'd heard from people that she'd be like slagging me off behind my back . . . I heard some story that I was in front of her house and really slag-ging her off on the phone to her friend . . . when I don't even know her phone number, and so we weren't talking, and then she was like going round telling everyone else this story. I don't like that so one day I went in and I said 'I want a word with you'. So she comes up to me and I told her what I thought, and I didn't say it 'cause I haven't got your number, and she goes 'well that's what my friend said to me' and bleurgh, bleurgh,

bleurgh. So I said 'don't you think you should have come and asked me, instead of telling everybody else but me?', and she goes, 'well I didn't think you were talking . . . bleurgh, bleurgh . . .' and we got into an argument. Then she started putting her finger up in my face so I sort of like got up and I pushed my hand in her face, and then we just started fighting. It was only a little one, and then the teacher came in and stopped it . . . apparently her friend had gone up to her before and tried to split her up from her friends, and she might have been doing it again.

Fights Arising Out of 'Mucking About'

Sometimes fights occurred because mucking about, often at breaktimes, went too far. As 'mucking about' is often rooted in physical actions, progression to a physical fight can be easier than in the case of retaliation to verbal comments. There can be different interpretations of the same behaviours, so that one pupil can still be mucking about, not realizing that the other is actually fighting.

Here is an example of how messing about can lead to one person feeling that things have gone too far, and that for them their sense of injustice could only be settled by fighting the person who had caused their distress.

> **P** It was when it was snowing and we was having snowball fights, and the snow was all ice . . . Me and my friend was there. The pips had gone, and I like said 'right, stop throwing it now, because I'm going up to my class now'. And this Asian girl said 'ok', and I was walking, and my friend was walking, and a snowball missed her. 'Cause this Asian girl was throwing it at her, and she (the friend) was going like, 'don't, don't'. And I was coming round the corner and I went, 'don't throw the snowball'. And she went 'ok then', and she put her hand out, and as soon as I carried on walking she threw the snowball and it hit me on the side of my face and it runned all my face, and my friend saw that I was getting angry and she said, 'No don't, don't, 'cause you're going to get in trouble'. And I just went crazy and I went, 'Why did you throw the snowball?'. I asked her first, I asked her nicely, 'Why did you throw the snowball?', and she said because she wanted to. And I got a really short temper, and I really snapped, and I started hitting her, and I could see my friend, my other friend in the classroom, jumping up and down, going, 'No, no, no'. So I beat up the girl.

In the next extract, a girl loses her temper with a boy who she felt went too far.

> **P** Once I fighted a boy who was in the classroom. He was being stupid, throwing people, and I was like keeping out of his way, 'cause I didn't want to get involved. I warned him, he carried on, he started getting closer and closer, I ignored him and then I just went crazy . . . I just kept fighting him — wouldn't stop because he wouldn't stop when I told him to, why should I? And then a teacher came and stopped it.

Fights Arising Out of Playground Games

Games often involve quick and competitive physical actions, and misunderstanding of intention can occur, as the following extract from a 16-year-old shows.

> **P** There was a whole group of them, they were playing this game called 'Russian', they all run up to some boy, and they were giving him some punches, and the boy who was getting the punches didn't like it, and he punched some boy, and the other boy said 'it's only a joke, only a joke' . . . But the boy just started to swear and said 'it's no joke for me', and they started to fight. And the boy that done the fight, in the end he got kicked in the face and he got beaten up. And then the teachers started to come, but everyone was running, going mad so she (the teacher) got like moved out the way a bit, she got pushed around, and so other teachers came and got involved, broke it up and took the boys away.

It seems likely that fights beginning in this way will be more likely at primary level, and to some extent at the beginning of secondary school, when playground games are more common, as we saw in Chapter 4. In the course of the case study of the 8–9-year-olds, examples were collected of arguments, that sometimes led to fights. Arguments between friends were over who should play, who should do what in the game, and who was in charge. The arguments were often fierce, and it was inevitable that fights would sometimes occur. But on the whole, disputes were settled without fighting. In most cases, friendships appeared not to be affected, as a result of subsequent efforts to find a way of reconciling their disagreement. Arguments between non-friends seemed different in character, and typically were not in the context of a game.

We have seen that breaktime is the main forum for fights in school, and, in this sense, there is a situational effect on fights. But within breaktime itself, certain contexts and activities may be more likely than others to be the setting or cause of fights. With regard to the 8–9-year-olds, particular games were cited. As one boy put it: 'football's an arguing game isn't it'. This is in line with Boulton's (1993) finding that most fights occurred because of disputes over games, commonly involving boys playing football. Some games and activities seem to lend themselves more than others to dispute. This possible connection warrants more study.

Misinterpreting an Accident

Fights could arise as a result of one pupil interpreting a behaviour as deliberate, when another pupil thought it was accidental.

> **P** The kid was running with the football and he accidentally ran into some kid and he said, 'Sorry, mate, but it was an accident', and the kid sort of

like said, 'You're a fool, you're an idiot,' and he pushed him and they actually started fighting from there.

Once again, we see that it is a particular breaktime activity — football — that is the setting for the fight. The speed and intensity of the game make dispute and misunderstanding more likely.

Even messing about, and joking between friends, can go too far. The last extract, and the extract above involving the snowball incident, were not between friends, and behaviour is read in a different way to what would have been expected had they been friends. But friends can also interpret playful behaviour differently, and this misunderstanding can lead to a fight.

> **P** I was sitting down and the teacher just kept bothering me the day before my essay, and when I went to break I was sitting down and one of my friends came over and just slapped me on my head, joking. And I said 'don't, I'm not in the mood' and he done it again. And then I stand up and I punched him and we started to fight.
>
> **I** Right and how did it end then?
>
> **P** My other friend stopped it. The teacher came over and didn't really tell us off 'cause he knew that we were friends.

It appears here that teachers can also judge fights between friends as being less serious than between non-friends.

Fights Arising Out of Protecting Brothers and Sisters

Another way in which protective feelings towards one family can affect fighting, is when an elder brother or sister feels they must protect their younger sibling. Here is a 16-year-old girl:

> **P** She (my sister) was called the names under the sun by some girl in my year. And that was last year, so I was in the fourth year, and my sister was only in the first year. So I beat her up and got suspended for it. 'Cause she started on my sister . . . she started calling my sister a slag and everything else . . . And they phoned my mum up and my mum said 'I don't care, she shouldn't start on her sister then should she'. 'Cause I told my mum I was going to beat her up.
>
> **I** When your sister was being teased and all that, was she quite upset by that?
>
> **P** Yeah, I used to walk through the playground and see her sitting there crying. That's why in the end I beat her up 'cause it was winding me up that every time I was walking round my sister was sitting there crying.

and boy:

> **P** Well it started 'cause some boy in the fifth year above us, the year that just left, was troubling my little brother, asking him for money and things like

that. So obviously I stepped in to say well you ain't doing this. Then he decided that he didn't want to talk no more, he wanted to push me, so then push come to shove and I weren't having him pushing me, and then like he lost his temper and tried to hit me and then we started to fight.

Fights Resulting from Bullying

Some comments from pupils indicated ways in which bullying was the reason why fights started. In contrast to some approaches to bullying, which tend toward a static explanation, couched in terms of characteristics of bullies and victims, these comments indicated that bully–victim relationships could be subject to change. The victim may, for example, feel they can take no more and may be driven to some dramatic expression of their unhappiness, and this may shift the dynamic of the relationship, and the breaking of the power held by the bully.

Fights could also arise in the early stages of what might have become a bully–victim relationship.

P There was this kid, he thought because I'm a new kid in his class he could bully me, so he started trouble with me the first day. So I just left it for a while, and then he came up on that day and hit me, so I just had to hit him back, because my dad told me don't let them do these things to you. Because I already had one person who bullied me before that and I weren't going to let it happen again.

Fights Arising Out of the Way an Earlier Fight Had Been Reported

The meaning of a fight to the participants can be largely in terms of the way the outcome is seen by others. Accordingly, there can be manipulation after the fight, in order to affect the public perception of the outcome, and some accounts showed how upset a participant could be at the way a fight had been portrayed, and how they felt obliged to take steps to correct the impression.

P It was when she was going round saying that I never gave her a chance to hit me, so I offered her again, and she said 'no I never said it, I never said it'.
I You actually gave her another chance, but she didn't want it then?
P She went round saying that I frightened her, I come up behind her and I smacked her one. I went up to her and said, 'well if you want a chance to hit me back, do it now', and she said 'no I don't want to'. So now it's just left there.

P A boy in my year . . . my sister had just started in the first year, and they started to call her names when we were walking down to school, and we actually had a fight outside the school which got stopped by two passers-by. This boy had a 10 minute head start to get to school while the other two had to try and calm me down. And when I got into school, he was in the playground boasting to his mates about how he was supposed to have knocked me out and across the floor. That particular morning I wasn't very happy anyway so basically we just started another fight in school, which ended up with me nearly being suspended, and him nearly being suspended as well.

I And are you friends with this bloke now?

P No, not really, we tend to keep out of each other's way.

Individual and Social Factors in Fighting

I want now to look more closely at two aspects that emerged from pupils' accounts of fights. These were, first, personal characteristics of participants — why is it that some people are more prone to fight than others? And, second, social and situational factors in fights — to what extent do fights involve groups or individuals, what is the role of the crowd in fights, and what is the role of inter-group and between school rivalries?

Personal Characteristics of Fighters

In the case of the 8–9-year-olds, conflicts could be caused by someone who was well known to often get cross and annoyed with people, and had developed a reputation as someone who was 'moody'. This moodiness could often be shown and judged in the course of breaktime games.

> **P** Fallen out with her lots of times over quite a lot of things. It's difficult to play with people who are moody, like her. With football she won't play unless she's with me. You have to ignore her sometimes.

The last extract involves someone known to be moody, but who was accepted, or at least tolerated, as a friend. But other conflicts at this age were caused by the behaviour of a particular child that upset others, and which did not usually involve friends. Two types of characteristics that were mentioned were aggression and spitefulness. Two boys, in particular, were seen as aggressive, and I profiled these in Chapter 6.

In the national breaktime survey, teachers felt that a main and growing problem at breaktime was the poor and difficult behaviour of a few individual children. We asked questions of pupils at 16 years in order to obtain complementary information on the personal attributes of those involved in fights. In one introductory question, we asked if it was the same people who tended to be involved in fights. More than half (55 per cent) said it was not, but one in four (24 per cent) of the pupils said that the same pupils tended to be involved in fights, indicating that certain pupils could be the cause of fights in school.

P It does tend to be the same people. You get certain people who always like to fight, like even if you looked at them, they'd be like 'what are you looking at?' and come over to you and start arguing. You get that sort of people in this school.

The following extract is from a 16-year-old boy, who disturbed the interviewer by the flat and unconcerned way he described the pain he had inflicted on another boy.

P Well some white boy come up to me . . . shouting after me and stuff, and I weren't having it, so we just started fighting. I punched him in his chest twice, then I walked off when he was on the ground. I didn't know what's wrong with him.
I And then what?
P He was on the ground and I didn't know what was wrong with him, there was a big crowd and everybody walked off and he was just there. And the next day I found out he went into hospital 'cause I broke his ribs. That's it.
I And were you friendly with this boy before the fight?
P I never knew him.
I You didn't even know him. And what was he saying to you then, what was so bad?
P He was shouting, making a load of noise in my face.
I Like 'cause he said anything that was very annoying or?
P No, he was shouting, making noise.
I Do you feel then that you started that fight, or he started it?
P I did.
I Do you never get worried that somebody might really hurt you or injure you permanently?
P No.

This account, abbreviated here, is troubling. There is no insight here into motive or consequences. Though we have no evidence that this boy was involved in more fights than others on a regular basis, or that the account he gave was accurate, it was the interviewer's impression that aggression was for this boy an easy option, not subject to much control.

I have already looked at how one girl caused a serious fight by the way she kept calling others 'slag' in the lunch queue. The girl was very provocative, and had been on other occasions, and incited normally passive girls to fight her. In this case the fight, and ensuing suspensions from school, seemed to be attributable to one exceptionally aggressive girl.

Social Factors in Fighting

In this chapter we have already alluded to several social or situational factors affecting fights in school. These have included the breaktime context itself, and particular activities that occurred then, such as football. We have also seen the way, as with teasing, that the nature of the relationship between participants could affect the course and outcome of fights. I now look, on the basis of questions asked at 16 years, more closely at other social factors in fighting.

Social Group Context of Fights

Most fights at 16 years were seen to consist of individuals fighting each other (68 per cent); only 4 per cent thought fights consisted of groups on individuals, and 7 per cent thought fights started with individuals fighting but then progressed into groups fighting individuals or other groups.

The Role of the Crowd

I have already referred to the role the crowd can play in fights at breaktime. This was evident in the interviews with 7- and 11-year-olds. As one 11-year-old boy said:

> **P** I don't like it very much, but it is quite exciting when in a crowd — like a boxing match with everyone cheering the one they want to win.

We were interested in exploring in more detail with the 16-year-olds the action of other pupils when a fight developed. By far the most prevalent action taken by others was said to be watching and gathering around the fight, doing nothing to stop it (78 per cent). The crowd can also play a more active role; one in three pupils thought the crowd encouraged and cheered the fighters on, sometimes guessing who would win (31 per cent). And one in ten pupils said others would take a more active role, joining in, for example, if they did not like one of the fighters involved. But one in four pupils (26 per cent) thought that the crowd would discourage a fight and try to get the participants to stop.

So the crowd has an effect on fights in several ways. In the first place the crowd can be non-involved but an audience. Status and image in the eyes of others is important and the gathering crowd accentuate this for the fighters. This influence, though pervasive, is indirect. Being a member of a crowd in these contexts can involve an exciting sense of witnessing events, known to be wrong, but with a sense of anonymity that frees them from the threat of sanctions. It is a way of enjoying the spectacle of a fight, without the pain of involvement, or the possibility of punishment by teachers. But the effect of the crowd on a fight can be more direct. With the full force of crowd on them, the participants can become reluctant, as if fearful of where this influence might lead them. It is a powerful force and history and fiction show many instances when it has led to disastrous consequences.

> **P** These two people said they was going to fight, but when they actually saw each other they sort of made it up. Then all these people like gathered round them and started saying, 'you said you was going to beat him up, why don't you?' and all that, and then it started a big fight.

I And then they had a fight, just to please the crowd?

P Yeah, they wound her up, wound her up, wound her up, and then they just started to fight. And we heard about it in assembly. And the teachers told us about it, and we was a bit sort of shocked when they said it.

I So in that case do you think it was actually the crowd getting the fight instigated again?

P Yeah.

I Other pupils — what do they do if there is a fight?

P They all rush down the corridors and go 'fight, fight fight' . . . 'Cause once they hear about a fight, that's it, the whole school will know, then it'll be like the other one will say, meet outside at the top, or outside at the other gate, and they start fighting and the girls will go 'hit her, hit her' and the other girls will go 'no', and she hits her, and that's the way it starts into a fight.

P Someone from the crowd pushed one of the fighters against my mate, so obviously that would start friction . . . I do think it is the crowd that pushes it . . . and then they just started fighting, so the crowd did start that one.

As we have seen, pupils can also take a constructive role in stopping a fight. It is not easy to stop a fight on one's own, and in opposition to the social forces described in this chapter. Here a 16-year-old girl describes the dilemma that arose when faced with accusations of not having stopped a fight.

P There was a fight . . . we didn't know it had happened, we just went up there and there was this fight, and me and my friend went back to the school and we told our head of year, and . . . he said, 'there was a fight, why didn't you stop it?'. It wasn't really for me to go and stop it. Say if I'd got hit if I'd tried to stop it?

I Yeah, it's a difficult one isn't it, 'cause you could have got hit yourself.

P 'Cause you can't go in saying 'stop fighting' 'cause they aren't going to listen to you are they?

But some did try to stop fights:

P And people liked to egg them on, 'go on, go on' . . . But like when they started to fight, a couple of people like us, we got in and we like split them apart . . . sometimes, quite a lot of us do try to split up fights, but when there's a whole gang (and) there's not a lot of us then we can't really do nothing. Or else it will be an even bigger fight. We usually try to stop fights.

Fighting between Groups within School: racist fights

We have already seen that racist comments at 16 years were thought to be one cause of fights in school. It is possible that some references to name calling, teasing and cussing as causes of fights would also have involved racist comments. But for whatever reason, there were few descriptions of fights between ethnic groups, or which arose out of racist comments. There seemed to be recognition that people were sensitive about racist comments, and that such comments could lead to extreme reaction and fights. Pupils recognized differences between ethnic groups, and these differences could provide the basis for separation between friendship groups, but there was little evidence of outright hostility between groups, though, as has been said elsewhere, the interview situation may have underplayed the degree of conflict and ill feeling. Pupils in most schools seemed aware that school staff were clear about the unacceptability of racist comments.

However, there are many ways in which membership of an ethnic group is a significant factor in pupils' self identity, and which affects relationships between groups, and peer relations more generally. Pupils at 16 years were developing views on relations between and within groups, and these views sometimes provided a context for their accounts of fighting in school. I can only touch on the complexities of pupils' accounts here, and the issues involved.

I give just one of many possible extracts, in which the interviewer tries to get to grips with the intricacies involved. The extract links teasing, racist comments, fighting and ethnic group affiliations.

I What kind of things would you say to other people to hurt them?

P All different things, like swearing and cussing or something like that. If they do anything then it's your own fault.

I What, would you make racist remarks?

P Sometimes, it all depends if it's Asian, blacks or whatever, Chinese or whatever. The only thing is you want to be careful with the black boys in this school 'cause if you say something really racist, that's it, all hell would be let loose.

I But if say you made a remark to an Asian boy what would happen?

P They won't really say nothing because the blacks respect the whites the most, they don't like Pakis, if you know what I mean, and if a fight would let loose, the blacks would like hit the Asian boy and so in a way you're alright, but in a way it's not fair, if it's like you and the other boy fighting.

I So if say you fought, you yourself fought with an Asian boy right, black boys will back you up and not him, is that the way it works? If one of the boys was going to take sides, would they take sides with you or the Asian boy?

P It all depends. If your attitude is good and you ain't like been racist to the other boy then you're alright . . . the other boy would most probably get more stick on his back.

I Right, and if you have been racist to an Asian boy, how will black boys respond to that?

P It's like the same, if you know the black boys well then you're alright, it's like my mate who's got excluded earlier on in the year, he had a fight with this Asian boy, and when this Asian boy was loud mouthing him all the black boys were just kicking the boy in the head. 'Cause they didn't like the boy at all and I would have thought it would have been my other mate who would have got kicked in the head, but I was very surprised to see him not.

> **I** It sounds very complicated really.
>
> **P** Well no it's not complicated. Once you've been a year in the school, you know what it's all about. You know first year, when I came to the school I didn't know what to say or nothing . . .

This extract indicates that a main part of the socialization process and ordering of social relations in school is through ethnic group affiliations. Pupils' understanding of status differences between groups can be tested, reinforced, and then accepted. The extract indicates that it is not so much whether racism exists or not but that with years of co-existence behind them the groups have arrived at a kind of understanding of difference. Open hostilities, including fighting, can arise when the accepted order is seen to be questioned or not understood.

Fights between Schools

On a wider level there were also accounts of fighting between schools. These showed another set of group affiliations and considerations about status between groups. Pupils' social identities could be tightly linked to their sense of their school status, rather like football supporters favouring their own team in opposition to others. As one boy said: 'All Barnet School boys stick together.' It seemed clear that within school rivalries and hierarchies could be put aside, in the interests of the larger unit of the school, when there was a suspected threat from another school. Rivalries between schools could be vicious, though accounts of inter-school rivalries are prone to exaggeration, perhaps because the lack of day to day contact means the accuracy of reports is not tested. The threat from another school could be discussed with relish, and be accompanied by a fierce defence of one's own school prestige. There was also a kind of awe about the violence threatened between schools, and, as I remember from my own school days, a folklore can develop around notable incidents that had occurred in the past.

But some accounts indicated that the outcomes could be dangerous. Fights between schools would take place out of school, where the normal rules about fighting do not obviously apply, and this can add to the potential for getting out of control. In the next extract we see something of the rationale, from a pupil's point of view, of intense within-school affiliation, and the need for not losing face in relation to other schools.

> **P** 'Cause this is the hardest school now, it used to be Cheddar Grove but all our year went over to (there) and had a fight with knives and things like that, and they beat them all up, so we're the hardest school.
>
> **I** And why is it so important do you think for one school to want to be seen as harder than another?
>
> **P** In a way we don't want other schools on our backs saying you lot are the silliest school ever, once they know who's boss, you know what I mean. We're boss, no one can say nothing to us.

I   Right, ok, but why is that important, that's what I want to know?

P   If a school challenge us, that is it, all hell lets loose, I guarantee all the boys, all our Bett boys will go home and get their knives and everything and that would be it. There would be blood everywhere. This is what this school is like . . . they don't really care any more, they don't care what they do.

I   Why do they not care?

P   I don't really know, in a way I think they just like to feel big, but in a way I think it's really stupid 'cause I can't see the point of all us going over to another school and like cutting them and like all things like that. I don't know why they do it.

I   Ok, and do you think if you were at another school things would be different. You know, if you were in Cheddar Grove, maybe they have a different attitude there?

P   Yeah but the situation is if I go to Cheddar Grove and there would be another fight, I would be the one who would get stabbed, but if I was in Bett, I'd be alright, 'cause you know all Bett boys stick together.

The Role of Parents and Teachers in Fights

Parents

Some pupils felt that their parents expected them to defend themselves — to answer aggression toward them by retaliating in kind.

At 11 years:

A boy:

P   If they call me names — they annoy me and I start on them. Sometimes I don't like fighting because I know I will get into trouble. But sometimes my mum says if anyone hits me I've got to hit them back.

At 16 years

P   Yeah, they always let your parents know . . . but mum said, if they start, just defend yourself, don't worry about it.

P   I told my mum I was going to beat her up.

I   And did your mum try to tell you not to do that?

P   At first my mum said well do it then, 'cause, my mum knows what she's like, and then she turned round and said leave it, but I didn't listen, I went and done it. So she said, I told you to leave it, you should have done it out of school. So you wouldn't have got suspended for it.

There can appear to be two very different moral codes operating in schools. In contrast to that in the classroom, on the playground pupils can feel driven to respond in kind to aggression or threat, and this can be reinforced by parents, who can appear unconvinced by school policies that reject this.

The Role of Teachers

I turn, lastly in this chapter, to pupils' views on teachers' reactions to fighting in school. Teachers were not seen as an immediate resource when it came to halting a fight that had started. Only three pupils at 16 years thought that others would call a teacher or get help. If teachers were not seen as a presence during the fight itself, what about their actions afterward, and the way that fighting was dealt with more generally? In response to a question at 16 years, concerning how teachers responded to fighting, pupils most commonly said that teachers would suspend the culprits. Teachers were also said to split the fighters up, presumably if they arrived as a fight was in progress. Less frequently, pupils said that teachers would contact parents, exclude pupils, investigate the matter further, and report pupils, or give them a detention.

Teachers could sometimes be involved in the heat of a fight:

> **P** And then Ian goes, 'Shut up Terry'. And then I goes 'Ian don't tell me to shut up', and he told me to shut up. So I grabbed him and I threw him into the lockers and then he gave me a couple of times in my chest. Then some teacher came, I went to punch Ian and I punched her instead.
>
> **I** You punched the teacher?
>
> **P** Yeah, not in her face, in her arm and I broke her bracelet thing. And then the teacher got all fussed and took us to the office, and they excluded both of us.
>
> **I** How long were you excluded for?
>
> **P** Just for that day.

As we have seen, from a pupil's perspective there are strong reasons for committing themselves to a fight, and it is a strong sense of being wronged that ignites them. Dealing with fights is difficult for teachers, not the least because pupils can feel they are justified, and that teachers should have dealt with the wrongdoing that was the cause of the fight in the first place.

Sometimes teachers were seen to act in a way that recognized that a pupil was, to some extent, justified in their anger.

> **P** I also had a fight with a boy for calling me a slag, hit the teacher as well.
>
> **I** Why did you hit the teacher?
>
> **P** He called me a prostitute in my maths class, so he run out of the class, and the teacher stood in the doorway, so I couldn't get past, and he just wound me up so much I just hit the teacher to get out, and then got hold of him. But all she said was not to do it again, she never even took it to the Head.
>
> **I** It's a terrible thing for someone to say isn't it?

P   Yeah, I think that's why she never took it to the Head, 'cause she saw my point, and why I got wound up so much. He'd been doing it all lesson, and it was the end of the lesson and I'd just had enough

There was a general view that teachers did take fighting seriously, and the consequences of being caught were known and to be avoided.

Conclusion

In this chapter I have examined pupils' views about fighting in school. I have looked at the significance of fights to pupils, some ways in which fights are caused, the social and situational context of fights, and characteristics of individual children involved in fights.

Prevalence of, and Age Changes in, Fighting

Involvement in fighting was at its height at 7 years, though, even at 11 and 16 years, about a half of the pupils said they were involved in fights. At each age, pupils were for the most part unhappy about fighting, though some age differences were evident. There was a more ambivalent attitude at 7 years, with more saying they liked fighting, but still half felt very negative about fights. Children at 11 years were more negative about fights, and at 16 years in some respects more indifferent. Fighting in the primary school years can arise in the context of playground games and physical activity. The intensity of activity at primary breaktimes can lead to misunderstanding and slippage into fights, even between friends. This might explain the greater prevalence of fighting at 7 years. With age, fights could increase in terms of impact and consequences, and appeared to arise mainly as a reaction to threat or humiliation.

There appeared to be a recognition that fighting solved nothing, was an unusual event, and that, in the normal course of things, efforts would be taken to avoid them. As with other aspects of pupils' social lives in school, it is difficult for an outside observer to get an accurate picture, and easy to underestimate the concerns of young people. The level of physical contact at breaktime, aggressive in appearance, may give staff an inflated view of the extent of fighting, and it is possible to exaggerate the general willingness of pupils to engage in fights. It is correspondingly easy to underestimate their wish to get along with each other, and the everyday and skilful steps they routinely take to avoid confrontation and fights. By concentrating on pupils' accounts of a particular incident, this chapter itself stands the risk of over-stressing the significance of fights in school. It becomes clear from talking to 16-year-olds that fights are often distressing and entered into reluctantly, or because social forces around them drive them to fight. There appears to be little gratuitous fighting, though it is possible that the interview method used in the study could underestimate this.

Causes of Fights

The main reason for fighting was a response to provocation, and the wish not to be seen to be dominated or humiliated by another. Particular causes of fights, examined in most depth with the older secondary pupils, were provocation by name calling, teasing and cussing; stirring and spreading rumours; fights arising out of mucking about and games; misinterpreting an accident; protecting brothers or sisters; as a result of bullying; and over the way an earlier fight was reported. There is some overlap with the causes of fights identified by Boulton (1993), with regard to 9-year-olds, though the prevalence of disputes over rule governed games reflects the age of children in his study.

Individual Factors

Some fights came about because of particularly aggressive and provocative individuals. This would be consistent with the views of staff in schools that the main problem at breaktime, at both primary and secondary level, is the poor behaviour of a few pupils. Teachers in the national survey also felt that breaktime behaviour had declined in school because there were now more individual pupils with difficult behaviour.

Social Factors in Fights

Pupils' accounts of fighting showed a number of ways in which social and situational factors were important. Perhaps most obvious was the breaktime context itself. Breaktime is the main forum for unsupervised activities in school and inevitably the main forum for fights. We have seen that particular breaktime activities, for example, football, could lend themselves more than others to conflict and disagreement. The immediate social context at breaktime could affect fights. A fight can have a magnetic pull on others in the playground, attracting crowds who will gather round, sometimes cheering on the participants, and even joining in, but sometimes trying to get the fighters to stop, though only rarely calling a teacher and getting help.

As with teasing, the nature of the relationship between pupils, for example, whether friends or not, could affect the course and outcome of fights. Examination of fights involving children from different ethnic groups highlighted ways in which fights, like other aspects of social relations at breaktime, can be underpinned by inter-group relations. The indication was that, by the end of secondary school, years of co-existence had led groups to a kind of understanding of difference, and fighting only arose when the accepted order was seen to be questioned or not understood. Membership of an ethnic group, and of a particular school, can be a significant factor in pupils' self identity, and affect peer relations. At times within-school rivalries and hierarchies could be put aside, in the interests of the larger unit of the school, when there was a real or, one suspected, exaggerated perception of a threat from another school.

It is interesting to note that, while pupils' motivation toward school work, and an interest in the school's academic standing, may seem muted, they can identify closely with the school, in terms of an informal understanding of dominance and threat between schools. Again, it is the informal world of school that can occupy pupils. Fights between schools are of interest not so much for what they say about violence in society. Indeed, the sense we had was that such fights were rare. They are of interest for what they say about pupils' inter-group relations and affiliations. Fights between schools are best understood not as a depersonalized loss of control, in the manner of some accounts of urban riots, so much as the result of identification with a school, and in terms of dynamics that underpin pupils' social experiences in school.

It seemed that inter-group relations — both within school and between schools — became more important as pupils got older. I do not have an exact test of this, but the impression was that fights at primary school are more likely to be inter personal, that is between individuals, rather than between groups.

Implications for Schools

As many teachers will recognize, there can appear to be two very different moral codes operating in schools. School policies on behaviour have as an aim the reduction of aggression, and the setting in place of non-retaliatory solutions to conflict. Yet, out of the classroom, pupils can appear to feel driven to respond in kind to aggression or threat. This out-of-classroom moral code seems to have at its heart a strong sense of reciprocity, and a sensitivity to any perception that they have been slighted or humiliated. For boys, especially, the test is often physical, and the fight is the most direct and threatening challenge to their status in the eyes of others. It is most natural for them to retaliate, and parents can reinforce this. It can take a strong and unusual individual to stand apart from this, and they will find it particularly difficult if not supported by an alternative non-retaliatory moral stance, that has meaning and application in pupils' everyday dealings with each other, especially experiences at breaktime. This is why the role of schools in setting a moral context, for pupils and parents, is so crucial.

Pupils' accounts indicated that schools differed in the degree to which they attached value to aggression and dominance in terms of physical prowess. It seemed that in some schools the need to attain dominance over others was stronger than in other schools, and this need appeared to permeate relations between groups, and made more likely the possibility of fights ensuing from conflict in schools. As we saw in Chapter 2, pupil culture in school is in some senses independent from adults and classroom life, but it also develops in the social and moral context of the school. It was our impression that pupils' rejection of aggressive solutions to conflict, and willingness to intervene constructively in fights, was affected by the lead set by schools. This raises important questions about the role of the school in relation to peer culture and we return to this in the last chapter of this book.

Chapter 10

Conclusion

In the first chapter of this book, the current place of breaktime and lunchtime in school life was described. It was argued that there is a predominantly negative view about breaktime, and that this has led to a reduction in time spent at breaktime and lunch, and more deliberate management and closer supervision of breaktime behaviour. Current trends in education, such as greater competition between schools, a concern with covering the National Curriculum, maximizing academic success rates, and worries about security in schools, though understandable, appear to be contributing to the marginalization of traditional breaktimes and lunchtime in school.

In contrast to this trend, in Chapter 2 I reviewed psychological and sociological research, and suggested that breaktime can offer valuable opportunities for social contact with peers and friends, and the development of social skills. In this book I have examined the pupils' perspective on breaktime and social life then, throughout the school years. In this final chapter I will seek to identify some main lessons that have been learned, and seek to draw conclusions about the role of breaktime experiences, and what schools can do.

Each chapter of this book has examined a facet of pupils' experience at breaktime. Let me briefly review the main conclusions from each area covered.

Pupil Views about Breaktime

We have seen that the great majority of pupils throughout their school careers expressed a positive view about breaktime. This was despite their recognition, especially at secondary level, of the sometimes unsatisfactory nature of the physical environment provided for breaktimes. Main reasons for a positive view were similar at primary and secondary school: they liked the opportunity to socialize with their friends, and having a break from work. At primary level, the other main reason for liking breaktime was the opportunity it gave for playing games. By the end of secondary school they liked breaktime because of the opportunities it provided for independence from adults. Their accounts showed how valuable breaktime and lunchtime could be for talking openly about school and teachers, in a way that would not be possible in lesson time, and for allowing them to behave in way freed from the constraints expected in school. Breaktime can therefore be of value to pupils throughout the school years, though the nature of the value changes from primary to secondary.

Breaktime Activities

Study of activities at breaktime showed a main difference between primary and secondary stages. At infant and junior school, much time is spent in games, while over the secondary years, involvement in games declines and pupils are more likely to talk to friends and walk about, and work and sit at tables playing cards. The vitality of primary school breaktimes contrasts with the more covert and seemingly desultory activities of the last years at school. But one needs to be cautious about concluding that secondary breaktimes are less important to pupils. Breaktime can be a main forum for social contact and friendships.

Closer study of the origins and changes in playground games of 8–9-year-olds, showed a gradual narrowing of the range of games, and the emergence of a few dominant ones. The influence of developmental and school influences was examined. There was evidence that in their play they were acquiring a distinctive culture, with particular activities and rules of engagement, that were particular to the school, though seemingly independent of staff. In the case of some activities, such as making camps, they were in a sense acquiring a history of the school's informal life.

Friendships

A main feature to emerge from the study of 8–9-year-olds, over the first year after entry to junior school, was the important ways in which breaktime games and children's friendships and social networks were interconnected. Soon after entry, one function of games was the facilitation and support provided for entry into social relationships, while at a later point in the school year the social function changed to one of supporting and maintaining friendship groups. The early days in a new school can be a time of uncertainty for children, and it seems likely that new friendships can help reduce uncertainty and thus help adjustment to school. Children as young as 8 years showed considerable skill in creating, and then managing complex social networks, and gradations of friendship status.

Pupils' accounts at 16 years showed that friendships were also developed at breaktime, but in different ways. If for the younger children, activities and games are a mediator and support for friendship, by the end of secondary school friendships are furthered in the context of 'hanging around' — by, in a sense, an absence of activity. It is relatively easy for adults to overestimate the lack of useful activity, and underestimate the value to pupils' social relations. One function provided by friendship groups at this age was the support provided to pupils as they moved toward their final exams and a life beyond school. So friendships, which can often only be enacted at breaktime, can be of value throughout school life, though the nature of the value changes.

Teasing

Study of teasing showed its ubiquitous place in peer interactions throughout school. The majority of children at all ages said that teasing occurred. The point was made that one needs to be careful not to see all teasing and name calling in a negative light. Pupils were keen to say at 11 and at 16 years that much teasing was understood not to be hurtful, but more a part of everyday banter, often between friends. Some teasing no doubt serves a social purpose, helping to denote limits, showing off sharpness in social discourse, and jostling for status. Pupils showed that considerable skill could be required in determining what form of teasing was appropriate with particular people. But, on some occasions, teasing could really upset people, and the effects could be harmful emotionally, and could adversely affect school progress, though this might not be appreciated by the teaser, for whom it could be just an act of harmless fun.

Pupil accounts showed the importance of considering teasing in the context of more general social relations between peers; for example, it can help to define and consolidate friendships, it can function to define power relations, and it can be used to strengthen group cohesion, sometimes by the taunting of a scapegoat. It is, in other words, subservient to the intent and purpose of peer relations, both affiliative and aggressive.

Fighting

Fighting can reflect a troubling school peer culture, involving power and dominance, reinforced by physical aggression, particularly, though not exclusively, involving boys. But pupils' accounts of fighting in school also show a recognition that fighting solved nothing, and was an unusual event. There is a danger, by examining fights that do occur, that we can underestimate pupils' desire to get along with each other, and the everyday and sometimes skilful steps they take to avoid confrontation and fights. From the pupils' perspective at least there often seems to be a logic to the cause of fights.

The Social Value of Breaktime

So the research described in this book, taken together with the review of peer relations and peer cultures in Chapter 2, indicates a number of features. Breaktime in schools can be a forum for enjoyment and activity, play and games, socialization into adult roles, and cultural transmission; the development of friendships, social networks, social skills and competence; the opportunity for independence and freedom from teachers and classrooms; and the management of conflict, aggression and inter-group relations. It can also be a site of harassment, cruelty and domination.

It is important to recognize the limitations on claims that can be made on the basis of the evidence reported in this book. The descriptive nature of the data means that the social value of breaktime cannot be proved as such. The research did not set out to prove or test a particular theory in any strict sense; rather it had a more exploratory aim, and attempted to describe pupils' experiences and views, in both quantitative and qualitative terms, and then draw what appeared to be the most likely interpretations and conclusions. It is actually difficult to envisage research that, whilst attempting to describe everyday school behaviour, *could* establish causal connections in such a clear way, though it is possible to target particular aspects of pupils' breaktime experience for example to test the effects of specific factors.

What one can say is that in a number of ways throughout the book the social value of breaktime for pupils has been strongly suggested, and that breaktime is an important context for pupils' social life throughout the school years. Breaktime is also important, and surprisingly underused, as a research site for close observation of a number of facets of social development during the school years. These conclusions can be contrasted with results from the national survey, which showed that breaktime in some schools was being reduced, and that, from the point of view of school staff, the main value of breaktime for pupils, at both primary and secondary level, was relatively low level, and expressed in terms of time for pupils to relax and have a break from classroom activities, and to 'let off steam'. There is a danger that these factors may underestimate the importance of breaktime, and its value to pupils. Pupils, also, may find it difficult to articulate the value of experiences so everyday as meeting and talking to their friends. The situation is troubling because there appears to be little appreciation of the potential value of breaktime. Current changes and developments in education are affecting breaktime experiences because there is little regard for something considered to be as marginal as breaktime. The danger is that we may recognize the value of breaktime to pupils long after changes have severely altered or reduced it.

There is a danger that developments within schools, and worries about children's safety out of school, may be inadvertently constraining young people's social development. This point has been developed by the journalist Ros Coward:

> The logic is obvious. With too much fast traffic, attacks on kids and the temptations of crime, the world is not a safe place for unsupervised children . . . There is something soulless about this regulation and restriction of the child's world. It responds to the problems of parents, not children . . . and our inability to order our community so that its open spaces and streets are safe places to play. Why shouldn't children go home alone, or hang about with their friends in parks? In a slightly better world (not just an ideal one), with cheaper leisure facilities, restricted traffic, and park-keepers, there's no reason why children shouldn't play unsupervised. If schools are becoming achievement-orientated, why should children be constantly supervised in 'constructive' activity . . . We should recognise children's rights to be bone idle, to encounter boredom,

thereby finding resources and creatively within themselves. (*Guardian*, 9 June 1997)

and by Mayer Hillman:

> The increasing circumscription of the lives of children may be well-intentioned, but it is also damaging. This generation of children are increasingly being denied opportunities for learning how to make their own decisions, how to act responsibly and how to assess the motives of those they do not know. They are prevented from having adventures, extending personal frontiers, being mischievous, taking risks, and suffering the consequences . . . These are basic elements of growing up best learned when children are on their own. (*Times Educational Supplement*, 20 June 1997)

These quotes raise difficult questions about the appropriate role of children's unsupervised activities out of school, and it is worrying that a proper consideration of these questions seem to be bypassed in the face of immediate worries about children's safety. More generally, there are concerns over a kind of moral panic seen in views about childhood, current among many politicians, media commentators and other public figures, not least because this is bound to affect teachers' and parents' views on children's social lives. A dominant view is of children at risk — as victims and perpetrators of crime, as liable to abduction and danger on roads. Little wonder that parents worry about their children and protect them from unsupervised activities. In line with Hillman's view above, Moss and Petrie (1997) conclude that: 'An examination of children's lives shows children as increasingly segregated from wider society, less visible in public places . . .' Current views about children therefore appear to be affecting children's social lives both out of school and within school. In the face of this, there is a need to consider a coherent and holistic policy towards childhood, and a respect for children's rights. This is, or should be, an important part of a public policy towards children and towards children's services, including schooling (Moss and Petrie, 1997). There is not space here to discuss further the situation out of school, but in the case of social life in school, much hinges on the view taken about the balance between pupil independence and school control, and I return to this at the end of the chapter.

In this book I have considered a number of facets of breaktime experience, and each has been considered in terms of four main themes: developments with age, individual differences, group differences, and social and contextual influences on behaviour. Let me now review some main conclusions from each of these themes.

Developments with Age in Breaktime Experiences and Behaviour

The case study of one year 4 class, after entry to junior school, showed a number of changes over the course of their first year in school. Changes in breaktime games and friendships were examined in Chapters 5 and 6, along with processes that seemed to explain these changes.

The most obvious changes over time, though, were revealed in the longitudinal study of pupils from 7 to 16 years. Some of these age differences have already been referred to in this chapter. The most noticeable change, for example, with regard to activities at breaktime, was a change from the physical activities and games of the primary years, to more sedentary activities at secondary level. Friendship relations changed accordingly, as we have seen. Some other less obvious aspects of friendships also showed changes with age. By secondary school, we saw the emergence, for some pupils, of a mistrust of close friendships, because of negative experiences of previous friendships in school, and a preference for maintaining a distance from others. More positively, other pupils, nearing the end of their secondary school lives, spoke for the first time of the cohesion and closeness of friendship groups, sometimes of a whole class in school. Teasing and name calling developed through the school years, as we saw in Chapter 8, and this was revealed not just in the prevalence and types of teasing, but in the role of teasing in peer relations. There was sign of a decline in teasing by the final years of secondary school, and this may have been partly because of the cohesiveness of social relations within groups. Fighting in school also changed with age. The intensity of physical activity during primary breaktimes could lead to fights, while secondary aged children had come to learn the serious consequences of fights, and fights appeared to arise mainly as a reaction to threat or humiliation. Relationships with adults also changed, though this was not directly studied. At primary level, breaktime activities can be pursued with equal enthusiasm, whether or not adults are around, but by secondary level, pupils place more importance on independence from adults.

An important issue concerns the reasons for changes in breaktime activities and experiences; in particular, to what extent they are the result of developmental changes within the child, or affected by outside factors. This issue was addressed in Chapters 4 and 5, with regard to changes in breaktime activities. Developmental factors within the child are bound to be important, but school based factors, such as the influence of peers, were also identified as important, for example, in the onset of an inhibition about playing games, and the development of a seemingly exaggerated and growing inactivity, through the secondary years. A feature of this study, seen in Chapter 4, was the analysis of pupils' own explanations for changes in their breaktime activities.

Individual Differences

In a number of ways, differences between pupils were found in their experiences and behaviour at breaktime. There were some pupils who had worries about breaktime, even though their overall judgment was a positive one, and there were a minority of pupils who had a predominantly negative view about breaktime, and who could find the experience distressing. In Chapter 6, I looked at characteristics of 8–9-year-old pupils who had difficulties forming friendships and being involved in breaktime activities. In Chapter 9, we saw that some fights could come about because of particularly aggressive and provocative individuals, and this is consistent with the views of staff in the National Survey that a main problem at breaktime, at both primary and secondary level, is the poor behaviour of a few pupils. These differences bring to light a darker side to breaktime life, and there clearly are steps that need to be taken to help those for whom breaktime is a difficult time.

However, it is also important that the difficulties experienced by some pupils are not used as the basis for judgment on *all* children's breaktime experience, nor the basis for policy on breaktime, which will affect all children. It does not even follow that the solution to difficulties faced by some children is to reduce breaktime, and therefore their opportunities for social interaction. Rejection by peers may still occur in other settings. An alternative interpretation is that for some children much could be gained from closer attention by teachers and supervisors to their breaktime experiences, because this may help reveal more about the nature and extent of their difficulties with peers, and strategies for intervention.

More positively, in Chapter 5, I examined characteristics of children who were 'key players' in breaktime life and games. Their influence was felt through suggesting, maintaining and ending games, and they were a main force around which the groups and their games functioned. Some characteristics appeared to be shared by these 'key players', but they also differed in other ways, and it was suggested that further study of the influence of such individuals on the development of playground games would be profitable.

Group Differences

Gender Differences

Previous research has highlighted sex differences in breaktime behaviour (Smith, 1994; Evans, 1989; Pellegrini, 1995). Throughout this book a number of differences between boys and girls were identified. There were, for example, differences between boys and girls in their views about breaktime. Girls were on the whole less positive about breaktime and had worries, for example, about the cold and having nothing to do. They were more likely than boys to express a preference for coming into the school buildings during breaktime.

A feature of the present study was the opportunity to study sex differences over a longer time period than previous research. It was shown in Chapter 4 that the consequences of changes in breaktime activities seemed different for boys and girls. Although boys and girls became less active with age, there was more continuity in boys' activities from primary to secondary levels, for example, in the case of football and active games. There was also a wider continuity into the world of adult male culture, where football of course has a main place. In the case of girls, by comparison, there was less continuity between the games played at primary level, and the mainly social and non-active activities preferred at secondary. The sense of a lost or buried world of childhood, noted by commentators on children's culture, is more noticeable in the case of girls.

Breaktime offered a context within which girls and boys could form separate groups but could also be drawn together. In Chapter 6 I found that 8–9-year-old girls and boys had mainly separate friendship groups, with a different style and composition. Relations between boys and girls at breaktime changed with age and preferences in breaktime activities. The play and active pursuits of the primary years could separate and also bring boys and girls together — a process that has been described by Thorne (1993) — while the more sedentary 'hanging around' of older pupils could draw them more fundamentally into social contact. The situation, though, was complex with some pupils describing a greater ease of contact with the opposite sex, while others appeared more self conscious, and still preferred separate pursuits.

Boys appeared a little more likely to tease girls than vice versa. Boys could taunt girls, for example, about their appearance, supposed sexual activity, as well as academic performance in lessons. For girls, 'slagging' each other seemed a main form of insult. Teasing during the secondary years sometimes reflected a growing awareness of sexuality, and one function is likely to be regulation of the amount of contact with the opposite sex.

In contrast to inter-ethnic relations, we formed the impression that relations between boys and girls were more implicitly dealt with in schools, and a clear lead on unacceptable behaviour was not provided. It was therefore more possible for stereotypical views, and a social distance between groups, to go unremarked, and for gender group differences to be more taken for granted and acceptable.

Ethnic Differences

In parallel research, involving the same pupils' views on school work and their own attainments, we found that by 16 years there were noticeable ethnic differences. White children were less positive than black children about their own attainments, and less positive about themselves at school and generally (Blatchford, 1996; Blatchford, 1997). In contrast, as we have seen in this book, we did not find clear differences in their views about breaktime and their breaktime activities.

Most pupils in these mainly ethnically diverse schools said they spent time, often at breaktime, in ethnically mixed groups, and some were keen to say that their choice of friendships was on the basis of individual characteristics of others rather than on the basis of their ethnic group. Accounts of friendships indicated a degree of separation between ethnic groups, but an overall lack of hostility and conflict, which some pupils explained in terms of different groups having co-existed together over the formative school years. Separation between groups seemed to be based on having different interests and concerns, many revealed at breaktime.

Special attention was paid to the place of pupils' ethnic origin in their accounts of teasing and name calling, and fighting. While it is important not to underestimate or underplay the importance of racism in children's lives at school, it is also likely that conflict between ethnic groups is part of a more general tendency, well understood in social psychology, for conflicts to arise between clearly defined groups. As Milner (1997) has said:

> It is certainly not that racism in the childhood years is a trivial matter. It is that the 'seeking', absorbing and reproducing of racist ideas may have rather more to do with the developing identity needs of the child than with the objects of these attitudes; that they function to bring positive increments of self-definition during a period in which the child has little else from which to fashion a positive identity; and that they may rapidly be superseded by other sources of status and self-esteem when they present themselves. (Milner, 1997, p. 125)

In this sense ethnic group differences provide categories, much reinforced by factors outside school, by which 'in' and 'out' groups are defined, and it can be this which is primary, rather than anything intrinsically disliked in the out group. Ethnic classifications are a convenient tool for children in their attempts to order and simplify their social worlds.

Nevertheless, a child's ethnic origin is likely to be a main force in their view of themselves, and we have seen in this book many ways in which within-group affiliation and identification affected breaktime behaviour, particularly teasing and fighting. As with gender differences, one purpose of teasing and name calling between ethnic groups is regulation of differences between groups.

As with other areas, it also appeared that pupils differed in the perceived importance and significance of racist teasing. Some felt it was not a problem and not an issue, while others recognized it occurred but saw it as an inevitable part of social life, and yet others considered it was serious and a part of hostility between groups that adversely affected everyday life in school. Some pupils no doubt are hostile to other groups, whether different ethnic groups or the opposite sex, and hold stereotypical views about them. There are unlikely to be natural laws, of a social psychological kind, governing inter-group relations, because relations between groups can vary, and are affected by the context within which they occur. As I shall point out soon, it also appeared that the school provided an important context for, and influence on, inter-group relations, and this could set the tone for contact between ethnic groups, as well as boys and girls.

Social and Situational Factors

Throughout this book a number of social and contextual factors, influencing breaktime behaviour, have been discussed. A main theme has been the importance of the breaktime context itself, in its effect on pupil behaviour and activities. There is a common assumption that breaktime and the outside grounds are a forum for unacceptable behaviour, but breaktime can just as easily be a forum for the development of social sensitivity, peer regulation and the management of potential difficulties with others. Breaktime provides the opportunity for qualitatively different playful behaviours, forms of social relations, and conversation to that found in the school. To use Sutton-Smith's (1990) image, the school playground can provide the context for a unique sense of 'festival'. More specifically, social situations and breaktime activities at breaktime can affect types of behaviours, for example, the likelihood of conflict and the possibility of fights. 'Hanging around', a main feature of secondary school breaktimes, can be a context for important social contacts.

Other social influences at breaktime, identified in the book, are the force of peer pressure in shaping breaktime activities; more particularly, the role of other pupils in affecting the course of playground fights; and the way that friendship relations are vital in pupils' interpretation of actions at breaktime, including teasing and fighting. Reference has already been made to the interconnections between breaktime games and friendships. A main influence on changes in breaktime activities in the class of 8–9-year-olds, stemmed from social processes such as those involved in getting to know other people. As friendship groups stabilized, the games played became narrower in range and more stable themselves. Pupils also talked more, unaccompanied by play, as they found out more about each other.

We have also seen how breaktime behaviour could be affected by intergroup affiliations. Inter-school identification could also affect pupil social behaviour, and in Chapter 9 I referred to pupils with little obvious enthusiasm for school academic success, treating very seriously any perceived threats from other schools to the school's non-academic reputation.

A Summary of Influences on Breaktime Behaviour and Experience

In this book I have therefore worked toward a description of pupils' experiences and views on breaktime in schools. As a way of summarizing the approach and some of the findings, Figure 10.1 has been drawn up. In this figure each 'cell' gives some examples of the results and are only meant to be illustrative. The book has concentrated on four main themes, and these are shown in Figure 10.1, but other influences on breaktime behaviour were also suggested. I have already looked at the influence of peers, for example on changes in breaktime activities over time. Another influence on breaktime behaviour and

Figure 10.1: Influences on pupils' breaktime experience and behaviour

Aspects of Pupil's Breaktime Experience	Age Differences	Individual Differences	Group Differences			
			Group (Ethnic and Gender) Differences	Between and Within Group Factors	Situational Factors
Views on Breaktime	Positive at all ages More ambivalence at 7 years	A minority negative about breaktime	Boys more positive than girls		More positive about breaktime than other aspects of school
Activities: Games	Active (e.g. chasing games) ⇒ sedentary	'key players'; rejected players	Boys football; girls less continuity over time	girls and boys exploring boundaries in play	playground context
Friendships	Through activities/games ⇒ hanging around	some popular, have close friends; some unpopular, no close friends	Girls more likely to have best friends, more exclusive friendships	Mixing but also tension and separation between ethnic groups	Breaktime v. classroom context; different games with friends
Teasing and Name Calling	Frequent at all ages but declines by 16 yrs	Some individuals more likely to tease, to be teased	No clear ethnic or gender differences	Boys tease girls; girls 'slag' other girls	Breaktime context; nature of relationship affects impact of teasing
Fighting	Arises through activities ⇒ through spreading rumours	Aggressive individuals start fights	Boys more than girls	Between group and school fights	Role of playground crowd

experience is likely to be parental and family influences, for example in pupils' attitudes to fighting and aggressive behaviour, and the influence of siblings on a pupils' knowledge of games. Another key dimension, which affects breaktime behaviour, is connected to the nature of the relationship between pupils, and in particular the extent to which they are affiliative or aggressive. This affected, for example, the nature and interpretation of teasing and name calling.

Quality of Play/Behaviour at Breaktime

As we saw in Chapter 1, it is the view of some teachers that traditional games are in decline and the quality of play has declined. Elsewhere I have considered the evidence concerning historical changes in the quality of outside play (Blatchford, 1994). A general point to make is that it is easy to exaggerate the extent of a decline in quality of outside play. As the Opies (1969) remind us:

> . . . the belief that traditional games are dying out is itself traditional; it was received wisdom even when those who now regret the passing of the games were themselves vigorously playing them. We overlook the fact that as we have grown older our interests have changed . . . we no longer have eyes for the games, and not noticing them suppose them to have vanished. (Opie and Opie, 1969, p. 14)

From a distance, games and activities may appear impoverished, but it may be that activities have changed, and young people have found new forms of expression.

But the main point I wish to make here is that consideration of social and contextual issues makes more complex the debate over general trends in the quality of play, and that it may be more profitable to consider play behaviour in the context of social forces within schools. In Chapters 5 and 6 we saw the influence of social influences such as other pupils and the informal culture in the school; the influence of particular 'key players'; and connections between developments over time in breaktime activities, particularly games, and friendship formation. We also saw how the quality of breaktime pursuits of 16-year-olds may seem very low level but may in fact be subservient to other social ends, such as the formation of friendships. Any consideration of the general quality of outside play and games would need to consider these factors.

Differences between Schools

But there was another likely influence. Though the research described in this book was not designed to examine school differences, pupils' accounts indicated that even informal social experiences were affected by the wider school context. Examination of pupils' accounts of teasing and fighting indicated that schools differed in the degree to which pupils attached value to aggression and dominance in terms of physical prowess. It seemed that in some schools the need for attaining dominance over others was stronger than in other schools, and this need appeared to permeate relations between groups, and made more likely the possibility of aggressive name calling and fights. Pupil culture in school is in some senses independent from adults and classroom life, but it also develops in the social and moral context of the school. I return to this theme shortly.

Implications for Schools

At the end of each chapter I have identified some implications for schools, arising out of each particular aspect of breaktime behaviour examined. I want now to draw out some main themes concerning the management of breaktime.

School Improvement and Peer Culture: A Dilemma

From the point of view of the material presented in this book, there are dilemmas for school management and improvement. As we have seen, the main problem arises out of the growing restrictions on pupils' unsupervised activities within school, on the one hand, and the likely benefits of these activities for their social development, on the other hand. There is a tension, in other words, between a greater control of pupil behaviour, on the one hand, and the likely value of pupil independence, on the other. This tension is reflected in some awkward questions. Will unacceptable behaviour decline and peer relations necessarily benefit from policies to improve schools? Or will pupils' social freedoms and relations suffer? Are social experiences at breaktime an irrelevance, of little consequence to school learning? What if, as we have seen, peer cultures can run counter to a learning orientation within school? Or, importantly, is there something important in peer relations and peer culture that should be recognized and supported?

Although this dilemma, concerning the balance of control and independence, may not be addressed directly within schools, policies adopted and actions taken will represent an answer in practice. And steps taken within schools, as they bear on school breaktimes, largely hinge on the stance taken with regard to a main question: what is the appropriate role of adults with regard to breaktime? There are two extremes of view. The first, which might be called an 'interventionist' view, characterizes the growing trend toward more deliberate management of pupils' behaviour at breaktime, and changes to the playground environment. In a similar vein, in some primary schools the supposed decline in traditional games has been approached by teaching children games.

At the other extreme is an alternative, what might be called a 'non-interventionist' view. The Opies (1969) were very clear that adults had no role at all in children's play activities, no matter how well meaning their intentions: '. . . nothing extinguishes self-organised play more effectively than does action to promote it' (p. 16). They argue that it is appropriate that adults do not share children's interests and leisure activities, and vehemently object to attempts to organize and tame children's games. In a strong and well constructed warning the Opies say this:

> If children's games are tamed and made part of the school curricula, if wastelands are turned into playing-fields for the benefit of those who conform and ape their elders, if children are given the idea that they cannot enjoy themselves without being provided with the 'proper' equipment, we need blame only ourselves when we produce a generation who have lost their dignity, who are ever dissatisfied, and who descend for their sport to the easy excitement of rioting, or pilfering, or vandalism. (Opie and Opie, 1969, p. 16)

This view can be considered to be over-romantic, and to conveniently ignore ways in which peer culture can reflect negative aspects of adult culture. The non-interventionist view can find particular application at the primary stage, where the value of unsupervised play is more obvious. Even so, it could be justified at the secondary stage when, as we have seen, pupils attach growing importance to independence from adults and classroom life.

Interestingly, sociological and ethnographical research has tended to portray relations between the two cultures of pupils and school as coexisting by virtue of a collaboration between pupils and teachers, based on pupils being rewarded or not criticized if basic rules of classroom procedure are adhered to (Woods, 1990). Pupils may not therefore like school or school work but will collude with teachers in order to avoid outright conflict. This kind of view therefore sets limits on the degree of intervention in peer culture, and does in a sense passively accept it.

There are difficulties with both extremes. The interventionist stance, which is gaining dominance, as we have seen, risks overrunning pupils' freedoms and the positive aspects identified in the review above, while the non-interventionist stance risks allowing anti-school cultures to develop and dominate, and have a destructive effect on school learning. It needs to be said that the role of peer interaction and pupil culture in schools cannot be simply ignored. As Epstein (1989) has said: 'Teachers and parents have been hesitant to interfere in children's friendships . . . But tacit acceptance of typical environmental conditions is, in fact, "passive interference" in students' opportunities for social and educational experiences that lead to choice of friends' (p. 183).

An important challenge facing schools, therefore, is getting the balance between the two polarities right, that is, the balance between control and independence. Pollard (1985) has pointed to the need for an 'acceptable' balance of three major child interests — self, peer group membership and learning — which will affect coping in school. But how is this balance to be achieved and what are current policies and actions toward breaktime telling us about the current balance? Is it possible to reconcile the value to pupils of free assembly with the understandable wish of schools to ensure control over behaviour and learning? Is there, in other words, a third approach that avoids the extremes of passivity and intervention just identified?

What Can Be Done?

There is now greater awareness of breaktime experiences in school. Even a few years ago it was possible for me to argue that, 'playtime has received very little attention. It could lay claim to being the forgotten part of the school day' (Blatchford, 1989). But recently there have been a number of initiatives (Blatchford and Sharp, 1994). School grounds are being improved and opportunities for environmental education have been encouraged by organizations such as Learning Through Landscapes (Lucas, 1994). Environmental improvements have included: installing play equipment; making the playground more attractive, for example, through murals, plants etc; and all manner of green initiatives such as the creation of ponds, wildlife areas and other habitats. Sheat and Beer (1994), have described ways of involving pupils in the design and improvement of playgrounds. In an effort to reduce bullying, there are initiatives to improve the school grounds in a collaborative way with pupils (Higgins, 1994). Titman (1994) has described ways of changing and developing school grounds based on awareness of pupils' 'readings' of the school grounds.

Another direction of recent work has been the introduction of a number of schemes to train supervisory staff and improve dialogue between lunchtime and teaching staff (Fell, 1994; Sharp, 1994). A main message underlying recent breaktime initiatives (see especially, Ross and Ryan, 1994), is that breaktime improvements should involve the whole school, that is, they should, as far as possible, involve all in schools — teaching staff, of course, but also ancillary staff, pupils and parents — and they should also be whole school approaches, in the sense that what is discussed and decided with regard to breaktime is consistent with what goes on in the school. Expectations about behaviour which are not seen to operate once pupils go outside to the playground are unlikely to be effective (Sharp and Blatchford, 1994).

As well as initiatives directed at breaktime and the playground, there have also been more specific initiatives to help and encourage inter-personal relations between pupils. These include techniques such as collaborative conflict resolution, peer counselling and assertiveness training, which have been used as part of preventive work to reduce conflict and bullying (Sharp and Cowie, 1994; Sharp, Cooper and Cowie, 1994). Roffey, Tarrant and Majors (1994), drawing on a wide range of applied work, offer many examples of action in schools to help young pupils' social relations and friendships, including role playing exercises, activities to learn and practise social skills, group work strategies, and exercises to improve classroom social climate. These and other developments are to be welcomed. But they do not offer full solutions to the dilemma just posed. The problem still remains that breaktime experience and peer culture can be left untouched, ignored and separate.

On the basis of my research, visits and discussion within schools, and the literature, the following four general principles are offered as ways of connecting breaktime experiences and school policies.

Understanding Pupils' Breaktime Experiences

One first step is to encourage better descriptive information on, and better understanding of, the meaning and value of pupils' breaktime experiences. Better information is a necessary first step on which to build school policy. As Pollard has said: 'In my view wise teachers will do everything they can to understand the children's culture and social structure. If this is done policy decisions can be made which will make it possible to work *with* the children and to harness their energy and enthusiasm to educational and social goals' (1985, pp. 245–6). Titman has expressed a similar point: 'The absence of clarification of the purpose and value of the Informal Curriculum amongst pupils . . . has been seen to lead to assumption and confusion in terms of management policy and practice. It may also result in playtime being a less positive and enjoyable learning experience for everyone concerned' (1994, p. 118).

The challenge for schools is to pay more attention to peer relations and culture, and the need for peer affiliations. Teachers will often be the first to admit that they have little knowledge of what pupils do at breaktime. Teachers do, after all, understandably want a break themselves. But, in any case, there are inherent difficulties in accessing information about a world away from the classroom, and separate from adults. School projects on the playground may help to begin better mutual understanding, though these can miss essential realities of the playground from the pupils' point of view. One primary teacher, described in Blatchford (1989), took very seriously time outside with her pupils in order to become more familiar with their games, and became almost an honorary playground member. Involvement at secondary level will be different, and not so based on an interest in games and activities. There are unlikely to be any clear rules here. The basis of a dialogue may flow from simply showing an *interest* in pupils' outside experiences, in contexts in which they feel control over information given, and in which they see their experiences are recognized.

Involvement of Pupils

There is evidence of the benefits of pupil involvement in school decision making. Jennings and Kohlberg (Schneider, 1993) found that participation in the governance of school enhanced the moral judgments of adolescent delinquents.

Epstein (in Schneider, 1993) found that a more participatory secondary school style had a positive effect on friendships between pupils; for example, more students were selected as best friends, fewer were left out, and there was less evidence of small enclosed cliques.

But our research has suggested that pupils had little sense of involvement in decision making, especially at secondary level. Despite efforts in some schools toward pupil involvement, these can be relatively superficial and short lived, and pupils are likely to be quick to spot token gestures toward involvement. Forums like School Councils can be a valuable means of pupil involvement (Blatchford, 1989), though pupils should be able to see their participation has purpose, that recommendations are responded to and have impact. Further, ways could be devised to give responsibility to pupils for such things as planning improvements to playground, and in planning rules of behaviour at breaktime.

The involvement of pupils in decisions concerning breaktime offers many opportunities, because, as has been said, they are the main participants and experts. They have, after all, to live their lives on the playground, and the nature of the issues at stake, and the consequences of decisions made, are very apparent to them, if not always to adults. Productive involvement offers the basis for greater responsibility toward the school community.

Facilitating Peer Relations at Breaktime

It may be appropriate to consider a more active role in facilitating breaktime activities. Clearly, given what has been said so far, this would need to be sensitive to pupils' views on breaktime and to avoid being over prescriptive. The approach taken is best considered in the context of particular school activities and school grounds. In the study of the playground activities of one junior school class (Chapter 5), it was found that activities had a history that predated many members of staff. The complex rules of engagement and alliances derived from accumulative developments over time, and were well understood by pupils who appeared to have passed knowledge to each other. There was, in other words, a long standing informal playground culture, and any suggestions by adults would need to be sensitive to this.

If there are dangers from an interventionist approach to breaktime activities, there are equal dangers from a *laissez-faire* approach. Sutton-Smith (1981), as we have seen, is a sensitive defender of the importance of breaktime in children's school lives, but even he has said: 'The older view that we need only leave children alone and their spontaneity will do the rest no longer holds. Children can be spontaneous, but only in the limited, traditional ways of the world which were already given' (p. 289). In the *Playtime and the Primary School* book (1989) I tried to offer a balanced view in which, for example, games and activities are presented to pupils as possibilities. Many primary schools now provide equipment and suggestions for breaktime activities. Children must enjoy the activities — any imposition is unlikely to be successful for long. Experience suggests that adults can facilitate breaktime activities, but this role is a modest one, and activities once taken up are bound to change and be adapted. The type and form of facilitation will differ from primary and secondary. At primary level, as we have seen, breaktime is active and dominated by games, and a facilitative role for adults is more obvious. But at secondary level the more covert nature of activities, and the wish for independence from adults, will alter what adults can do; it will be more appropriate for adults to provide conditions and resources for pupils themselves to make decisions about activities.

Providing a Moral Context

We have seen that peer relations in school at breaktime can be viewed negatively within schools and that opportunities for pupils to meet are being reduced. Breaktime in school is dealt with implicitly, taken for granted, and marginalized, especially at secondary school. Nevertheless, pupils *will* interact in school; this is inevitable. Furthermore, social and moral lessons are being learned at breaktime, whether this is recognized within school or not. Two separate and conflicting moral codes can develop in school — that relevant to the classroom and that to the playground.

But there are likely to be differences between schools in the moral codes that operate. It is easy to convey an over-general view of 'peer culture', as if it is in some mysterious way similar across schools. Though we did not set out to examine school differences, we have seen ways in which schools differed in, and affected, breaktime experience and peer culture. Schools are likely to differ in the extent to which darker aspects like harassment, bullying and aggression are a feature of peer relations. In some schools more than others, peer relations seemed to be governed by malice and victimization, seemingly driven by a few powerful individuals, unchecked by the school. And pupils' accounts indicated that some schools — especially secondary — seemed not to have considered pupils' breaktime experiences or the outside school grounds at all. It was not clear to the pupils where they were supposed to go or what they were to do. The message they received was that neither breaktime, nor their experiences then, were of interest or valued. Titman (1994) has made the point that the design of the school grounds and the nature of breaktime experience can affect pupils' view of the school ethos.

Pupil culture and peer relations are therefore likely to be best conceived as something emerging in context and affected by the school culture and environment. As Epstein (1989) has said: 'It is no longer feasible to study or explain the selection of friends with attention only to psychological constructs and child development terms. It is also necessary to give attention to the designs of the school, classroom, family, and other environments in which peer relations and the selection and influence of friends take place' (1989, p. 183). But in fact very little is known about ways in which schools differently affect breaktime experiences and pupil relations, and this is an important area of future research. Schneider (1993) argues that in sharp contrast to knowledge about the impact of family factors on peer relations, research on school effects appears limited and fragmented. Schneider is interested in peer relations in connection with school and classroom based features such as teacher characteristics, staff cohesiveness, and classroom grouping practices. All of these are of course important, but from the viewpoint of peer relations at breaktime are too limited. There is a need to consider school effects on peer relations in settings such as breaktime, which, as we have seen, involve different processes and experiences to the classroom context.

But, in the meantime, if there are differences between schools in effects on pupil culture then this indicates that negative aspects of peer relations need be neither inevitable nor acceptable. The challenge within schools is to consider the most productive way of approaching pupils' social world. We need to think through our approach to breaktime experiences and peer relations. In my view, schools must consider how to set a moral context for breaktime activities and social relations, at both primary and secondary level. Of course, in many schools, a concern with moral issues is a part of school policy and management. But this concern may not derive from, or be couched in terms of, the realities, from the pupils' perspective, of social life in school and at breaktime. Schools can set a moral context that provides a general framework for peer interaction, whilst not prescribing forms of interaction or limiting contexts for peer contact. It could focus on specific features of breaktime, without this being only used to criticize or draw attention to negative aspects of pupil behaviour. The worlds of classroom and playground may well continue to be separate and unique, but it is possible to aim for a degree of trust and dialogue in order for them to co-exist in one community.

References

BALL, S. (1981) *Beachside Comprehensive*, Cambridge: Cambridge University Press.

BARBER, M. (1994) 'Young people and their attitudes to school: An interim report of a research project in the Centre for Successful Schools': Keele University.

BELLE, D. (1989) 'Studying children's social networks and social supports', in BELLE, D. (ed.) *Children's Social Networks and Social Supports*, New York: Wiley.

BERNDT, T.J. (1989) 'Obtaining support from friends during childhood and adolescence', in BELLE, D. (ed.) *Children's Social Networks and Social Supports*, New York: Wiley, pp. 308–31.

BERNDT, T.J. (1996) 'Exploring the effects of friendship quality on social development', in BUKOWSKI, W.M., NEWCOMB, A.F. and HARTUP, W.W. (eds) *The Company They Keep: Friendships in Childhood and Adolescence*, Cambridge: Cambridge University Press.

BERNDT, T.J., HAWKINS, J.A. and HOYLE, S.G. (1986) 'Changes in friendship during a school year: Effects on children's and adolescents' impressions of friendship and sharing with friends', *Child Development*, **57**, pp. 1284–97.

BLATCHFORD, P. (1989) *Playtime in the Primary School: Problems and Improvements*, Windsor: NFER-Nelson, London: Routledge.

BLATCHFORD, P. (1992a) 'Academic self assessment on 7 and 11 years: Its accuracy and association with ethnic group and sex', *British Journal of Educational Psychology*, **62**, pp. 35–44.

BLATCHFORD, P. (1992b) 'Children's views on work in junior schools', *Educational Studies*, **18**, 1, pp. 107–19.

BLATCHFORD, P. (1993) 'Bullying and the school playground', in TATTUM, D. (ed.) *Understanding and Managing Bullying*, Oxford: Heinemann.

BLATCHFORD, P. (1994) 'Research on children's school playground behaviour in the UK: A review', in BLATCHFORD, P. and SHARP, S. (eds) *Breaktime and the School: Understanding and Changing Playground Behaviour*, London: Routledge.

BLATCHFORD, P. (1996) 'Pupils' views on school and school work from 7 to 16 years', *Research Papers in Education*, **11**, 3, pp. 263–88.

BLATCHFORD, P. (1997) 'Pupils' perceived academic attainment at 7, 11 and 16 years: Effects of sex and ethnic group', *British Journal of Educational Psychology*, **67**, pp. 169–84.

BLATCHFORD, P. (in press) 'The state of play in schools', *Child Psychology and Psychiatry Review*.

BLATCHFORD, P., BURKE, J., FARQUHAR, C., PLEWIS, I. and TIZARD, B. (1987) 'An observational study of children's behaviour at Infant school', *Research Papers in Education*, **2**, 1 (Reprinted in WOODHEAD, M. and MCGRATH, A. (eds) (1988) *Family, School and Society*: Open University/Hodder and Stoughton).

BLATCHFORD, P., CREESER, R. and MOONEY, A. (1990) 'Playground games and playtime: The children's view', *Educational Research*, **32**, 3, pp. 163–74, Reprinted in

WOODHEAD, M., LIGHT, P. and CARR, R. (1991) (eds) *Growing Up in a Changing Society*, London: Routledge/Open University.

BLATCHFORD, P. and SHARP, S. (1994) (eds) *Breaktime and the School: Understanding and Changing Playground Behaviour*, London: Routledge.

BLATCHFORD, P. and SUMPNER, C. (1996) 'Changes to breaktime in primary and secondary schools', Final Report to Nuffield Foundation.

BLATCHFORD, P. and SUMPNER, C. (1997) 'What do we know about breaktime?: Results from a national survey of breaktime and lunchtime in primary and secondary schools', *British Educational Research Journal*.

BOULTON, M. (1992) 'Participation in playground activities at middle school', *Educational Research*, **34**, 3, pp. 167–82.

BOULTON, M. (1993) 'Aggressive fighting in middle school children', *Educational Studies*, **19**, 1, pp. 19–39.

BOULTON, M. (1994) 'Playful and aggressive fighting in the middle-school playground', in BLATCHFORD, P. and SHARP, S. (eds) *Breaktime and the School: Understanding and Changing Playground Behaviour*, London: Routledge.

BOULTON, M. (1996) 'Lunchtime supervisors' attitudes towards playful fighting, and ability to differentiate between playful and aggressive fighting: An intervention study', *British Journal of Educational Psychology*, **66**, 3, pp. 367–81.

BROWN, B.B. (1989) 'The role of peer groups in adolescents' adjustment to secondary school', in BERNDT, T.J. and LADD, G.W. (eds) *Peer Relationships in Child Development*, New York: Wiley.

BROWN, B.B. (1990) 'Peer groups and cultures', in FELDMAN, S.S. and ELLIOTT, G.R. (eds) *At the Threshold: The Developing Adolescent*, Cambridge, MA: Harvard University Press.

BUKOWSKI, W.M. and HOZA, B. (1989) 'Popularity and friendship: Issues in theory, measurement and outcome', in BERNDT, T.J. and LADD, G.W. (eds) *Peer Relationships in Child Development*, New York: Wiley.

COHN, T. (1988) 'Sambo — a study of name calling', in KELLY, E. and COHN, T. *Racism in Schools: New Research Evidence*, Stoke-on-Trent: Trentham Books.

CRICK, N.R. and DODGE, K.A. (1994) 'A review and reformulation of social information-processing mechanisms in children's social adjustment', *Psychological Bulletin*, **115**, 1, pp. 74–101.

DAVEY, A.G. (1987) 'Inter-ethnic friendship patterns in British schools over three decades', *New Community*, **14**, 1, 2, Autumn, pp. 202–9.

DAVIES, B. (1982) *Life in the Classroom and the Playground: The Accounts of Primary School Children*, London: Routledge and Kegan Paul.

DEPARTMENT FOR EDUCATION AND SCIENCE (DES) (Swann Report) (1985) *The Report of the Committee of Inquiry into the Education of Children from Ethnic Minority Groups, Education for All*, London: HMSO.

DEPARTMENT FOR EDUCATION AND SCIENCE (DES) (Elton Report) (1989) *Discipline in Schools: Report of the Committee of Enquiry*, Chaired by Lord Elton, London: HMSO.

DENSCOMBE, M. (1983) 'Ethnic group and friendship choice in the primary school', *Educational Research*, **25**, 3, pp. 184–90.

DEVRIES, R. (1997) 'Piaget's social theory', *Educational Researcher*, March, pp. 4–17.

DUNN, J. (1993) *Young Children's Close Relationships: Beyond Attachment*, Newbury Park, CA: Sage.

EDER, D. and HALLINAN, M.T. (1978) 'Some differences in children's friendships', *American Sociological Review*, **43**, pp. 237–50.

EPSTEIN, J.L. (1989) 'The selection of friends: Changes across the grades and the different school environments', in BERNDT, T.J. and LADD, G.W. (eds) *Peer Relationships in Child Development*, New York: Wiley.

ERWIN, P. (1993) *Friendship and Peer Relations in Children*, Chichester: Wiley.

EVANS, J. (1989) *Children in Play: Life in the School Playground*, Geelong, Victoria: Deakin University.

EVANS, J. (no date) 'Cutting playtime in response to behaviour problems in the playground', Unpublished manuscript.

FAULKNER, D. and MIELL, D. (1993) 'Settling into school: The importance of early friendships for the development of children's social understanding and communicative competence', *International Journal of Early Years Education*, **1**, 1, pp. 23–45.

FELL, G. (1994) 'You're only a dinner lady!: A case study of the 'SALVE' lunchtime organiser project', in BLATCHFORD, P. and SHARP, S. (eds) *Breaktime and the School: Understanding and Changing Playground Behaviour*, London: Routledge.

FREDERICKSON, N. (1994) 'An investigation of the social status of integrated children with moderate learning difficulties', Unpublished PhD thesis: University College London.

FURLONG, V.J. (1984) 'Interaction sets in the classroom: Towards a study of pupils knowledge', in HAMMERSLEY, M. and WOODS, P. (eds) *Life in School: The Sociology of Pupil Culture*, Milton Keynes: Open University Press.

FURMAN, W. (1989) 'The development of children's networks', in BELLE, D. (ed.) *Children's Social Networks and Social Supports*, New York: Wiley.

GOODNOW, J. and BURNS, A. (1985) *Home and School: A Child's Eye View*, Sydney: Allen and Unwin.

GRUDGEON, E. (1993) 'Gender implications of playground culture', in WOODS, P. and HAMMERSLEY, M. (eds) *Gender and Ethnicity in Schools: Ethnographic Accounts*, London: Routledge.

HARGREAVES, D.H. (1967) *Social Relations in a Secondary School*, London: Routledge and Kegan Paul.

HART, C.H. (1993) *Children on Playgrounds: Research Perspectives and Applications*, Albany, NY: State University of New York Press.

HARTUP, W.W. (1989) 'Behavioral manifestations of children's friendships', in BERNDT, T.J. and LADD, G.W. (eds) *Peer Relationships in Child Development*, New York: Wiley.

HARTUP, W.W. (1992) 'Friendships and their developmental significance', in McGURK, H. (ed.) *Childhood Social Development: Contemporary Perspectives*, Hove: Lawrence Erlbaum Associates.

HARTUP, W.W. (1996) 'The company they keep: Friendships and their developmental significance', *Child Development*, **67**, pp. 1–13.

HARTUP, W.W. and LAURSEN, B. (1993) 'Conflict and context in peer relations', in HART, C.H. (ed.) *Children on Playgrounds: Research Perspectives and Applications*, Albany, NY: State University of New York Press.

HIGGINS, C. (1994) 'Improving the school ground environment as an anti-bullying intervention', in SMITH, P.K. and SHARP, S. (eds) *School Bullying: Insights and Perspectives*, London: Routledge.

HILLMAN, M. (1993) 'One false move . . .', in HILLMAN, M. (ed.) *Children, Transport and the Quality of Life*, London: Policy Studies Institute.

HIRSCH, B.J. and DUBOIS, D.L. (1989) 'The school-nonschool ecology of early adolescent friendships', in BELLE, D. (ed.) *Children's Social Networks and Social Supports*, New York: Wiley.

HOWITT, D. (1989) (ed.) *Social Psychology: Conflicts and Continuities,* Milton Keynes: Open University Press.

Journal of Research in Childhood Education (1996) Special edition on 'The Place of Recess in School', **11**, 1, pp. 14–24.

KELLY, E. (1988) 'Pupils, racial groups and behaviour in schools', in KELLY, E. and COHN, T. *Racism in Schools: New Research Evidence,* Stoke-on-Trent: Trentham.

KELLY, E. (1994) 'Racism and sexism in the playground', in BLATCHFORD, P. and SHARP, S. (eds) *Breaktime and the School: Understanding and Changing Playground Behaviour,* London: Routledge.

KWO, S.L. (1994) 'Verbal playfulness as a rapport-building strategy: Conversation among Chinese female friends', Paper to Sociolinguistics Symposium 10th, Lancaster, UK.

LABRELL, F. (1994) 'A typical interaction between fathers and toddlers: Teasing', *Early Development and Parenting,* **3**, 2, pp. 125–30.

LACEY, C. (1970) *Hightown Grammar,* Manchester: Manchester University Press.

LA FONTAINE, J. (1991) *Bullying: The Child's View,* London: Calouste Gulbenkian Foundation.

LADD, G.W., KOCHENDERFER, B.J. and COLEMAN, C.C. (1996) 'Friendship quality as a predictor of young children's early school adjustment', *Child Development,* **67**, pp. 1103–18.

LADD, G.W. and PRICE, J.M. (1993) 'Playstyles of peer-accepted and peer-rejected children on the playground', in HART, C.H. (ed.) *Children on Playgrounds: Research Perspectives and Applications,* Albany, NY: State University of New York Press.

LUCAS, B. (1994) 'The power of school grounds: The philosophy and practise of learning through landscapes', in BLATCHFORD, P. and SHARP, S. (eds) *Breaktime and the School: Understanding and Changing Playground Behaviour,* London: Routledge.

MACDONALD, B. (1989) *Murder in the Playground* (Burnage Inquiry) London: Longsight Press.

MARSH, H.W. (1990) 'Self description questionnaire 11 (SDQ11) manual', University of Western Sydney, Australia.

MILNER, D. (1997) 'Racism and childhood identity', *The Psychologist,* March, pp. 123–5.

MOONEY, A., CREESER, R. and BLATCHFORD, P. (1991) 'Children's views on teasing and fighting in junior schools', *Educational Research,* **33**, 2, pp. 103–12.

MORTIMORE, P. (1991) 'The nature and findings of research on school effectiveness in the primary sector', in RIDDELL, S. and BROWN, S. (eds) *School Effectiveness Research,* London: HMSO.

MOSS, P. and PETRIE, P. (1997) *Children's services: time for a new approach.* A discussion paper. London: Institute of Education.

MOYLES, J.R. (1989) *Just Playing: The Role and Status of Play in Early Childhood Education,* Milton Keynes: Open University Press.

OLWEUS, D. (1993) *Bullying at School: What We Know and What We Can Do,* Oxford: Basil Blackwell.

OPIE, I. and OPIE, P. (1959) *The Lore and Language of Schoolchildren,* London: Oxford University Press.

OPIE, I. and OPIE, P. (1969) *Children's Games in Street and Playground,* London: Oxford University Press.

PARKER, J.G. and ASHER, S.R. (1987) 'Peer relations and later personal adjustment: Are low-accepted children at risk?', *Psychological Bulletin,* **102**, 3, pp. 357–89.

PARKER, J.G. and GOTTMAN, J.M. (1989) 'Social and emotional development in a relational context: Friendship interaction from early childhood to adolescence', in

BERNDT, T.J. and LADD, G.W. (eds) *Peer Relationships in Child Development*, New York: Wiley.

PELLEGRINI, A.D. (1995) *School Recess and Playground Behaviour: Educational and Developmental Roles*, Albany, New York: State University of New York Press.

PELLEGRINI, A.D. and SMITH, P.K. (1993) 'School recess: Implications for education and development', *Review of Educational Research*, **63**, 2, pp. 51–67.

PLEWIS, I. (1991) 'Pupils' progress in reading and maths during primary school: Associations with ethnic group and sex', *Educational Research*, **33**, 2, pp. 133–40.

POLLARD, A. (1985) *The Social World of the Primary School*, London: Holt, Rinehart and Winston.

PRICE, V. (1994) 'The best part of the school day: A gender and age study of lunch break in a secondary school', MA in Education (Psychology) Report, Institute of Education, University of London.

REYNOLDS, D. (1991) 'School effectiveness in secondary schools: Research and its policy implications', in RIDDELL, S. and BROWN, S. (eds) *School Effectiveness Research*, London: HMSO.

ROFFEY, S., TARRANT, T. and MAJORS, K. (1994) *Young Friends: Schools and Friendship*, London: Cassell.

ROSS, L. and NESBETT, R.E. (1991) *The Person and the Situation: Perspectives of Social Psychology*, New York: MacGraw-Hill.

ROSS, C. and RYAN, A. (1994) 'Changing playground society: A whole-school approach', in BLATCHFORD, P. and SHARP, S. (eds) *Breaktime and the School: Understanding and Changing Playground Behaviour*, London: Routledge.

RUDDOCK, J., CHAPLAIN, R. and WALLACE, G. (1996) *School Improvement: What Can Pupils Tell Us?*, London: Fulton.

SAVIN-WILLIAMS, R.C. and BERNDT, T.J. (1990) 'Friendship and peer relations', in FELDMAN, S.S. and ELLIOTT, G.R. (eds) *At the Threshold: The Developing Adolescent*, Cambridge, MA: Harvard University Press.

SCHNEIDER, B.H. (1993) *Children's Social Competence in Context: The Contributions of Family, School and Culture*, Oxford: Pergamon.

SHANTZ, C.U. and HARTUP, W.W. (1992) *Conflict in Child and Adolescent Development*, Cambridge: Cambridge University Press.

SHARP, R. and GREEN, A. (1976) *Education and Social Control: A Study of Progressive Primary Education*, London: Routledge and Kegan Paul.

SHARP, S. (1994) 'Training schemes for lunchtime supervisors in the United Kingdom: An overview', in BLATCHFORD, P. and SHARP, S. (eds) *Breaktime and the School: Understanding and Changing Playground Behaviour*, London: Routledge.

SHARP, S. and BLATCHFORD, P. (1994) 'Understanding and changing school breaktime behaviour: Themes and conclusion', in BLATCHFORD, P. and SHARP, S. (eds) *Breaktime and the School: Understanding and Changing Playground Behaviour*, London: Routledge.

SHARP, S., COOPER, F. and COWIE, H. (1994) 'Making peace in the playground', in BLATCHFORD, P. and SHARP, S. (eds) *Breaktime and the School: Understanding and Changing Playground Behaviour*, London: Routledge.

SHARP, S. and COWIE, H. (1994) 'Enpowering pupils to take positive action against bullying', in SMITH, P.K. and SHARP, S. (1994) (eds) *School Bullying: Insights and Perspectives*, London: Routledge.

SHARP, S. and SMITH, P.K. (1994) *Tackling Bullying in Your School*, London: Routledge.

SHEAT, L.G. and BEER, A.R. (1994) 'Giving pupils an effective voice in the design and use of their school grounds', in BLATCHFORD, P. and SHARP, S. (eds) *Breaktime and the School: Understanding and Changing Playground Behaviour*, London: Routledge.

SLUCKIN, A. (1981) *Growing Up in the Playground: The Social Development of Children*, London: Routledge and Kegan Paul.

SMITH, P. (1990) 'The role of play in he nursery and primary school', in ROGERS, C. and KUTNICK, P. (eds) *The Social Psychology of the Primary School*, London: Routledge, pp. 144–68.

SMITH, P. (1994) 'What children learn from playtime, and what adults can learn from it', in BLATCHFORD, P. and SHARP, S. (eds) *Breaktime and the School: Understanding and Changing Playground Behaviour*, London: Routledge.

SMITH, P.K. and SHARP, S. (1994) (eds) *School Bullying: Insights and Perspectives*, London: Routledge.

STOLL, L. and MORTIMORE, P. (1995) 'School effectiveness and school improvement', *Institute of Education Viewpoint*, London: Institute of Education.

SUTTON-SMITH, B. (1981) *A History of Children's Play: New Zealand, 1840–1950*, Philadelphia: University of Pennsylvania Press.

SUTTON-SMITH, B. (1982) 'A performance theory of peer relations', in BORMAN, K.M. (ed.) *The Social Life of Children in a Changing Society*, Hillsdale, New Jersey: Lawrence Erlbaum Associates.

SUTTON-SMITH, B. (1990) 'School playground as festival', *Children's Environments Quarterly*, **7**, 2, pp. 3–7.

TATTUM, D. and LANE, O.A. (1989) *Bullying in Schools*, Stoke-on-Trent: Trentham.

THORNE, B. (1993) *Gender Play: Girls and Boys in School*, Buckingham: Open University Press.

TITMAN, W. (1994) *Special Places: Special People: The Hidden Curriculum of the School Grounds*, Godalming, Surrey, World Wildlife Fund for Nature/Learning Through Landscapes.

TIZARD, B., BLATCHFORD, P., BURKE, J., FARQUHAR, C. and PLEWIS, I. (1988) *Young Children at School in the Inner City*, Hove: Lawrence Erlbaum Associates.

TROYNA, B. and HATCHER, R. (1992) *Racism in Children's Lives: A Study of Mainly-White Primary Schools*, London: Routledge.

WALVIN, J. (1982) *A Child's World: A Social History of English Childhood*, Harmondsworth, Middlesex: Penguin.

WHITNEY, I. and SMITH, P. (1993) 'A survey of the nature and extent of bully/victim problems in junior/middle and secondary schools', *Educational Research*, **35**, pp. 3–25.

WILLIAMS, B.T.R. and GILMOUR, J.D. (1994) 'Annotation: Sociometry and peer relationships', *Journal of Child Psychology and Psychiatry*, **35**, 6, pp. 997–1013.

WILLIS, P. (1977) *Learning to Labour*, Saxon House.

WOODS, P. (1983) *Sociology and the School*, London: Routledge and Kegan Paul.

WOODS, P. (1990) *The Happiest Days?: How Pupils Cope with School*, London: Falmer Press.

YOUNISS, J. (1980) *Parents and Peers in Social Development: A Sullivan-Piaget Perspective*, Chicago: University of Chicago Press.

Index

academic ability, 61
  popularity, 74
  Robert, 84
  teasing, 121–2, 125
accident misinterpretation, 144–5, 156
activity levels, 48–9
affiliation, 94
Afro-Caribbean children, 91
aggression, 4
  breaktime fears, 33, 39
  fighters, 147
  Grant, 84
  overestimation, 110
  psychology, 136
  rejection, 17
  teasing, 127–8
AH1 Perceptual Reasoning Test, 61, 75, 84
ancillary staff, 5, 40
appearance, teasing, 117, 120–1, 131
Asher, J.R., 17
Asian children, 91
assertiveness training, 173
Australia, 6

ball games, 44, 62
Ball, S., 12
Barber, M., 9
Barker, R., 21
Beer, A.R., 173
Belle, D., 73
Berndt, T.J., 16, 17, 73, 74, 91
best friends, 73, 76–8, 79, 86, 91, 92, 93
between group fighting, 150–2
between group processes, 119–20
borderwork, 88
boredom
  breaktime views, 33–4, 36, 53
  games, 67

Boulton, M., 11, 15, 18, 22
  aggression overestimation, 110
  fighting, 111, 136, 137, 144, 156
  football, 68
  mixed age groups, 76
  mixed age playing, 70
  teasing, 112
Brown, B.B., 90, 91–2, 95, 107
Bukowski, W.M., 73, 74
bullying, 3, 8, 12, 33
  initiatives, 9
  leading to fights, 146, 156
  playground design, 173
  teasing, 131
    difference, 109–10
    verbal, 18–19
Burns, A., 72

camps, 62, 67–8, 70
Candy, 75
catching games, 44, 62
Celia, 75, 78, 80, 82
chasing games, 44, 62
childishness, 68, 70
Childs, K., 87
choice, 52, 91, 95–8
chum friendships, 90
Cindy, 77
cliques, 90
clubs, 37, 38, 40
cognitive development, 42
Cohn, T., 3, 109, 111, 112
cold teasing, 111
Coleman, C.C., 16
Colin, 78
collaborative conflict resolution, 173
conflicts, 18–19
Cooper, F., 173
coorientation, 87

Coward, R., 162–3
Cowie, H., 173
Creeser, R., 109, 138
Crick, N.R., 116
criminality, 17
crowds, 90, 149–50, 156
cultural transmission, 14
culture
    gender differences, 15
    peer, 12–13, 42, 171–3, 176
    playgrounds, 14

Davey, A.G., 91
David, 84
Davies, B., 16, 72, 109
Denscombe, M., 91
depth of selection, 86
developmental changes, 20, 41–57, 59,
    69, 90, 163–4
DeVries, R., 16
dinner ladies, 5, 63
Dodge, K.A., 116
dominant games, 67–8
dropping out of school, 17
Dubois, D.L., 72
Dunn, J., 16
duration of breaktime, 2, 5
dyads, 90

ecological psychology, 21
Eder, D., 73, 75
Edinburgh Reading Score, 61, 64, 75,
    84
Edna, 77
effectiveness of schools, 9
Eifermann, R., 69–70
eight year olds, 24–5, 160, 163–4
    fighting, 144, 147
    friendship formation, 72–89
    games, 58–71, 160, 168
    personal characteristics, 165
Elaine, 75, 76, 77, 78, 79, 80, 82
eleven year olds
    crowds, 149
    developmental changes, 41–57
    fighting, 155
        causes, 140
        frequency, 138

opinions on, 139
parents' role, 153
pupils' views, 26–40
teasing and name calling, 109–35, 161
Elton Committee, 3
Enquiry into Discipline in Schools, 3
environmental factors, 86
environmental improvements, 38, 173
environmental projects, 6
Epstein, J.L., 76
    friendship intervention, 172
    pupil involvement, 175
    school effects, 176
    sex segregation, 92
    similarities, 73, 86
equipment, 6, 38, 66
equipment games, 62
Erwin, P., 22, 73
ethnic bias, 91–2
ethnic differences, 21, 166–7
    breaktime views, 29
    fighting, 156–7
    name calling, 167
    sixteen year olds, 106, 107–8
    staying in school, 30
    teasing, 114, 133, 167
ethnic groups
    see also racism
    mixed friendships, 98–102
Evans, J., 11, 110
    fight frequency, 137
    fights, 19
    gender differences, 21, 165
    social context, 42
    teasing, 131, 132

family insults, 111, 120, 122–3, 132,
    145–6, 156
Faulkner, D., 16
Fell, G., 173
fighting, 8, 18–19, 136–58, 161
    breaktime views, 33
    changes with age, 164
    different types, 111
    ethnic differences, 167
    Grant, 84
    individual differences, 165
    name calling, 140, 141–2, 156
    teasing, 112

food, 35
football, 47, 66
  breaktime views, 32, 33, 38
  dominant games, 67
  eleven year olds, 44
  gender differences, 56, 57, 165–6
  leading to fights, 144, 145
  popularity, 68
  sixteen year olds, 45, 46, 102, 103,
    104, 106
Frederickson, N., 60–1
freedom, 30, 31, 52
friendship groups
  formation, 66, 80, 87
  games, 70
  gender differences, 75
  sixteen year olds, 90–1, 92–5
  stability, 81–2, 87
friendships, 8, 15–17, 160
  changes with age, 164
  chum friendships, 90
  fights, 145
  formation, 72–89
  gender differences, 73, 92
  mixed ages, 76
  similarities, 73, 79, 86, 101
  sixteen year olds, 90–108
  talking to, 31–2
  teasing, 116–17, 132
  why children are friends, 73–4, 78–80,
    86
Furlong, V.J., 12
Furman, W., 73, 86, 87

games, 4, 14, 32
  see also football; play
  ball games, 44, 62
  boredom, 67
  catching games, 44, 62
  changes with age, 44–50
  chasing games, 44, 62
  cross-gender games, 82
  development, 65
  dominant, 67–8
  equipment games, 62
  friendships, 70, 72, 88, 160
  gender differences, 44, 45, 46, 47
  home made, 62, 68
  interventionist view, 171, 172

junior school, 58–71, 160
  leading to fights, 144, 156
  non-interventionist view, 172
  play quality, 4, 170
  primary school children, 39
  racing games, 62
  rules, 69
  seeking games, 44, 62
  skipping, 44, 62, 63
  traditional, 4, 41, 59, 62, 66, 67, 69,
    170
gender
  boys teasing girls, 125–6
  cross-gender games, 82
  cross-gender interaction, 133
  girls teased as slags, 123, 126–7, 132,
    141–2
  girls teasing boys, 125, 126
  girls teasing girls, 126–8
  separate sex friendships, 103–5
gender differences, 21, 56, 165–6
  best friends, 92
  breaktime locations, 43–4
  breaktime views, 27, 29, 39
  fighting, 138–9
  friendship groups, 75
  friendships, 73, 92
  games, 44, 45, 46, 47
  mixed friendships, 92, 102–3
  name calling, 111, 112
  sixteen year olds, 105, 106
  staying in school, 30
  talking to friends, 31
  teasing, 114, 133
gender identity, 15
George, 77, 78
Gillian, 75, 76, 77, 78, 80, 82, 85
Gilmour, J.D., 17
Goodnow, J., 72
Gottman, J.M., 16, 59, 74
Graham, 77, 79
Grant, 78, 84
Green, A., 12
groups
  see also ethnic differences; gender
    differences
  between group fighting, 150–2
  between group processes, 119–20
  differences, 21, 27, 165–7

fighting, 149
processes, 119–20
teasing, 132–3
within group processes, 119
Grudgeon, E., 14
Gump, P., 21

Hallinan, M.T., 73, 75
Hannah, 77
Hargreaves, D.H., 12
Harre, R., 109
Harriet, 77
Hart, C.H., 7
Hartup, W.W., 16, 18, 73, 74, 75, 87,
    88
Hatcher, R., 13, 21, 109, 111, 112, 133
Hawkins, J.A., 73, 91
Helen, 75, 77, 82, 85
Higgins, C., 173
Hillman, M., 6, 163
Hirsch, B.J., 72
home made games, 62, 68
homework, 54
hot teasing, 111
Howitt, D., 136
Hoyle, S.G., 73
Hoza, B., 73, 74

independence, 30, 31, 33, 34, 35–6,
    39
individual differences, 21, 164–5
Inner London Education Authority,
    107
intelligence, 17
inter-group relations, 156, 157
interests, 104
interventionist view, 171, 172, 175–6

Jamie, 78, 79
Janet, 75, 77, 78, 82
Jennings, 174
John, 75, 77, 79
Josh, 84
junior school, 2
    see also eight year olds; eleven year
        olds; nine year olds
    breaktime activities, 160
    friendship formation, 72–89
    games, 58–71, 160

Katherine, 85
    academic ability, 75, 80
    friends, 76, 77, 78, 79
    group stability, 82
Kelly, E., 3, 13, 109, 111, 112, 123
key players, 63–4, 69, 165, 170
Knapp, M. and H., 110
Kochenderfer, B.J., 16
Kohlberg, L., 174
Kwo, S.L., 110

La Fontaine, J., 3
Labrell, F., 110
Lacey, C., 12
Ladd, G.W., 16, 17, 22, 64, 74, 76
laissez-faire approach, 175
Lane, O.A., 3
Lara, 77
Laursen, B., 18
leadership, 63, 83
Learning Through Landscapes, 173
Lewin, K., 21
lifestyles, 97
'Like to Play With' (LITOP), 60–1, 63, 64,
    81, 83, 85
'Like to Work With' (LITOW), 60–1, 81
Linda, 85
LITOP *see* 'Like to Play With'
LITOW *see* 'Like to Work With'
Lucas, B., 173
Lucy, 79

Macdonald, B., 3
Macdonald Committee Inquiry, 111
Majors, K., 173
Malcolm, 76, 80, 84, 85
Markus, H.J., 74
Marsh, H.W., 61, 75
Martin, 76, 78, 79, 84
Matthew, 76
maturity, 50–1, 55, 113
Miell, D., 16
Milner, D., 21, 167
mixed age groups, 70, 76
Molly, 76
moodiness, 147
Mooney, A., 3, 24, 109, 122, 138
moral context, 176–7
moral judgements, 174

Morgan, J., 109
Mortimore, P., 9
Moss, P., 163
Moyles, J.R., 15
'mucking about', 143, 156
music, 97, 101, 121

name calling, 8, 18–19, 109–35
    changes with age, 164
    ethnic differences, 167
    fight provocation, 140, 141–2, 156
    racist, 3, 13, 111–12
Nesbett, R.E., 21
networks, 80, 105, 160
nine year olds, 24–5, 160, 163–4
    fighting, 144, 147
    friendship formation, 72–89
    games, 58–71, 160, 168
    personal characteristics, 165
Noreen, 77, 79, 82
Nurius, P., 74

Olweus, D., 3, 8, 110, 111, 131, 137
O'Neill, C., 109
Opie, I. and P., 9, 14, 44, 58, 109, 170, 172
out of school, 6, 96

parents
    fighting encouragement, 137–8, 153–4
    influence, 170
Parker, J.G., 16, 17, 59, 74
peer
    acceptance, 17
    adjustment, 17
    counselling, 173
    culture, 12–13, 42, 171–3, 176
    influence, 68–9, 70
    intervention, 150
    nominations, 74, 81, 83
    pressure, 51, 98, 103, 168
    ratings, 60–1, 81
    regulation, 128–9, 134, 137
    rejection, 17
Pellegrini, A.D., 11
    breaktime value, 27
    development, 20
    friendships, 16

gender differences, 56, 165
observation methods, 22
psychology, 15
socialization model, 42
teasing, 110
US recess, 3, 6
personal characteristics, 74, 79–80, 137, 147–8
Petrie, P., 163
Piaget, J., 15–16, 42
play, 15
    see also games
    friendships, 16
    quality, 4, 56, 59, 170
playgrounds, 3, 6, 38, 43–4, 168
    equipment, 66
    improvements, 173
Plewis, I., 21
Pollard, A., 12, 13, 21–2, 172–3, 174
popularity, 17–18, 63, 74, 81, 83
prestige, teasing, 119
Price, J.M., 17, 22, 64
Price, V., 29, 44, 47
primary school, 2
    see also seven year olds
    breaktime activities, 160
provocation to fight, 140–2, 156

racing games, 62
racism, 21, 98–102, 109, 167
    fights, 150–2
    name calling, 3, 13, 111–12
    peer regulation, 128–9
    school policy, 130
    staff regulation, 134
    teasing, 3, 13, 123–5, 129–30, 133
reciprocal nominations, 76
rejection, 17–18, 64, 75, 83
Reynolds, D., 9
Robert, 83–4
Roffey, S., 173
romantic interest, 103
Ross, C., 173
Ross, L., 21
Rubin, K.H., 16
Ruddock, J., 10
rules of games, 69
rumours, 142–3, 156

Ruth, 75, 77, 80, 82, 85
Ryan, A., 173

safety, 6, 162, 163
Sandra, 75
Savin-Williams, R.C., 16, 17, 91, 137
Schneider, B.H., 174–5, 177
School Councils, 175
schools
    differences, 57, 157, 170–1
        effects on culture, 176–7
        teasing and bullying, 134
    effectiveness, 9
    fights between, 152–3, 157
    improvement, 9, 26, 171–3
    policy, 8–10
        on racism, 130
    rules, 34–7
SDQ *see* Self Description Questionnaire
Sean, 77
seasonal changes, 66
secondary school, 2
    see also eleven year olds; sixteen year
        olds
    breaktime activities, 160
seeking games, 44, 62
self awareness, 84
self concept, 61, 74–5, 84, 85
self consciousness, 51
self defence, 140
Self Description Questionnaire (SDQ),
    61, 64, 75, 83, 84
self esteem, 74, 84, 85, 90, 136
self identity, 91
self understanding, 51, 55
self worth, 74
Selman, R., 86
seven year olds
    developmental changes, 41–57
    fighting, 155
        causes, 140, 141
        frequency, 138
        opinions on, 138–9
    pupils' views, 26–40
    teasing and name calling, 109–35
sexual harassment, 13
Shantz, C.U., 18
Sharp, R., culture, 12

Sharp, S., 7, 57, 173
    bullying, 3, 8, 9
    playgrounds, 6
    supervisors, 87
    teasing, 131
Shawn, 79
Sheat, L.G., 173
siblings, 63, 64
similarities, 73, 79, 86, 101
Simon, 77, 79, 80
situational factors, 21–2, 43–4, 87, 148–9,
    156, 168
sixteen year olds
    crowds, 149, 150
    developmental changes, 41–57
    fighting, 153, 155
        causes, 140, 141, 144, 145
        frequency, 138
        opinions on, 139–40
    friendships, 90–108, 160
    pupils' views, 26–40
    teasing and name calling, 109–35, 161
skipping, 44, 62, 63
Sluckin, A.
    games, 58
    name calling, 109
    social skills, 14, 18, 42
    teasing, 116
Smith, P., 7, 11
    bullying, 3, 110
    developmental changes, 69
    gender differences, 21, 165
    play, 15
Smith, P.K.
    breaktime value, 27
    bullying, 3, 8, 9
    development, 20
    teasing, 131
smoking, 32
socialization, 14–15, 39, 41–2, 46, 54,
    102
socialization model, 42
sport, 34
staff, 63
    see also teachers
    ancillary, 5, 40
    dinner ladies, 5, 63
    influence, 71

racism regulation, 134
  training, 173
staying in school, 29–30, 53–4
stirring, 142–3, 156
Stoll, L., 9
sub-cultures, 12
Sullivan, H.S., 15, 74, 90
Sumpner, C., 5, 9, 40
supervisory staff, 173
surface of selection, 86
Sutton-Smith, B., 69–70
  breaktime views, 29
  playground culture, 12–13, 16, 168
  social skills, 41, 42
  spontaneity, 175
Swann Report, 111

Tarrant, T., 173
Tattum, D., 3
teachers
  see also staff
  fight frequency, 137
  interventionist vs non-interventionist
    view, 172
  parents encourage fighting, 137–8
  pupils' experiences, 174
  reaction to fighting, 154–5, 156
  teasing regulation, 129–30, 134
Teachers Union, 3
teasing, 8, 18–19, 109–35, 161
  changes with age, 164
  clothes, 120, 121
  cold, 111
  ethnic differences, 114, 133, 167
  fight provocation, 140, 141–2, 156

gender differences, 166
hot, 111
racism, 3, 13, 123–5, 129–30, 133
romantic interest, 103
Thorne, B.
  cross-gender games, 82, 88
  gender differences, 15, 21, 166
  teasing, 112, 133
Tim, 75, 77, 79, 85
Titman, W., 173, 174, 176
Tizard, B., 21, 23, 24
  games, 32, 44
  seven year olds, 12, 13, 32, 33, 44, 109
  teasing and name calling, 109
traditional games, 4, 41, 59, 62, 66, 67,
  69, 170
Troyna, B., 13, 21, 109, 111, 112, 133

United States, 2, 3, 6

violence, 3

Walvin, J., 14
weather, 33, 39
Whitney, I., 3, 110
William, 77
Williams, B.T.R., 17
Willis, P., 12
within group processes, 119
Woodhead, C., 9
Woods, P., 16, 172
work, 46, 54, 55, 125
Wright, H.F., 21

Youniss, J., 15